THE RUBBISH-PICKER'S WIFE
AN UNLIKELY FRIENDSHIP IN KOSOVO

ELIZABETH GOWING

For Eleanor
from a fellow
teacher!

Elizabeth Gowing

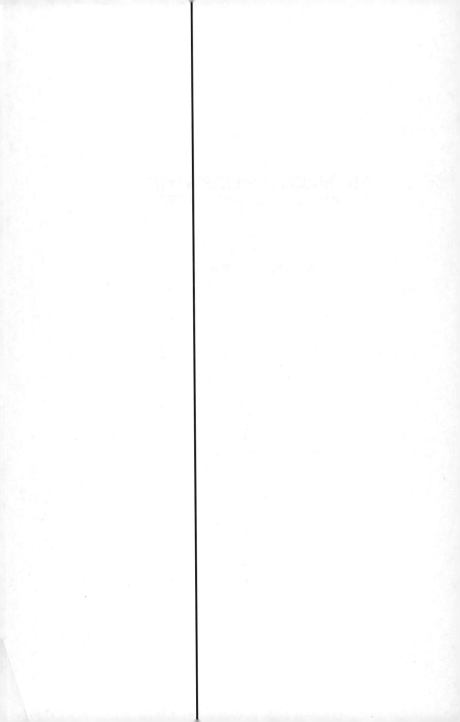

Dedicated to my own and the world's teachers, meaning not only the committed men and women who work in schools, but also parents, grandparents, volunteers, civil society activists — and nine year-old Ashkali girls — from whom I've learned so much.

First published in 2015 by Elbow Publishing

Copyright © Elizabeth Gowing, 2015

The right of Elizabeth Gowing to be identified as the author of this work has been asserted by her in accordance with the Copyright, Designs and Patents Act, 1988.

A catalogue record for this book is available from the British Library

ISBN 978-0-9574090-3-3

Cover design by Su Jones and Paddy McEntaggart incorporating photographs taken by children of Neighbourhood 29 in Fushë Kosovë and used by them with permission. The photographs were taken as part of a summer project with children aged six to sixteen and a larger selection of the work of these talented young photographers can be seen at www.thisisneighbourhood29.com

Inline photographs © Elizabeth Gowing, except where others are acknowledged alongside the photograph

Design & typesetting: Sally Ellis

Printed and bound in Great Britain by
TJ International Ltd, Padstow, Cornwall

THE RUBBISH-PICKER'S WIFE
AN UNLIKELY FRIENDSHIP IN KOSOVO

ELIZABETH GOWING

Elbow Publishing
Cornwall

CONTENTS

This book has failed if it doesn't give a proper picture of the huge and varied team of people who made possible the education of the families of the rubbish-pickers of Fushë Kosovë and beyond. So many people gave their time, their skills and their money to make the events narrated here happen. I am enormously grateful to the Krasniqi family and to all their neighbours and community for making me feel welcome, but also to all those who have supported me and others of The Ideas Partnership charity in our work there. Chief among them is the man who has bankrolled so many of my untested ideas, who said 'we could do that' with not a second's hesitation when I suggested working in Fushë Kosovë, and who wakes me every morning with a cup of green tea and enthusiasm for the day ahead. Thank you, Rob.

The Ideas Partnership is going from strength to strength, and its impact has developed even further from the work narrated here. This is due to the enormous commitment of our staff and volunteers, many but not all of whom are mentioned by name in the book. We have also been lucky to have support from a wide range of private and institutional donors, many of them also friends. Thank you!

Others have helped with the production of this book – whether encouraging me to write it (thank you, Louise and Charlie), reading extracts of it in draft (thank you, Chris Gowing, Joanna Jepson, Marie Kreft, Sam Lucas, Rob Wilton, Moira Ashley and the other members of Liz Cleere's Itinerant Writers Club), creating such gorgeous cover art for it (thank you, Su Jones and Paddy McEntaggart and Órlagh) and making it look lovely inside (thank you, Sally Ellis) or proofreading (thank you Hannah Brandley, though any errors that remain are my own). I would like to thank the Raphael family for all that they have given throughout the process of its writing, and beyond, in Kosovan levels of hospitality, and support of every kind to me and to our work in Fushë Kosovë.

In a few places in the text, names have been changed to protect the privacy of individuals, but the events recounted here are true.

1 The turning away

I had never been this far into Fushë Kosovë before. It's a
suburb I'm familiar with: every foreigner who comes to
Kosovo passes through it because it's the municipality that
lies between the airport and Kosovo's capital city, Prishtina.
It's mainly a strip development: for me Fushë Kosovë was
the Scandinavian furniture store where we'd bought lamps
and cushions for our new home here, and the supermarket
where I'd bought canned coconut milk like a burst of exotic
sunshine in my wintry Balkan home cooking. But today the
taxi drove me past these well-lit stores and I realised we were
heading for the train station.

Fushë Kosovë railway station is grim. Not just because it's
a brown 1970s whimsy floored with broken tiles and pools
of brown liquid, probably – though not certainly – from the
leaking roof. Also because it was to this station that Prishtina's
Albanians were herded by Milošević's Serbian forces in the
freezing days of April 1999. In their thousands they were
gathered in this station and held for twenty four hours (long
enough for a baby to be born, and an old man to die – I
imagined moans and wailing) while they thought about their
history books and the Jews of the 1940s, before being forced
onto trains and dispatched to the Macedonian border.

In fact my taxi drove past the station too. This was deep into
another part of Fushë Kosovë, another side to Kosovo. At a
corner stood a staring group of young men, dark-skinned.
They eyed our car and me, unsmiling. They looked like
trouble waiting to happen.

We left the long shadows of Fushë Kosovë's high-rise strip development, and a new neighbourhood unfolded – on one side the railway lines in the colours of oil smears and industrial decay; on the other side shacks and single-storey homes, fenced with old car doors also the colour of rust. Smoke that smelled of shit rose from behind the houses. There were words spray-painted on walls, 'for sale', 'lime in stock', 'pipes and drums for weddings'. More young men loitered, blowing on their hands to keep warm.

The community was clustered around an enormous rubbish heap, like old English villages centred their homes round a green and a duckpond. Children shouted, toddled or rummaged the rubbish heap. Some of them were barefoot; some had the swollen bellies of malnutrition. Women whipped into doorways with a whisk of a headscarf. After four years living in Kosovo this country usually seemed familiar to me; here I felt I was in a foreign land, and in another time. A grubby-faced boy came out of an alley bowed low under a sack of metal salvage. It was like being in a dark-faced Dickens novel.

The car pulled up at a community centre – Portakabins surrounded by a huddle of children. Some of the kids tried out their English on me as I walked through them with my bulging sacks of clothes. 'Hello. Ow arry oo?' I hate the fact I am so obviously not from this country. I replied in Albanian, '*Si je?*' – how are you?

The children were confused, embarrassed; they hid their faces and turned away.

I was here to meet with the head of the Balkan Sunflowers Learning Centre offering homework support for the neighbourhood's schoolchildren. I'd heard about his work and it seemed that this was the main force for changing the life-chances of the children in this community. I was here because our charity had run an environmental education camp which had left us with a surplus of sleeping bags, plates, and equipment that might be useful for families in need, and my bags were stuffed with things we wanted to give away. Rrahmon, the head of the Centre, was going to take me to some families he considered most in need, in this community where need was a default.

His office was crowded with two desks and a scramble of chairs. I inched round the sharp edges with my plump bag of donations and found a place to sit. He greeted me with the elaborate welcome I've got used to in Kosovo, asking after my health, my family, my work, and sitting me down and offering tea. But his attention wasn't all on me – even as he welcomed me the door was opening and pixie-faced children were coming in with questions or requests. Some wanted to borrow books from the centre's 'library' sitting on a few shelves above Rrahmon's desk, and they carried in carefully battered school primers or books of cartoons on cheap paper, and Rrahmon wrote down their names and details in a ledger and they chose another book to carry out just as carefully. Members of staff interrupted us too with queries, problems, timetabling concerns. These were familiar rhythms to me, and more than I had since arriving in Kosovo I felt nostalgic for the little primary school in Hackney where I'd worked as a deputy head.

I'd visited other educational institutions in Kosovo in the years that I'd lived here – as part of my work with local NGOs and international charities, working on a British Council grant, and through the charity my partner and I had set up with a friend here. When I'd been a visitor in Kosovan schools before, I'd been struck by many things indicating the desperate needs of the under-funded system, but also by the atmosphere of leisure in headteachers' offices and staffrooms. They're certainly not places of luxury: the average teacher in Kosovo earns three hundred euros a month, and while the cost of living in Prishtina is less than in London, costs aren't so wildly different that this is an acceptable wage. But these were people who seemed to feel none of the pressures of their clients' needs. Teachers turned up (but often late), and as long as it didn't interfere with other demands on their lives they would teach, but if a friend phoned in the middle of a lesson, they would take the call. If a foreigner turned up for a visit to the headteacher, the children and their library books were generally required to wait while the head hosted coffee, sometimes in a nearby café. I love the Albanian prioritisation of hospitality and I've learned a lot about shaping my life better around the concept that your home 'belongs to God and the guest'. But there are some things that I feel have an even higher call than hospitality, and education is one of them.

Rrahmon obviously agreed with me: in this Centre, while I was courteously served a welcome chamomile tea against the cold (though really, in this underheated Portakabin, one plastic cup of warm water wasn't going to make much difference – it was like being offered a flowery light cotton scarf to wrap round me in the snow), it was clear what the priorities were. I got to the point: how could I find the families that Rrahmon was suggesting would benefit most from the bags I had with me? Would he give me names so I could find them? Given how obviously under pressure he was, I didn't want to take any more of his time.

No, he assured me; he would take me himself. Right, then – we should get on with it. I bolted the last sugary slug of tea and we went out with the bags to his car.

We were soon off the asphalt and squelching through mud. The corpse of a puppy lay by the side of the road, split like a fallen fig by passing car tyres. We drove down a path until we reached a dead end and Rrahmon stopped the car, got out and banged on the metal panelling surrounding a home. I got out with him, nervously holding the bags with our donations in them. Children who had been playing in the street gathered like a gang. Where they had shoes, the shoes didn't fit. Most had dirty faces. Some were sullen and silent but others were curious, asking me my name, where I was from, what was in the bags. Rrahmon tried to shoo them away and I smiled at them apologetically, and held the bag tighter. I remembered what I'd read about food drop workers in Africa being mobbed by hungry people. These kids looked hungry, though they didn't look like they'd mob me.

In the midst of such obvious need, I didn't feel the weight of my generosity in the fat bag in my arms. This was no Father Christmas act; instead I felt keenly how pathetic the bag contents were. I remembered as a teenager seeing a homeless guy on the street in London slumped next to a bowl for donations. He, like the people I'd seen today, had looked in need of vitamins and calories. On impulse I had gone to a fruit stall across the road from him and bought a bulging bag filled with oranges and bananas. I had taken it over to him and he'd ripped it open.

'Oh darlin', nah, nah, that's a waste o' money. The fruit guy gives me leftovers for free when he goes 'ome each day. Nah, nah. Why djer do tha'?' He had been genuinely frustrated, angry with the situation – with the world – and I had felt foolish and angry too.

'Well, that's all I can give you,' I had said as I had walked away with my eyes smarting, though it had been a lie of course.

Remembering that experience twenty years ago, a new fear came to me as the children circled nearer and Rrahmon continued banging on the panel, 'O Agron, are you there?' Maybe when this Agron came out, and took the bag, he'd rip it open like his brother on the other side of Europe had done on that street corner, and the same look would cross his face when he saw the unnecessary sleeping bag, the useless china. Maybe he'd sneer at me with the Albanian equivalent of 'nah, nah', and all the while I'd be taking Rrahmon's time and the little girls in the Portakabin would be waiting outside his office to exchange their library books.

The children were shifting around me, starting to kick their ball again. I sized them up; they didn't look like they needed old sleeping bags and second-hand china; they needed indoor bathrooms and nit combs, a decent pair of shoes, and health care. Agron wasn't answering anyway; I guessed he was out scavenging through the garbage, which was how most families here seemed to subsist, and the pointlessness of my visit here was excruciating. With my arms full of the unwieldy bag, and hampered anyway by my poor footwork skills, I couldn't even respond to the kids' friendly dribbling of the ball around my feet. I turned to get back in the car.

With a creak, the panel door Rrahmon had been knocking at swung back and a dishevelled woman stood there, streaks of henna showing in the grey hair escaping from her headscarf. Rrahmon greeted her and explained who I was and why I was there. Grateful to be offloading something, I handed the bag over and awaited her response.

She was polite, far from sneering. She took the bag and thanked me, 'May Allah reward you,' she said as she moved back inside.

Phew. I felt better – lighter not just from losing the weight of the bag, but from the relative elegance of the transaction. In fact, I felt good. I had clothed the needy, done something close to feeding the hungry. Get me! The glow of charity warmed me up better than a sleeping bag. I smiled at Rrahmon and stepped towards the car.

A woman's voice called out from behind the door. A flicker of anxiety came back with the memory of the man inspecting my misguided offering of fruit twenty years ago. Had she been disappointed in the contents of the bag? Was this how the mobbing started?

The rusty panel swung back again but it wasn't the older woman I'd given the bag to – this was a slight, fine-featured woman younger than me. In her arms she held a mournful-faced toddler.

'Stop!' she cried. 'You have to help my son.' And with that she pulled down the tracksuit trousers he was wearing, to reveal tiny brown legs shiny with recent burns. The scar tissue covered his legs almost entirely, from groin to shin. It was patched and taut, painful just to look at.

'I'm sorry, I'm not a doctor,' I said. 'I can't help with medical needs. I just wanted to give you that bag.'

'Three hundred euros, the doctor told me. I don't have three hundred euros,' she said.

'I don't have three hundred euros either,' I said, though it was as untrue as what I'd said that day to the man on the London street.

And I walked away.

2 The salve

In fact I didn't go very far. It's not the same as throwing away a leaflet that's come through your door telling you about child poverty. It's not the same as bustling past one of those charming guys on a busy shopping street with a collection tin or a request for a small monthly direct debit. I thought of the tight skin of the little boy, shiny like butter that's melted and re-formed, the mother standing bravely in the mud thrusting him at me, the sure knowledge that I did, in fact, have three hundred euros … and I couldn't have lived with myself if I hadn't stopped.

But another instinct was fighting in me too – the delicious Father Christmas feeling of going to the cash machine a few miles away at the roundabout and bringing back to this fierce, desperate mother the means for her child to be cured. The idea battled with others – would the money really go to help her frail damaged son? Worse fears, fuelled by every racist article I'd ever read … was the woman one of those 'professional beggars' you read about? Might her son even have been deliberately injured to play on the easy sympathies of well-meaning people like me? Would I be Father Christmas or a patsy?

I asked Rrahmon to stop the car and made a phone call, to Mary – a British doctor who had been in Kosovo for longer than I had. She would know what I should do.

Mary said that if the family had already been told they needed a particular sum of money then that meant they had already been to the hospital. They should therefore have the discharge papers which would set out exactly what was needed. She said I should go and ask for those.

It wasn't quite the role I'd had in mind. You don't hear about the chap in the red suit conducting needs assessments with the professionals involved in the cases of children whose stockings he climbs down the chimney to fill. It seemed a little elaborate, but certainly wise. So I suggested Rrahmon should go back to his Centre, and I returned to the house.

Yes, Agron's wife (whose name, she told me shyly, was Hatemja) did have the papers. She asked me to wait outside while she got them, and she splashed through the puddles of mud (and worse – I saw that I was standing by the family's outhouse) to the opening in the corrugated iron which was the entrance to her home. I stood feeling self-conscious, and grinned nervously at the children who stood watching me from a distance.

Hatemja returned with a plastic bag and from inside it she unfolded a wedge of greasy papers. There in her hand was the grubby summary of the state's engagement with her and Agron and their five children – birth certificates, bills from the state electricity company, and plenty of evidence of doctors' appointments, hospital appointments, tests, prescriptions … the bewildering paperwork system so beloved of a post-communist regime. She thumbed through them, scanning each one carefully, and I tried not to appear nosy, not to look over her shoulder as she did so. It seemed that she couldn't find what she wanted though, and after some tense minutes I asked, 'Can you not find it?'

'Can you help me?' she asked. And suddenly, and with a rush of embarrassment at my insensitivity, I realised why she had been so slow and uncertain in her scanning of each dirty form and certificate: Hatemja couldn't read.

But if she was functionally illiterate, then in this case so was I. Yes, I could decipher the handwriting and the letters, and spot the names of members of her family on the different documents. I could understand the Albanian too, but I knew nothing of the system – the difference between a *fletëlëshim* and a *fletëudhëzim* (a 'release sheet' and an 'order sheet') – as I had never been ill in Albanian. And I had no medical background to know whether it was good or bad news contained in the blood pressure figures or the measures of micrograms per millilitre of various substances that should or should not have been present in Hatemja's son's urine and blood. I asked why some of the test results were priced, as I'd understood that the Kosovo health system was free to people on social welfare (and there was the social card as proof that Hatemja's family should qualify). 'The machines at the hospital were broken,' she explained – 'so unless we were willing to wait for them to be fixed, we had to do it privately.'

I leafed through the documents, asking for explanations, some of which Hatemja was able to give me, but in some cases she was as confused as I was – or more so. At least I knew what haemoglobin was (I tried to explain about iron, remembering biology teachers, and gesturing to the old bits of railings which were propped in Hatemja's front yard, but she looked sceptical that any of this could be circulating in the fine tubes of her son's blood vessels). As I rummaged through the pile I felt the terrible violation of the privacy of this family, as I scanned all their administrative secrets – information that they themselves couldn't read – and spied on their naked bodies.

One of the few useful bits of information I did learn from the stack of documents was that the boy was called Ramadan, named for the month of fasting that's one of the five pillars of

Islam. Looking at his skinny frame I wished he'd been named for something with more calories in it.

As Ramadan clung to his mother's skirts, she and I stood frowning and bewildered over the papers that were trying to describe his little body to us in a language neither of us could properly understand. I seized on another piece of information that was on the papers – the stamp of a surgeon at Prishtina hospital who seemed to have done some skin grafts on Ramadan. Hatemja confirmed the surgery, pulling the boy's trousers down again, and describing more slowly the twin damage done by boiling water – a pan of macaroni he'd pulled over himself – and the messy patchwork of transplanted skin. As she talked, Ramadan glared silently up at me as I guessed he had learned to look at the many people who tried to read the history he now carried with him across his spindly thighs, his painful groin, the gleaming sticks of legs covered with new skin. I felt I was adding to the terrifying indignity of that scalding splash, the wave of pasta and pain that had unexpectedly washed over him, with a new indignity as I stared at where his mother gently traced what seemed to be botched surgery that had left a concave pouch tucked into his groin, painful when he walked, because of how it pulled at every step.

On the surgeon's stamp was a name and a mobile phone number, and with Hatemja's permission, I called it. Awkwardly, I tried to explain who I was. 'An Englishwoman,' I began – as if that explained it. 'A friend of Hatemja's,' I went on, and I saw Hatemja smile as I said it, though it wasn't really true. 'I just want to help Ramadan …' I ended, but the doctor didn't quibble. Perhaps the punishing fees and costs of Kosovo's health system meant that he was used to strangers getting in touch and offering to support members of this community. He agreed to Hatemja and I meeting him at the hospital. 'Come early in the morning,' he said.

I asked Hatemja whether she had a car, and she looked at me pityingly. 'I don't even have a proper house.' No, she didn't have a car.

Although I did have a proper house, I didn't have a car either, so I suggested that I'd come to Fushë Kosovë by taxi and then we could travel to Prishtina together to the hospital. 'Would ten o'clock suit you?' I asked Hatemja, but she shook her head.

'We have to be there early, like the doctor said,' she explained. 'It opens at eight o'clock and he'll have packed up and gone to his private surgery if we don't get there early.'

So we arrived in good time. At the hospital gates we left the taxi (no point in paying the fee for cars to enter – I was feeling enough ill-will already toward the Kosovan health system) and Hatemja showed me the way to the surgical hut within the huge hospital compound. She was in charge here, and once we got inside the low crowded hut where the doctor had his room, it was she who shouldered through the people massed in the corridor, towards the door with the right number on it.

It seemed that all the people were waiting for the same doctor, but Hatemja knocked at the door anyway. There was no answer so she opened it. Inside was a doctor, his patient half-dressed and being examined, and a nurse. None of them seemed bothered by the interruption, and I felt a little less bad at having violated Hatemja's family's privacy with my rifling through their papers when I'd visited her; it seemed that there were different expectations of patient confidentiality here. The doctor recognised Hatemja and worked out who I was. 'Wait outside and the nurse will call you in,' he said, and returned to scrutiny of the exposed back of the burns victim he was attending to.

We spent an hour outside, with Hatemja constantly shouldering forward to ensure we were near the front of the scarred crowd of patients crowding outside the door. Her name in Arabic means 'determined' and her persistence, combined with my obvious foreignness, finally got us to see the doctor. He explained that the three hundred euros Hatemja had mentioned had been for some kind of net bodystocking to cover Ramadan's burns and keep air circulating to them while they were still new. The time for that had now passed, he said, but what was needed was a special cream – he wrote the name down on a scrap of paper – which should be used to massage Ramadan's scar tissue every morning and evening, to keep it supple, stop it hurting so much when it pulled, and prepare him for further surgery sometime in the future.

We left the doctor and went immediately to a pharmacy nearby where I bought a tube of the precious salve for nine euros. Placing it in Hatemja's hands I felt a return of the uncomplicated feel-good pheromone which had been crowded out by all the over-thinking since my phonecall to Mary, the rummaging through documents, and the complications of transport. I had a smug sense of having done the right thing, and having helped little Ramadan most appropriately without even having had to spend three hundred euros. And now the problem was solved, for a thirtieth of the original budget – it was a weird kind of charity bargain.

I gave Hatemja my phone number and said she should let me know when the tube of cream was used up. I paid in advance for a taxi to take her and Ramadan back to Fushë Kosovë, and sent her off with greetings to her husband to parry the repeated thanks from her. The problem was solved, her taxi set off, and I turned and walked away.

Photo: Arber Jashari

3 The pink trainers

'How are you? How is your husband? Your health? Thanks to God!'

It was about ten days after our trip to the hospital and I'd had a notification on my mobile of a missed call from a number I didn't recognise. When I'd called back, the phone had been answered by Hatemja and we were now parrying the approved Kosovan greetings and responses.

The cream was finished, she said. I was pleased to hear she'd been using it; I had wondered occasionally about her and her son, and had a new tug of compassion to think of the tight patch where Ramadan pulled at the surgery with every step, hoping it was now more comfortable.

'So I'll come round with some more,' I offered.

I bought the tube in Prishtina and took a taxi out to Fushë Kosovë again. The economics of this didn't make sense since the cream cost nine euros and the return taxi fare was ten. But I thought about the three hundred euros I could have handed over if I'd gone for the easy way of trying to help Ramadan. It would have been wasted money – at least as far as helping his burns. No doubt it would have been put towards something else for the family – Hatemja had told me how much she got in social welfare payments: a total of 75 euros per month.

When I arrived at their house she came out to greet me with a man I presumed was her husband Agron, and Ramadan ran towards me too in his lopsided way. He stopped short of speaking to me, hiding again in his mother's skirts as soon as we were face-to-face, but it was a nice welcome. Agron shook my hand and introduced himself. Hatemja kissed me, and I gave her the cream. She brushed it away for a moment, 'Come in.'

I didn't really have time, but I was curious to see the home of this family whose path had so randomly crossed with mine. So I went in, picking my way as I'd seen Hatemja doing on my first visit, past the outhouse, through the puddles, past the wheelbarrow of scrap metal to sell that Agron had obviously been out collecting from the bins that morning, and to a doorway giving onto a dark room.

I kicked off my boots; they were the fancy red and gold ones I'd bought in Istanbul and they sat glowing on the doorstep alongside the muddy, shitty, down-at-heel footwear that the rest of the family had scuffed off as they entered the house.

Hatemja apologised that there was no light as they'd had a power cut, and there was very little natural light either as the one window looked out across a narrow alleyway to the blank brick wall of the house next door. But it was possible to make out the people in the room – a baby and two young boys – and I smiled at them, peering curiously through the gloom to see beyond the room into the rest of the house.

There was no other part to Hatemja's home.

On Hatemja's invitation I sat down with her and Agron on the sponge mattresses against two of the walls. We exchanged more ritual questions and then I tentatively asked where … well, where the rest of their house was. No, they confirmed, there was no other space – just this room, that I judged to be two metres by two metres. So, umm, where did they sleep? Agron looked at me as if it was a stupid question – 'here'. There were seven of them – the two parents, Ramadan, the baby Elhame, the two boys aged six and seven, and an older girl, aged nine, who wasn't at home at the moment. I tried to imagine them laid out together in the darkness. They would just about fit. I tried to imagine what married life for Hatemja was like, and felt again that my concerns for privacy from my previous visit were bourgeois and irrelevant in the realities of this life.

The boys were messing around while we chatted, and their little sister, just old enough to stand, was tumbling around with them. They were less than a metre – less than a body-length – from the wood stove which was heating the room to a cosy fug, and where the family presumably did their cooking too. Ramadan's injuries suddenly made more sense – not a freak accident, not deliberate maiming by a professional beggar mother (yes, I felt ashamed of myself now for having thought it), but the natural consequence of overcrowding. Ramadan had been burned by poverty; I winced again at his injuries.

Agron was nodding vigorously at everything I said, smiling approvingly as Hatemja showed me off a little, like a curiosity she had brought to contribute to the family's well-being. I imagined Agron might have a similar approach to something unusual or potentially valuable that he found in the rubbish while looking for recyclable scrap. Hatemja presented the key facts about me – 'She speaks Albanian. She's married, and her husband's English too. They rent a house in Prishtina. They don't have children.'

In exchange, Agron gave his own CV. He'd been born in Fushë Kosovë, in this house. But in those days – before the argument with his mother (the lady with the alarmingly hennaed hair whom I'd seen on the first visit) – the whole building had been shared between him and his parents and his two brothers. Now the doorway between rooms had been boarded up, and they had a separate entrance.

He'd been to school – as he told me this, he got up and reached for a nail hammered into the wall. There was a familiar plastic bag hanging from it which I recognised as Hatemja's filing system that we'd rummaged through together standing outside their house on my first visit. Agron went through it with more confidence – the security of someone who'd been to school and could understand what was written on each sheet. It wasn't long before he found the piece he wanted – a certificate showing his school grades. They weren't bad and I complimented him on them. 'I'm a teacher by profession,' I told him, and he beamed.

'Education is the most important thing,' he said, and of course I nodded. 'Without education you're nothing.' Hatemja looked wistful at his side.

I turned to his boys. 'So what class are you in?' I asked, in my teacher's voice.

'We don't go to school,' the eldest of them replied.

It was an awkward moment. It seemed to show their father up as a liar and a hypocrite. It was a terrible tragedy for the kids themselves. They knew I was a teacher, and I wondered what I should say; wondered what I was expected to say.

I realised it would probably be better to say nothing. There must be reasons, and what I said wouldn't change anything. It wasn't for me to meddle; it was for me to be respectful of other people's culture and priorities. I've been a vegetarian almost all my life and I've got used to the same situation at dinner parties – if other people are eating meat, it's not for me to wave slaughterhouse images or ecological facts at them while they're enjoying their meal. I should keep silent.

I kept silent for about a minute.

'But …' I said, turning to Agron. 'You just said education was the most important thing … do you not want your children to go to school?'

His answer surprised me – I had expected defensiveness or quibbling, but he replied simply, 'Of course I want them to go to school. What father would not want their children to go to school?'

I didn't understand.

'But…?' I said again. Oh, what the hell,

'So why are they not at school?'

Agron gestured at the boys with the same look, of pointing out the bleeding obvious, that he had had when I asked about the rest of their house, and that Hatemja had used when I'd asked whether she had a car.

'They don't have shoes.'

I looked at the boys. It was true of course that they weren't wearing shoes, but we were in the house (indeed sitting on the same blanket where I could see a half-eaten loaf) so I assumed that was why they were barefoot, and that their shoes were outside the door like mine.

But perhaps this was just an excuse?

'Are you really saying that if the boys had shoes they would go to school?'

Hatemja nodded enthusiastically, and Agron too.

'Yes, shoes – and maybe some decent clothes. They couldn't go to school wearing those dirty trousers.'

Was this an elaborate ruse for the sake of some footwear for their sons? If it was, they were pretty desperate. But then Rrahmon had told me that this family was the most in need.

And what if it were true; what if all that stood between these kids and access to education was a quick trip to the shops?

I was still dubious, so it was with rather less grace than I would have liked, that I offered, 'OK then – we'll go now and buy them some.'

There was a pause and I looked carefully at Hatemja; was this reluctance? No, I realised; it was disbelief.

I got up, and she came with me. We walked together out of the Ashkali neighbourhood to the nearest shop that I'd seen selling shoes. There was a large basket full of trainers which seemed practical enough, so I pulled out a couple of pairs.

'What about these?' There was a blue pair and a purple pair. Hatemja took them from me and held them in her hand, massaging them as if they were her first-born son's feet.

'No,' she said, 'the purple ones are too small.'

OK then, the blue ones?

'But there's only one pair of blue ones.' She pulled out a couple of pink pairs. 'How about these?' she asked.

Really? Sending a pair of lads to join the local school in pink trainers? Thinking back to my time teaching in London it seemed an unlikely way to help them fit in; a guarantee of them being teased.

'It's the only one of the colours here that has two pairs the right size. I want them to have matching trainers so that everyone knows these were bought new, and not found in the bins.'

I realised then that there were more ways for children to be teased than I had imagined.

We bought new pink trainers for both Vehbi and Labinot, and some tracksuit trousers for each of them too. And then I said I needed to be getting back to Prishtina. I handed over the bulging bag with our purchases to Hatemja and said goodbye.

'But,' I added, about as ungenerously as it was possible to be, 'I'll be back. I'll come and see you in a month and check that the boys are in school – this isn't a gift; it's a deal.'

Labinot

4 Missing the train

A month later, my taxi pulled up at Hatemja's house. The oldest boy, Vehbi, was outside, playing with some of the neighbours' children, digging in the grey mud with sticks. He was wearing pink trainers. He looked up as the car pulled in and his face lit up with recognition. Then he ran off inside.

It wasn't an auspicious welcome, and I felt the return of the doubts that had been niggling me after my impulsive shopping trip with Hatemja. I guessed that Vehbi had rushed off just now out of shame, remembering the terms of the deal I'd left him with. Those boys weren't going to be tramping in their trainers to school every day – they were just going to be getting them muddy while they dug pointless holes in the front yard. It seemed like a metaphor. And I felt like a fool – of course it wasn't so easy to get two kids to school in the face of a whole community's culture and tradition.

But then Vehbi was back, tugging his mother out of the house and presenting me as if he was responsible for my arrival. His brother, Labinot, was there too, scuffing on his own pair of pink trainers as he came out of the house. Hatemja was beaming with baby Elhame in her arms, and Agron was a step behind her.

I smiled at Hatemja first, but it was to Agron that I addressed myself when I was out of the cab – we all knew how this was supposed to work, with the head of household standing before his guest.

I was impatient to follow up on the deal, but of course Agron was asking me how I was, how my health was, and I nodded the correct responses to the questions. They praised God that all was well; I did the same on hearing that their family was healthy.... And then there was a pause. I nodded to Vehbi and Labinot. 'How come they're not at school?' A nasty tone of accusation whined round the edge of the sentence; this was not a neutral question. Speeches (of persuasion, recrimination) were already beginning to form in my head.

'They've been today already,' said Hatemja with a smile, gesturing at her son, and I let out a small 'oh!' of joy, relief and apology for my doubts. I looked down and saw what Vehbi was holding in his hand: an exercise book rolled into a tight tube – like a telescope, or a weapon. The cover was scuffed as if it had been frequently rolled and unrolled and when he passed it to me it sat still half-coiled in my palm. It was a small spring, ready to launch.

I opened it up. The first page was covered in repeated ragged tracings of the number one. The next page was all twos. It went on, interspersed with letters, just as uncertain; just as extraordinary.

Vehbi had a new way of making sense of the world, putting things in the right order. He'd be able to scramble this new code in particular ways to tell people how he felt; or unscramble it to understand what other people wanted to tell him – not just people he knew, but people he would never meet; people on the other side of the world. He'd know the destinations of the buses he boarded, the promises of the politicians he voted for. He would be able to read Facebook and Tennyson, he could google the answers to questions that his neighbours or his parents wouldn't be able to tell him; he could decipher holy books. It was with these letters that Vehbi could now form that I'd learned to define myself, mark myself present; that I'd read the reasons to become a vegetarian, decided that I was an atheist. And for all the broken dreams

and ideas the letters had talked me through, they had left me
one powerful belief: in the might of that alphabet. I was one
of the people of the book, and I looked at Vehbi now with
all the zeal of an evangelist. As I got him parroting 'g – g – g'
while he traced the letters on a recent page, it felt like a lump
in my throat.

Labinot was chivvied indoors, and soon he reappeared too
with his own curled up notebook. I cooed congratulations
over the same grubby pages of serried digits, marching over
the paper like the footprints of some magic trainer.

photo credit: Janet Young

Agron and Hatemja were beaming at my praise and I asked
the parents more about how the boys were doing at school
and Agron explained. They weren't actually in school, because
he said they'd discovered the school would only accept
children in September (by now it was December). He talked
about it as if school was a train which set off once a year, and

if you weren't at the station with your ticket on 1 September you had to wait until the following year. It seemed a ludicrous system, and I made a note to check whether he'd understood correctly. But the boys were going every day to the Balkan Sunflowers Learning Centre, which meant that they would be helped into school in September. For now, this was all they could get. It didn't sound ideal, but Agron had definitely kept his part of the bargain. I wondered whether they'd attended regularly, and thought back to the pencil marks on the pages of the boys' notebooks – as far as I could see there had been no gaps in the alphabet they'd copied out day by day.

I gave Hatemja some more cream for Ramadan, and told the boys again how proud I was of them, and left, heading towards Rrahmon's Centre.

He was busy again, but I caught him in the corridor and asked about Agron's boys.

'Yes, yes, they've been coming every day,' he confirmed.

Excellent. 'And could they start in school now?'

'No, because they weren't there for the first of September. They can start in September next year. They'll only have missed one year.'

It was true – I'd read that the school system in Kosovo begins with a pre-primary class at age six, and the first grade for children aged seven, so the boys weren't as far behind their peers as they would have been in the British system.

'But a year is a lot to catch up!'

'Welcome to Kosovo!' said one of the women working in the Centre, who had stopped and heard our conversation.

She was being sarcastic of course. She was telling me not to be naïve: that this is how things are done here; that I should get used to it. It was my cue to leave; I thanked Rrahmon for his time, wished him the traditional farewell of 'propitious work' and set off home.

A few weeks later I got another abruptly terminated call from someone who turned out, when I rang back, to be Hatemja. She never had enough credit on her phone to call me, and the numbers she phoned from were always changing. It was part of the fragile, fluid infrastructure of a life lived off the rubbish bins and the second-hand market stalls. She said that the cream had run out again, and I said I'd come round with some more in the next few days.

In fact this time it wouldn't be me buying the cream — I had told a friend of mine, Lesley, about Ramadan and his family and she'd given me some money for the next time they needed the burns cream. I went into the nearest pharmacy in Prishtina to use her money, and they gave me the slim tube. Since it was her money I felt I needed to be responsible about proof of spending it, and I asked the pharmacist if I could have a receipt. It wasn't usual to get a receipt for purchases in small shops and she looked awkward when I asked. I understood that the till was probably not working. 'Don't worry — just a written receipt will be fine,' I said.

'For this?' she asked.

'Yes, for the cream I've just bought,' I repeated — wondering whether my Albanian was suddenly letting me down.

'I can give you a receipt for nine euros,' she said carefully.

'Yes, for the cream I've just bought,' I insisted, slightly grumpily now.

'Can I write it down as something else?' she asked. And then she explained. The cream I'd been buying for Ramadan on the prescription of the public hospital doctor, and from various different pharmacies, was in fact contraband. It wasn't on the list of medicines allowed for import so the pharmacy was selling it 'on the grey'. So if I wanted to prove my honesty to Lesley, I would have, instead, to prove my dishonesty.

The pharmacist wrote out a fictional receipt of aspirins, cough medicine and a packet of plasters, all imports licensed by the Ministry, and coming to nine euros. I thanked her, and screwed up the useless bit of paper in my pocket.

My visits to Hatemja and her family continued every few weeks, depending on the speed with which little Ramadan's body was anointed with the precious smuggled cream. I guessed the intervals must be getting infinitesimally smaller, as he grew and the amount of cream needed to massage him increased each day.

Now, it was automatically assumed that I would come into the house when I delivered the cream. I would sit on the sponge mattresses, and chat with the kids. I was teaching Elhame the 'round and round the garden' action song, and the other children a clapping game which they got better at each time I visited. I had started to look forward to the visits to this happy family. They were attentive hosts, working hard at friendship – learning my family structure (just one sister and no brothers? They were pitying of such a small family), asking after Rob by name, noticing if I had a cold – the tiny courtesies and connections that can bind people together.

In my turn, it was a treat to sit in a home so filled with love, despite the grim physical conditions in which it thrived. The older children were always holding the younger ones, lugging them around, playing with them, laughing at their silly mistakes, exultant at their triumphs ('Mum, Elhame took a step!'). The parents, too, were always holding one child or another, casually stroking or kissing or playing with them, and I was invited to do the same.

I was happy in my childlessness – it was a decision Rob and I had come to years before, and had never regretted. We loved our home as a haven for the two of us; we loved each other uninterrupted by night-time feeds, ballet classes, decisions about school catchment areas, squabbling and all the things we saw dominating the lives of our friends who'd had children. We were perhaps selfish in our self-sufficiency, but it gave us the solid base to go out from, full of energy, to other activities – which in my case had always, from the age of twenty, included daily professional work with kids. But that had come to an end just a few months previously when the work I was doing at a school in Kosovo had finished. I was busy with other consultancy work, writing training materials for headteachers, editing reports on projects against child trafficking, training people to be evaluators of kindergarten development projects … a range of fascinating stuff that gave me none of the day-to-day thrill of 'Mum, Elhame took a step'. So I would sit happily in Hatemja's home watching the children grow, checking Vehbi and Labinot's homework (rejoicing that Vehbi now did know how many fingers '5' was), learning about the lives in this unknown community, meeting neighbours as they stuck their heads round the door (were they coming to peer at me, or really 'just to ask …'?), and eventually handing over the little tube of cream that was my ticket to being a part of these lives for half an hour.

It was only after four or five visits that I finally met Hatemja's eldest child, Gjelane. On that first visit she'd been staying with her grandmother out of town, and at other times when I'd come round she'd been out playing with all the freedom of a nine year-old in a closed community of watchful neighbours. But on one winter's day when I brought a new tube of cream for Ramadan she was at home. She greeted me shyly but she had a smile and a watchfulness that blossomed into chattiness within a few minutes.

Perhaps it shows how the deputy headteacher had been buried in me, but it was only when presented with Gjelane physically in front of me that I realised how absent she had been from all my earlier conversations about schooling. Her education had never been mentioned, either by me or her parents, and it was with a sinking feeling that I asked brightly,

'So, do you go to school?'

No.

I felt terribly sad. I felt terribly guilty. I was frustrated – with everyone who should have been there ensuring that nine year-olds are in school. With her parents, with Rrahmon, ('welcome to Kosovo'), with the education system. With myself.

I could hear the edge in my voice when I asked Agron, 'Why isn't she at school?'

He knew me well enough now that he could hear it too. And he must have known me well enough to know that there couldn't be an excuse – if she didn't have shoes then he knew I'd have bought them ….

'It's too late,' he said.

'What do you mean? She's only nine!' Through my head there raced the words of the United Nations Declaration of the Rights of the Child, the Kosovo Constitution, common sense….

'The school says that if you don't register within two years of when you should have started then you're too late, unless you can pass a test. Gjelane won't be able to pass that test because she hasn't been to school. It's too late,' Agron repeated.

I looked at Gjelane. There was something like regret in her eyes, but no anger, no fighting. Welcome to Kosovo.

I was suspicious, 'Do you actually want to go to school?'

Her face broke into a smile, 'Yes.'

If it was a bluff I was going to call it.

Gjelane

5 The Ministry official's birthday

I checked Gjelane's birth certificate – she was indeed nine years old. I checked with her parents that she had never started school, checked with Gjelane herself whether she knew any of her basic letters – even the pages of copied symbols that made up Vehbi and Labinot's learning? No.

Then I went to see Rrahmon. To my surprise he confirmed that what Agron had said about Gjelane being too late to go to school was indeed true. I asked whether he knew what this test was that Gjelane would have to pass to be accepted at this stage, and he said that there was no fixed syllabus for the test – it was at the discretion of the teacher. He then said that as a special favour he could include Gjelane in a 'women's literacy' class that was run at their Centre. The curriculum wouldn't be entirely appropriate for her, though, he warned, as it was designed for young women and included information on sexual health and parenting, and she might have to leave the class for some lessons.

I imagined Gjelane scrabbling for details of the alphabet in between information on contraception. It was better than nothing, so I spoke to Agron and Hatemja and they agreed that Gjelane should start there. Meanwhile, I decided there must be a misunderstanding somewhere, when a nine year-old girl who wanted to go to school was told she was too late. I went to meet with the director of the local primary school.

I'd been to the school before to meet him when I was working with an organisation on an integrated schools programme. I knew the dehumanisingly huge building where 1500 children attended classes each day. Walking through the yard I was prepared for the scowl of the caretaker at the door – it was the same scowl I'd had from every caretaker at every school I'd visited in Kosovo. School front doors were, like prisons, habitually locked from the inside, requiring an elderly man or woman in overalls to stand there all day with a bunch of keys. They wouldn't open up to talk to you about the reason for your visit, so you had to shout at the glass until your persistence or your miming impressed them enough to wearily sort through the keys on their piece of string and unlock for you.

The caretaker took me along the empty corridors to the director's office and knocked for me at the door.

Inside sat the director. Above him was the obligatory picture of Scanderbeg, the Albanians' national hero from the fourteenth century. On another wall was a picture of Adem Jashari, a more recent Albanian hero who was killed, along with almost all of his extended family, defending his compound in Kosovo against Serb forces in 1998.

A picture of the Albanian flag hung above a rubber plant; this was a patriotic office and it seemed awkward to remind the director that we'd met as part of a project for the inclusion of Roma and Ashkali children along with Albanians in Kosovo's mainstream education. He recognised me, though, and I was offered tea. I guessed that he thought my coming marked the beginning of a project, that I was the harbinger of cash or – better still, and what every Kosovar involved in a foreign-led project apparently most prizes – a study trip abroad.

I explained that I was here about a little girl aged nine who wanted to go to school, and his enthusiasm dimmed a little. His answer was immediate.

'She's too late.'

This time, thinking that the director might understand better than Agron – indeed, knowing that he'd attended training days focused on this kind of thing – I quoted the United Nations Convention on the Rights of the Child, the Kosovan constitution.

'Only if she can pass the test'.

And how could she pass the test if she wasn't allowed in school? It was like only allowing someone into hospital if they could prove they were healthy. The director shrugged and I screamed a little more inside, at the Kafkaesque conversation.

And the syllabus for the test?

No, the director couldn't say.

There must, surely, be some misunderstanding. The director was nodding vehemently; I could tell that he was saying what he honestly believed to be true, but Kosovo by this stage had been under UN administration for nearly twelve years. Countries all over the world had contributed aid efforts to rebuilding its education system, and drafting beautifully-crafted laws to the highest European standards. The implementation of the laws was often a mess, but surely there could be no legal basis for saying that Gjelane was too late to go to school.

I would have to ask someone else. Through contact with a Kosovan education expert with whom I was working on an EU project, I got the name of the official at the Ministry of Education responsible for children out of school. It was a Friday when I turned up at the Ministry. It's a new, purpose-built construction which I had watched go from brownfield to this impressive glassy block. I climbed the stairs high into the building until I was on the floor where I'd been told the relevant official sat. Slightly breathlessly, I knocked on her door.

I introduced myself and mentioned the name of the person who had given me her name. She greeted me politely and said she didn't have very much time right now as she'd be going home soon. I checked my watch – it was two o'clock.

'It's my birthday,' she smiled, as if this explained it.

'Well, happy birthday,' I offered, and started talking very fast about Gjelane. As I did so, the Ministry official put her coat on.

'I'm really sorry, but I'm going to have to go – you'll understand; it's Friday afternoon and I'm going out to celebrate my birthday.'

'Er, yes, I understand' (no I didn't; there was so much I didn't understand) 'but could you just help me as there seems to have been some misunderstanding – this nine year-old girl wants to go to school but the director says she's too late.'

The official nodded. 'Yes, she's too late; more than two years older than the age she should have registered. That makes children just too difficult to teach'. I imagined I could hear the sound of a train pulling out of a station far away.

'So what are the options for a nine year-old girl who can't read or write and who wants to go to school?' I asked the Ministry official. She looked at me and shrugged. She was by the door now with her coat on and her bag in her hand.

'I'm sorry …' she said.

I mumbled something, though I don't know what – the correct response to a Ministry official apologising that she has to go home at two o'clock because it's her birthday, but not apologising for the fact that the nine year-olds in her country who want to go to school are considered too late.

As we parted ways at the end of the corridor, I muttered insincerely the standard Albanian birthday greeting, *'ju bëftë edhe një qind'* – 'may you have one hundred more'. The other Albanian birthday tradition is to twist the person's ear as many times as they have lived years. It was tempting.

The next time I went to take Ramadan's cream to Hatemja, I took with me my friend Zsofia. She is Hungarian, brought to Kosovo by her husband's job with the EU, and studying for a Masters in International Development at the same time. We'd had a coffee and croissant at Prishtina's excellent French bakery the week before, picking with our forks at smart pastries while I told her about my emerging friendship with the family in Fushë Kosovë. I told her, too, about their desperate poverty – the family's tiny, dark and dirty home, Agron's daily rooting through the bins for stuff he could sell on or that the family could eat. She was the mother of two young children and suggested she could bring the family some of the things her kids had grown out of. She drove me out to Fushë Kosovë.

The children playing outside worked as the usual early warning system, skittering back into the house so that by the time we were out of the car, the family was assembled to greet us. The smiles were even bigger than usual – the Kosovo tradition is that it is genuinely the guest who does honour to their host by their visit, and this time I had done double the honour as a guest by bringing my own guest with me. I did the introductions and Zsofia bent immediately to Elhame, who was wriggling in Hatemja's arms. Elhame was close in age to Zsofia's own daughter, though the difference in their nutrition had already started to show in Salome's sturdy bones, the iron that bloomed in her cheeks, her glossy, protein-enriched hair. Holding the image of her in my mind

I realised just how ragged Hatemja's child was, saw the two girls' paths diverging already, along routes I could imagine the end of, as Salome travelled, studied, made choices, while Elhame learned – late – to walk the muddy paths of Fushë Kosovë.

We were excitedly being ushered inside, where Zsofia was asked about her family, her age, her health, and I translated where Zsofia's Albanian failed. For the first time in all my visits there, Hatemja asked if we wanted tea. She had some boiling on the stove in one of the Turkish 'xhugyms' like a figure of eight, with a stout round pot on the bottom for hot water, and a smaller vessel on top filled with strong tea. She served us in small glasses, using the hot water to make it the strength we each preferred.

But she was sorry, she had no sugar. They were waiting for Agron to come back with some money.... We assured her that it was no problem, that we preferred our tea like this, but she wouldn't believe us. She held a whispered discussion with Gjelane who went out and reappeared a few minutes later with sugar from a neighbour. A sickly mound of largesse was poured into each of our glasses and we stirred it in with tiny spoons making bell-like noises as we talked.

Zsofia was asking Hatemja about her children – their ages, and health; whether they had been inoculated. Hatemja wasn't sure – some of them, yes.

Zsofia turned to me, 'It's really important, you know. It could be the biggest way to change the lives of these children, saving them from those diseases. Can you ask which vaccinations they've had?'

I squirmed a little. It seemed too intrusive, as we sat drinking tea in Hatemja's home. But Zsofia leaned to Hatemja, one mother to another, and talked straight to her in English that Hatemja couldn't understand. She was telling her how important the jabs were – how they needed to happen at the right time, how there was a need not just for one but for repeated injections…. Hatemja should have a booklet where they were all recorded, she said.

They both turned to me for translation, so I obediently repeated in Albanian what Zsofia had said. Hatemja went to the nail in the wall and pulled down the now familiar plastic bag of papers. She found the vaccination booklets for each child, and Zsofia started scanning them with an expert eye. I helped with translation of some of the words but Zsofia was shaking her head. Elhame (by this time on Zsofia's lap) had missed some of her most important jabs, she said.

And she was curious about why one of the boys hadn't had the jabs he should have received in hospital when he was born. She asked me to translate the question to Hatemja, who explained: the oldest boy had been born at home. We looked around us – at the small dark space without any source of water inside, and outside only the standpipe which froze over during winter. 'Home birth' had conjured up cosy middle-class visions of a doula and your choice of classical music; here it meant a baby brought into the world in the cold and the mud of Agron's boots, and the afterbirth spilling onto the blankets where the family would later curl up together to sleep.

And as we could see, home births also meant less chance of the baby getting the first vaccinations that are given as routine in the hospital, and no automatic birth registration…. Hatemja confirmed that Vehbi didn't have a birth certificate.

While we were talking, someone came in. I guessed it was the neighbour who'd lent Gjelane the sugar for us. She squatted by the doorway and listened in on our conversation.

Zsofia was suggesting to Hatemja that we could take the children to the doctor to catch up on their jabs. We discussed what day would be possible, the importance of the vaccinations, how we could all fit in her car … and then the neighbour interrupted, 'Could my kids come too? They haven't had their vaccinations.'

'Have lots of children missed vaccinations round here?' asked Zsofia.

The women nodded, and I could see Zsofia was coming up with a plan.

6 'You do both'

Now I had headlice. I had felt I needed to tell Zsofia at the
beginning of our meeting, but now I could see that she was
squirming and a little revolted by me. I could see running
through her head if not the little feet of small blood-sucking
bugs, at least the words of her mother about dirty children
and not going to their part of town. The battle between those
words and her international development studies and her
huge heart – the hug with which she'd immediately wrapped
up Hatemja's children – was almost visible as she held back at
one moment, holding her head at more than insect-jumping
distance from mine, and then leant in seconds later to engage
with excited hand gestures in the discussion of what we could
do about vaccinations. With us were Jeta, a young Kosovo
Albanian ecologist whom I'd met when she had volunteered
to support the environmental summer camp, and Laura, a
British student volunteering for a few months as part of her
gap year. She'd come out to Kosovo because her father was
working here, and she was a small bundle of no-nonsense
energy. Whether it was about nits or poverty, she made me feel
old with her impatience and her suggestions for immediate
action.

We told her about the visit to Hatemja's house and the need
to organise vaccinations.

'Well we obviously can't just stop at these two families,' she
said. 'It's clearly a bigger problem. We need to help them all.'

'But....'

But we knew nothing about vaccinations, apart from what
Zsofia was learning on her course. It had nothing to do with

ecology or education – the things that between us we were specialised in.

'So,' Laura went on, 'we need to go to all the houses and find out what vaccinations each child has had. We should create a form where we can just tick the appropriate columns ...' she started sketching on a piece of paper. 'Name, surname, age ...'

'We could use the form to write down whether the school-age children are registered in school, too,' someone suggested. We added columns on Laura's piece of paper.

By the end of the meeting we had a plan – Laura and Jeta and I would spend an afternoon with Agron going to the houses of his immediate neighbours in the *mahalla* to collect some information about children who hadn't been vaccinated.

'Do you think he'll be able to help us?' Zsofia asked. 'He would normally be out with his wheelbarrow collecting scrap metal.'

We all thought of the children waiting for Agron's return with whatever he'd salvaged from the scrap; thought of Hatemja not having sugar until he brought in the euros he'd earned that day, and knew it wasn't fair to ask Agron to give up his time. Volunteering was a luxury, like sugar.

And we thought of the little group of us standing in the muddy lanes of Fushë Kosovë looking for unvaccinated children without a guide – it would never work.

'We could pay him?'

I had only a vague sense of the economics of Fushë Kosovë but I'd heard that a casual labourer was paid a minimum of ten euros a day. What if we paid Agron by results – a euro for every family whose details we could fill in on our form? We could get through more than ten in a day, so he'd make some extra money. And I could afford ten euros, or even double

Agron

that. I called Agron and he agreed. He seemed proud at the idea of being our guide in his community. 'And I know how to write,' he reminded me.

The next day the temperatures were sub-zero – hard weather for fieldwork. But even harder weather for going through garbage bins, I thought to myself, and as I got dressed, putting on extra layers, I wondered whether Agron was dressing with the same thing in mind.

At the first house our little research team visited, Agron, Jeta, Laura and I were met with bemusement and I saw the strange party we made – the pretty young Kosovan ecologist, the British student, Agron, and the older foreign lady with her strange unidiomatic Albanian. Nevertheless, we were welcomed in, out of the cold. I was surprised how warm the house was, in the one room where all the family was gathered. Unlike Hatemja's house where there was only one room, this family had options and I suddenly saw the strategy and the sense in having lots of children – if you gathered your family round you, and stayed in the same room where all your cooking was done, you could generate a meaty fug of blood heat. So when people here pitied my parents for our small family, they didn't just mean 'you must be poor' or 'you must be lonely', they were having an instinctive response, 'you must be cold in winter.'

Beyond the warmth of this one room, though, I saw that the house was in bad shape. It could have been over sixty years old, and in the hallway where we'd come in there was a gap in the ceiling through which you could see the sky. Chickens came in with us through the front door; the limits between 'in' and 'out', 'wild' and 'tame' were blurred here. Looking at the children, I realised the same could be said for some of them.

We went through our form: there were five children and we were told that some of them had been vaccinated. With Zsofia's example before us, we asked tentatively to see the vaccination card. In fact, only one child was up-to-date with all his jabs.

And school? No.

What, none of the children? Four of them were of school-age. 'Do you go to Rrahmon's Centre?' I asked. No.

'Would you like to go to school?' Yes, they said, faces animated with grins of excitement, as if at an undreamed-of adventure, and eyes wide at the boldness of the idea. Their parents nodded too.

I thought of Vehbi and Labinot and knew it could be true.

After that we split up and went according to Agron's directions to various families. On the way to the next house, we saw Gjelane in the street and she came skipping up to us. She slipped her hand into mine, 'Can I come with you?'

Her fingers were cold and I enfolded them in my gloved hand. Even through the insulating microfibres I could feel the chill of her and I took her hand between mine and chafed it, trying to transfer some of my bloodheat to her.

When we arrived at the next house and had a new form to fill out, Gjelane asked if she could help. I'd just taught her 'E' – the double point of similarity between her name and mine – and we did lopsided teamwork on the form, me taking the other letters and she proudly striping the paper whenever we needed an E. I thought again of the Ministry official telling me that children like Gjelane were 'too hard to teach'.

The day became a blur of families, each group huddled round a stove, each with staring children, bewildered mothers; each seemed to have a bag hung on a nail in the wall which they brought down in answer to our question about vaccinations.

None of them resisted, or questioned our right to be there, our motivation for asking. No-one asked to see ID. I couldn't work out whether this was a sign of the trust we'd built (Agron and Gjelane as our safe conduct passes) or the desperation of the community. I wondered how many other people came by asking these questions – were we the last in a long line, or had these families been entirely ignored by Kosovo's institutions and aid agencies?

I lost track of time and space, needing Gjelane again to help us negotiate the alleys, to distinguish one corrugated metal fence from another. I tried drawing a basic map, looking for points of reference that might endure, but everything seemed temporary, provisional, shifting. The houses were propped up with old bits of metal, flattened oil drums, old car doors. There was no street furniture, and the shops were people's front rooms opened to the street, usually with a lone display of lollipops or a single bright box of crisp packets on a dusty floor scattered with crates of old vegetables.

When we met back up with Jeta and Agron we were all drained. We shuffled from one foot to another to try to keep warm; our movements slowed by low blood sugar and dulled by the multiple layers we were wearing. But more than anything, we were overwhelmed by the information we'd found. Between us, we'd been to 21 houses, gathering information on families. There were huge needs for vaccinations – Zsofia would be happy that we had made these home visits. We discussed whether the vaccination problem could be dealt with in just one trip to the doctors – what if we hired a bus?

But a bus wasn't really the issue here; there was something much bigger that we'd found out that day: more than our questions about vaccinations, it was the answers to the question about education which were scary … out of the 21 houses we'd visited between us we'd found eighteen children in the same situation as Gjelane.

Eighteen children – more than half a class – who were of school age, and didn't go to school (or even to the Balkan Sunflowers Centre), but said that they wanted to. That wasn't including the children we'd met who didn't go to school but told us that they didn't want to. Those children were also a problem to worry about, but a different kind of problem.

There was approximately one child per household, then, who wanted to go to school. I asked Agron how many houses there were in this neighbourhood.

'Including the Ashkali neighbourhood over the railway, about five hundred houses,' he said.

Five hundred children?

Well, Laura reminded me reassuringly, Agron had deliberately taken us to the houses most in need because those were the ones we wanted to target. Maybe the rest of the neighbourhood was better off, and the kids were all in school. Maybe.

We all badly needed to warm up, to eat some chocolate, to take time to think. What had started as a conversation with Hatemja and the idea of helping one family was now looking like a systemic failing. And my response for one family – the little pink trainers, the conversations with the school and the Ministry about one nine year-old – seemed pathetic and hopeless in the face of such a huge problem.

The chocolate helped a bit in building our resilience, but it didn't really change anything. Through the rest of the day the images and the numbers bounced around my head. All those children, kicking around dirty homes, with no chance of a future anywhere different....

But what was bothering me more was my own position. I felt like a doctor must feel at the scene of a car crash – my whole professional life had been developing in me the skills to be able to deal with a situation like this. I was a trained teacher, I spoke Albanian, I knew something about the Kosovan system;

and I had just finished a consultancy contract and had no work on the horizon … there was absolutely nothing to stop me trying to meet this need.

Except a huge and unnameable fear. It was made up of components I could recognise – a fear of failure that was fed by pure vanity; fear of getting it wrong, fed by a more worthy sense of not wanting to let down a group of children; fear of losing my income – because to tackle this issue I would have to turn down consultancy work; though thinking about Hatemja and her kids living on their social welfare of 75 euros a month and whatever Agron could bring back from the bins gave me some healthy perspective on that. This last was compounded by a more subtle fear, since to do this I'd need to live off Rob's salary – maybe my biggest fear was the fear of dependence.

I slept very little that night. And in the morning I said to Rob, 'What if I didn't work for the next six months? That would take us until September, and by then those children should be in the mainstream school.'

'We could do that,' Rob replied.

I love him.

He went to work, and I got on the computer. Zsofia was on Skype and I told her about my disturbed night. I told her my idea – of taking six months to try to solve this problem. But I was still undecided – would it be most useful for me to use that time to teach the children (at the idea my heart leapt – I had been too long away from the classroom; I knew I could do this, and do it well) so they could pass the mythical test. Or was that a kind of cowardice, hiding myself in Fushë Kosovë with children sitting round my skirts (I had an image of the von Trapp family with their pretty Julie Andrews tutor) without making any difference to this ridiculous law that would condemn other children to the same exclusion forever?

In which case, should I use these six months to lobby for a change in the law? I knew lots of people and organisations who should care about this issue – I could spend the time having coffee with opinion-formers and decision-makers, write emails, lobby through the media, kick up a fuss; perhaps that was the best way to get Hatemja's daughter to school. Or was that a different kind of cowardice, sitting sipping tea in Prishtina's cafes while Gjelane and her friends still didn't know the letters of their names.

I asked Zsofia; what did she think?

Her answer was immediate and simple; you do both.

7 Cap in hand

The money I'd paid Agron for those 21 families for whom we now had details was 21 euros I would never notice the lack of. The next few times I went out to dinner with friends at a restaurant I'd go without a dessert, and I'd have made up the cost. It was easy to feel rich – and powerful – in Kosovo's economy.

But I wasn't stupid: if I was really going to stop work for six months in order to try to help Gjelane and her friends into school, I wouldn't have the money I was used to for eating out at restaurants, or even some of the more basic things my consultancy fees covered in our domestic arrangements. And although it wouldn't cost much (back to the image of Julie Andrews – teaching a small group of children round my skirts) we would need to hire a room somewhere in the community. I'd be travelling to Fushë Kosovë each day. We'd need some paper and pens and … actually, I couldn't think of anything else that was likely to be a cost of this project, but my maths was good enough to calculate that it could be tight to provide the rent of a space in Fushë Kosovë if you have no salary.

Laura wouldn't let a little thing like six months' rent get in the way of a good idea. 'People out here have money,' she said. I thought of the little girl I'd seen playing barefoot on the rubbish heap in Fushë Kosovë. Her clothes were too small and pulled up over a swollen belly. Not swollen with big dinners, but with that vile parody of obesity that malnutrition puffs into the poor.

But of course Laura wasn't talking about the people of Fushë Kosovë. She was thinking about her father's colleagues – the large community of ex-pats referred to as 'the Internationals'. It was true that not only was there a large group of such people in Prishtina, but also that they were a good group to ask to be midwives to this project we'd found ourselves unexpectedly gestating. Most of them were working for large institutions – the EU, the UN, governments' bilateral donor organisations – and, like Rob and I, they had come to a post-conflict country with dreams of doing Good.

Many of them did indeed bring Good with them but they were pushing it in Kosovo's direction email by email, one slow round-table meeting at a time. The aid effort targeting Kosovo's sustainable development was a relatively sophisticated but hugely cumbersome enterprise, and most of it took place in air-conditioned offices. Inside each of those offices was someone on an international salary whose mum and friends back home thought they were getting children like the girl on the rubbish heap into school. No mother, no voter, back home wants to hear about the education action plan you wrote; they want to know you're a human rights hero. Laura said this was our chance to give The Internationals an opportunity to be who they really wanted to be; we should invite them to throw down their action plans for an evening, jump out from behind their desks, and round their tables, and bring real physical money to a real, physical problem. She suggested a fundraising evening combined with a clothing drive.

Zsofia offered her beautiful house for the event and we sent out the invitations. Meanwhile, Rob and I went back to Fushë Kosovë to look for a room where a miracle could happen.

Right at the entrance to the community I'd seen an empty shop which I thought might be a good enough space for classes to be held, so we started by asking around for the owner. When we tracked him down, we explained our plan and asked his price. Five hundred euros a month....

The plan suddenly seemed less straightforward. The price was ridiculous by Kosovo standards – higher than the rent we paid on our two-bedroom home in the centre of Prishtina. Multiplied by six months, it was three thousand euros. We weren't going to be able to raise that from one drinks party. We thanked him and tramped on through the neighbourhood.

A child came skipping up to us and I smiled vaguely at him, still scanning for possible premises.

'What are you doing?' he asked.

'Looking for a room to rent,' I said.

'You should go and ask the miner,' he told me. It was an odd thing to say because there were no active miners in Kosovo any more, and besides, the well-known mines were thirty kilometres from here.

'Who's the Miner?' I asked.

The kid beckoned us on, and we followed him. Turning a corner we looked down another long street of properties fenced with flattened oil drums, past piles of burning garbage. At the end of the street was a white building, still only half-finished, that towered over its neighbours. It was the tallest construction in sight, and it was to this that our new guide was waving. 'The guys from the mines are building it.'

We walked closer and found that the ground floor was another shop. The same mean selection of produce sat on sticky shelves. A cardboard box of dry dark sausage gave off a pungent smoky smell; a bucket of pale cheese sat soaking in whey like old cloths someone was trying to get the stains out of. I noticed a shelf with a bold sign advertising Turkish delight, but all that sat there was cheap imported shampoo.

We introduced ourselves and explained what we were there for, and that our young informant had said they might have some appropriate space. The guy behind the counter was called Nexhat and he said he'd show us the room.

He took us downstairs to a basement. A little light filtered through dirty windows high up in the walls and showed a storeroom. Sacks of flour slumped at one end, and a huge snooker table took up most of the space.

I tried to imagine Julie Andrews here.

'We'd move the snooker table, obviously,' said Nexhat.

'Yes. Obviously….'

But was it enough? Could this little place really be a school for eighteen children deprived their rights? Would eighteen children turn up anyway? It was one thing to tell a well-meaning foreign lady when she comes to your house that yes, you'd like to go to school, and quite another to come and do battle with the intricacies of alphabets and arithmetic day after day. Perhaps the whole idea was stupid. Surely if these children really wanted to go to school they would be there already.

'How much would this be a month?' I asked, but Nexhat wouldn't say.

'You'll have to talk to my brother,' he replied. 'But let me show you the other space too.' He led us up two flights of stairs, to the floor above the shop, and unlocked a door. The floor inside was bare concrete but there was light, and plenty of space, in three separate rooms. One of them had the door closed and he knocked.

'Can we come in, Mother?' he asked, and incongruously we walked into an old lady's bedroom. From the concrete shell outside, we were suddenly in a carpeted room filled with furniture, and fuggy with an electric heater. The frail old lady we found looking at us seemed to be fully clothed, but tucked up in blankets against the cold. I smiled apologetically at her and explained why we were there.

'Yes, it's such a terrible shame to have so many children out of school,' she murmured. 'May God bless you for coming to help.' Her cool bony fingers unfolded from the bedclothes and clutched my arm. 'Thank you.'

I gulped a little. I hadn't done anything yet.

'Yes, yes, speak to my oldest son about renting this place.'

But ... I didn't like to point out that she'd be without a bedroom.

'No, no, I can move back to the old house next door. May Allah protect you,' she repeated, in benediction.

Nexhat was ushering us out of the room.

'This flat is too big,' said Rob. 'We don't need this much space. What did you say, eighteen kids? They'd fit in one room....'

Of course he was right, but I could feel the cool touch of the old lady still on my arm. Perhaps there really was an appetite for what we were going to be offering here. What if more children came? And the space in the basement was so dingy. Maybe the children wouldn't come at all if the classroom put them off. I looked around the concrete shell here. I imagined bright phonics echoing off the walls, with picture-books stacked on a table. I worked out where we'd display children's work. There was a clean bathroom where I'd make them wash their hands before they came to class...

We made a phone call to Nexhat's brother. 'How much would the flat be to rent for six months?'

He didn't want to talk on the phone but asked to meet for a coffee. I knew the routine – how agreements in the Balkans are signed and sealed not with ink, but with makiato. He said he was in Prishtina so Rob and I went back to town to meet him there.

But there was probably no point. If the other guy's price was five hundred euros, this wasn't going to be hugely different. And anyway, until the fundraiser evening, we didn't actually have any money. Perhaps this was all just whimsy and I was wasting everyone's time – including my own.

Idriz was a stocky, compact man (he said he'd applied for the police service, and I could imagine him as a dependable presence in uniform). We opened with small-talk – where I was from, how long I'd been in Kosovo, his own family's story, of how his father had worked in the lucrative Trepça mines in the north of Kosovo before moving to Fushë Kosovë. To my surprise, when we moved onto business he started not by asking about money, but by asking how we wanted to help his community. I suddenly realised this was a job interview, not a business negotiation.

I flustered, made mistakes in my Albanian, tried to tell the story of Hatemja's children, then worried that it sounded like we'd privileged one family, and assured him that these classes would be open to all families. Then I worried that it sounded like his house would be full of unruly youngsters…. 'But who knows how many will come?' I added.

Idriz was serious. 'It's true that our community needs this,' he said. 'And I want to help my people.' I breathed out, and remembered his mother's blessing.

'I could rent you the flat for two hundred and fifty euros a month.'

I multiplied by six. One thousand five hundred euros; it still seemed a lot. I explained that we would have to wait until the fundraiser that Wednesday night, and that then I would call him.

He paid for our drinks 'out of respect.' I thanked him, asked him to send my best to his mother, and said we would speak on Wednesday.

Word was spreading about Wednesday night. Friends of Zsofia's, friends of mine, Laura's father, colleagues of Rob's, all were getting in touch and saying they planned to come. A local church heard about it and shared the news through their congregation. The Internationals started to mobilise.

Hatemja and her family weren't going to be there, but we wanted people to meet them, and their neighbours somehow. We prepared a rolling slideshow showing some of the families we'd visited and with a couple of sentences telling the story of each of them.

Some students from a local high school asked to help us and printed out some of the photographs on the wall too. Laura found a box and chose the picture of the most mournful looking child to hang over it with a handwritten sign saying 'Donations'. Zsofia cleared her back room to make space for bags of clothes that people might bring with them. Jeta and I set out drinks and glasses and bowls of crisps.

At last all the preparations were complete. We put some music on to cover the terrifying hush that scares any hostess five minutes before a party is due to start. What if no-one came? What if no-one gave money? What if we had to go back to eighteen children and tell them that they weren't going to go to school?

The doorbell rang.

In fact, it kept ringing all evening. Over the next few hours we must have had over fifty people coming in twos and threes, some bulging with bags of donated clothes, some carrying nothing but slipping their hands quietly into their pockets and rustling something into that box under the picture of the mournful child. Some drank too much of the wine; others stood transfixed at the slideshow, wondering, like I had a few weeks before, how it could be that there was such need, such cold, such neglect just a few kilometres from where they lived. Sometimes these were the same people who turned away and drank too much wine.

When the last guest had gone, Zsofia, Rob, Jeta, Laura and I sank onto the sofas in Zsofia's living room. Laura opened up the box. It was reassuringly full.

She started counting. There were small piles of coins, but more notes and one big cheque that sat in a pile of its own.

'It's one thousand three hundred euros,' Laura announced.

I divided by six … It was enough for the rent in Fushë Kosovë if we could negotiate Idriz down to two hundred euros a month. That would leave a hundred for some bus fares, some pens and paper….

It was possible.

A friend of Zsofia's had heard about our project. An Uzbeki-Russian American, I guessed she had learned the hard way about negotiating, and when Zsofia told her that we needed to get the rent down from 250 to 200 euros she snorted. 'It should be less than that! Let me talk to the landlord.'

So for my next trip to Fushë Kosovë to the tall white building where a miracle might be about to happen, I went with Elena. We met Idriz in the flat. I smiled at him, asked after his family, thanked him. Next to me, Elena's face was stony.

I walked her around the property, pointing out where I thought we could have the story-book corner, the phonics display…. She knocked the wall and rubbed at the rough plaster. 'Nothing will stick on this,' she said. I looked at the powdery surface that had come off on her hands, and realised she was right.

'And there are no carpets?' she asked, as if I was an imbecile for having considered entering into any agreement at all for such an irresponsibly furnished property. Idriz and I were equally crestfallen. 'Well, no — just in the one room.'

We went into Idriz' mother's room and Elena kicked gently at the carpet on the floor. It wasn't fitted — just a thin sheet laid down. 'The kids will get cold sitting on that if there's no furniture.'

She was right.

Her inspection continued and at the end she said to me, 'You shouldn't take this place.'

I was astounded. She knew the dream — she knew about the kids. And if she doubted what we were trying to do, why hadn't she said so in the car on the way here?

Idriz was watching us. And I realised Elena was watching him watching us. She spoke no Albanian, and Idriz spoke very little English, but when someone scuffs at an inadequate carpet and runs disapproving hands over poorly constructed walls you don't need much translation. Rather late in the day I worked out what was going on.

'You're right, we can't afford it,' I said, shaking my head dramatically for the benefit of anyone who didn't speak English.

'How much did you say we collected at the fundraiser?' she asked, and I told her, counting out on my fingers elaborately too.

'You can only afford two hundred euros a month then,' she said pointedly.

'I know, I know. I'm sorry, Idriz, but we can't afford your flat,' I said in Albanian.

We got the flat for two hundred euros a month.

8 The half-finished alphabet

'I'll tell the parents,' Agron beamed. I had gone to tell him and Hatemja that lessons could start for Gjelane next Tuesday.

'And can I tell my friends?' asked Gjelane.

'Sure, tell everyone! It's for any child who's not in school and who's aged nine or over.'

'Can I come and see the school?'

She'd used the word! I hastened to correct her.

'It's not a school...' I wanted her to understand that a flat above a minimarket was not the educational summit she should be aiming at – there was more than this. I thought back to the 'it's too late' director. Bizarre though it seemed, this was who I wanted to be teaching Gjelane. In premises funded by the government of Kosovo, together with all the other children who were citizens of Kosovo.

'Can I come and see it?' We walked together back to the minimarket. I jingled the key in my pocket.

Gjelane offered to show me a shortcut between her house and our centre, as we were now calling it, and we climbed past a deserted house around which garbage was banked up in drifts. It was fetid – the rubbish discarded by those who go through other people's rubbish; the trashiest of the trash. Things oozed underfoot. Off to one side were the tarry remains of melted cables – I'd seen men and kids crouched over small toxic hearths of smouldering electrical wires, burning off the rubber housing so that the valuable copper inside could be sold to the scrap merchants. Elsewhere, the precious metals of stereo speakers or old computer monitors had been salvaged by smashing the harder plastics around them. Shards and smithereens of old hardware crunched when you stepped on them.

People were staring at us as we made our way back to Idriz' building. I felt conspicuous and uncomfortable. I could tell Gjelane had noticed the staring too, but she didn't seem to mind. I wondered about the 'shortcut' and whose house it was taking us past – I got the sense I was being toured.

Sure enough, a little girl came out of a doorway we passed, and Gjelane grinned proudly at her.

'This is Elizabeth I was telling you about.'

I smiled at the girl; we'd not met before. I asked whether she was at school.

A shy shake of the head.

'Then come to start learning with us on Tuesday!'

'At the miners' house,' added Gjelane, knowledgeably.

The girl skittered off. 'Do you think she'll come?' I asked Gjelane.

'Yes, I'll bring her,' Gjelane told me, and I wondered who exactly this miniature community advocate was, helping me to pick my way through her neighbourhood.

Suddenly the other little girl was back again.

'Can my brother come?'

'How old is he?' She held up her fingers – all of them. Yes, that was enough.

'Does he go to school?'

No. He was another candidate then.

I had the same conversation four or five times on the way to our new centre. It was exhilarating, offering education like this. Like giving candy to a baby. And I wondered – was it really this easy? All these children wanting to learn; me wanting to teach; the premises hired on the back of a drinks party.

Well, I had better get on and make sure we were ready for them.

The flat above the minimarket was starting to look a little more like a learning environment. Of course it helped that the old lady's bedroom had been dismantled, and the old lady had gone with it. I hoped her blessing remained.

We would hold our classes in that room, sitting on the thin carpet since there were no chairs. I had wondered what the absolute bare necessities were for a classroom, and had gone shopping with what I dared to spend of that one hundred euros that remained of our kitty from the fundraiser evening once the rent was allocated.

But our resources were going further than I'd ever believed possible. I said that I didn't believe in God – only in people – but these few weeks brought me closer than I had ever been to imagining some force co-ordinating events. It was as if the universe was wanting to sustain our desperate efforts, as if it was listening when I fretted to Rob that it wouldn't be feasible in the chilly temperatures of Kosovo's early spring to have children learning there without carpet underfoot and a heater. Rob pointed out that the ventilation didn't seem great and that with a heater there'd be a risk of carbon monoxide poisoning, and I only fretted more.

Later that night I'd found an email from my friend Louise – 'We've been clearing out, and we have some stuff which I guess might be useful for your teaching space. Would you be able to use a rug and a heater? We even have a carbon monoxide detector – is that any good to you?' It was a little freaky.

The same week, Joanna had got in touch and said, 'I have some play resources which are brand new and might be useful for the activities you're organising.' When she'd brought them over and we'd looked at the shiny plastic and the tempting toys, we'd realised we were going to need proper storage to keep them safe and clean: we were going to need lots of boxes, and we didn't have any. Twelve hours later there was an email in the inbox from someone called Judith. 'We've just moved to Prishtina and have a load of boxes to spare. We've heard about your project; could you use them?'

It's almost scary when you get the things you wish for. Maybe I should have been thinking bigger – world peace? Johnny Depp? But I had no time for Johnny right then. I was narrowing things down to the bare essentials....

I'd known we would need a clock. Perhaps no-one but me would be able to tell the time, but they would be taught, and a shared sense of when our day together started and when it ended would be important. But it seemed an indulgence.... I'd mentioned it to my parents and they'd said they'd pay for the clock. Idriz had come round with a hammer and banged a nail in the wall for it.

And an alphabet.... I had gone to a bookshop and bought a pack of alphabet cards with a letter on each one, together with a bright picture of something that started with that letter. They needed to go up on the wall.

I'd brought in some children's storybooks from home too. Some were in Albanian, but even those that weren't could be useful, I reckoned, since the children wouldn't be able to read. The story told in the vibrant illustrations of picture-books like *Handa's Surprise* had introduced children in my London classrooms to literacy, and I was sure they could work here too.

For maths I'd felt we needed counters. In England, every classroom I'd worked in had had a tray of centicubes, the small plastic cubes one centimetre high. They were accompanied by sticks of ten centicubes and slabs of one hundred which children could use for understanding the hundreds, tens and units of the decimal system. To me, from my own childhood to my years as a teacher, maths meant centicubes. They were ingrained in me not just figuratively – centicubes always get loose somehow in a primary school classroom and it's only when everyone is changing for PE that they get found underfoot, by small tender toes.

But I'd had no idea where I'd be able to buy centicubes in Kosovo, and anyway I wasn't sure I could justify our meagre one hundred euros being spent on them. Checking in my kitchen cupboards I came up with a better alternative, and spent a happy afternoon manufacturing dried bean ten-sticks. It sounded like a Chinese appetiser, but the strips of ten beans, snuggled one against the other like a series of quotation marks, and then held in place with wide sellotape made a deliciously tactile alternative to centicube sticks. Softer underfoot when you trod on them, too.

Soon I had a Tupperware pot of single beans and ten-strips, and reckoned we were ready for maths.

Gjelane fingered the resources neatly arranged in the classroom with a kind of hunger, mixed with wonder. Eventually she left me to the preparations – to get ready for literacy I just needed to stick up the alphabet cards. It was less easy than it sounds, not least because of what Elena had noticed on her visit; that shoddy wall surface was resistant to sellotape and to blu-tack.

Nevertheless, with inelegant cross-sticking of sellotape, more like dressing a wound than displaying a learning resource, I got A displayed on the wall. In English, A is for apple and it makes a nice start to the alphabet, the healthy fruit you'd traditionally give the teacher. There's something for everyone in A-for-apple.

In Albanian, I discovered, A is for *akullore* – ice-cream. Perhaps it's even more motivating than apples for the average child, but I wondered whether Gjelane had ever tasted an *akullore*. She was going to be getting access to all kinds of things through these letters stuck on the wall.

Once the colourful *akullore* picture was in place, I sifted through the shuffled pack of cards to find B. I measured out the space available on the wall and divided it by the letters in the Albanian alphabet, of which there are 36 (all the letters of our alphabet plus an Ë and a Ç and some digraphs like Rr, Sh and Xh). I worked out where B should go in order to fit all 36 letters along one wall. Then I continued to C. I went on like this until I'd rummaged through almost all the cards in the pack. With the repeated sticking it was a time-consuming and rather dusty task. Outside, it had got dark, and I realised Rob would be home by now; I should be finishing up soon.

It was when I had only a few cards left that I suddenly noticed the mistake I'd made. After N (for *nuse* – bride; setting those aspirations early) I'd gone straight on to O (for *ora* – clock – so nice to see my own priorities reflected in the learning materials). But in Albanian, there should be the letter 'Nj' between them. By the time I'd realised this I was almost at the end of the alphabet – to stick the Nj in the right place meant unpeeling from the wall about half of the little cards and then repositioning them. I sat down heavily, suddenly deflated. It wasn't just the tedious task of putting the alphabet up; it was the fact I'd made such an elementary mistake. I may have a degree in linguistics, and be functionally fluent in Albanian, but the fact was that I'd only known this language for four years; it wasn't in my blood. I had just made a mistake in the most basic unit of literacy knowledge; I didn't actually know my Albanian alphabet off by heart.

And I was intending to share my (partial, inaccurate) knowledge with these kids, palming off my ignorance to them as if it were an education. I suddenly doubted that I could do this at all.

It was time to go home and have some sleep. Before I left, I pulled down the offending letters so that the alphabet ended at N. I would come back tomorrow and finish it off.

I turned the light off and plunged the sad, curtailed alphabet into darkness, leaving it there like a metaphor of unfinished education, for me to come back to another day.

I came back of course, but I came back with reinforcements. It was becoming quite clear that I couldn't do this alone. But help was at hand – Laura was keen to teach, and through the church that had helped with advertising our fundraising evening, we'd been contacted by an American woman called Hope. She was in Kosovo with a Christian organisation called the Agape Foundation and had a Kosovan Albanian member of staff whom she suggested could help on our project. I bet Vlora knew her alphabet off by heart.

Without knowing how many children were going to come (I had an estimate – five on the first day, growing to twenty over the first week) it was difficult to know whether we would need Vlora, but it was too good an offer to miss. Vlora and

Hope helped with getting the centre ready and Vlora offered to come with me and Gjelane to visit six homes where we knew of kids who weren't registered at school, and who'd told us they'd like to learn enough to be able to register in September. Gjelane came with us, like a chatty, giggly nine-year old advert for the idea. She held Vlora's hand tight.

Mothers who stood gossiping in the sunshine nudged their neighbours as we passed, 'ask her, ask her,' and we confirmed. 'Yes, your kids can come.'

One twelve year-old whispered to us, 'but I can't write my name.' I told him that was exactly why we wanted him to come.

The day before classes were due to start, it seemed that everything was ready – the clock ticking on the wall, the resources stored, every letter of the alphabet in its proper place. All that was needed was children.

I popped round to Hatemja's house before leaving for Prishtina. Had Agron remembered that it was tomorrow?

'Yes, yes – I've been telling everyone,' he assured me. He walked me back to the market where the informal taxis parked. On the way he called out to people we passed, 'O neighbour! Your son's eleven isn't he? Don't forget – ten o'clock tomorrow'.

A little girl came up to us.

'Is it just for boys?'

'No, no, you can come too,' I told her, as if I was Mary Wollstonecraft. She grinned at me and scampered off waving as she ran,

'See you tomorrow'.

9 May we see each other for good

Was I right – would it be five children who came today? I hoped it wouldn't be fewer than that – with me and Laura and Hope and Vlora we would be in danger of volunteers outnumbering children.

In fact, now we had another teacher, too – thanks to Laura's unstoppable enthusiasm. Her cousin, another Rob (as a result of the need to distinguish them my Rob immediately got downgraded, or perhaps promoted, to being 'old Rob') was a law graduate who had recently left one job in England and was looking for another. She'd suggested that he should come out to Kosovo for a few months to get a bit of perspective on what he really wanted to do.

His plane got in at night; by 8.30 the next morning he was stumbling out of a taxi at the tall white building in Fushë Kosovë. By 9.45am he seemed in as much suspense as the rest of us about whether this project was going to work at all.

Would they come?

At 9.55 there was a knock on the door. I rushed to it; would I find on the other side of it one of the pixie-faced girls waiting for an education? (Would they come?)

I opened it looking out at what would be eye-level for a nine year-old, but as I saw who was standing there, I had to raise my eyes. No children – it was Agron.

'I just thought I'd come and see whether everything was OK.'

Coming in, he inspected the classroom we'd set up and nodded approvingly.

'Agron, will they come?'

'Oh yes, yes, I've been telling everyone,' he assured me.

We stood in the hallway together – the American evangelist, the unemployed British lawyer, the gap year student, the Kosovan Christian, and me. Despite the heater in the classroom, it was cold in the hallway. You could see puffs of fog as we all breathed out slowly. I felt slightly foolish.

There was another knock on the door. Behind me, I heard Hope muttering something under her breath. It was a prayer.

I went to open up, and outside saw not one, but a small gaggle of little girls. Their hair was unbrushed and their feet were in plastic sandals with no socks.

'We've come to learn,' one of them announced.

I wanted to hug her, but some deep training took over at this point. I'd never taught in a school above a minimarket; I'd never taught children too poor to buy socks; I'd never taught an alphabet with the letter Nj in it, but for fifteen years I'd been a teacher. And you don't hug your pupils; especially not on the first day. I solemnly shook her hand.

'My name's Elizabeth, I'm a teacher,' I said.

The solemnity worked – the two girls who'd been giggling behind her stopped.

'My name's Azemine,' she announced.

'I'm pleased to meet you. Come inside.'

I greeted each of the children and introduced myself. They walked in to where Vlora stood with an exercise book ready to write down their full names. Then we took them into the improvised classroom.

There were four of them. Less than my prediction, but it was good enough. I gave each of them a piece of paper and put a box of felt-tips in front of them.

'Draw a picture of yourself to go on the wall,' I suggested. 'And if you can, write your name.'

It seemed a simple task, but also something that would generate some pictures right away to display on our walls, and it was also a chance for a quick diagnosis of whether they knew their letters.

The girls smiled, and rummaged through the felt-tips, unable to choose between the jewel-like colours. When they each had a pen, they took off the lid and hovered over the paper.

There was another knock on the door. Hope went to answer it and reappeared with another three children. While she was settling them into place, the front door opened again. Vlora left to find out who was there, and when she came back, there were more children following her. I tried to count the heads but more kids kept on coming. Eventually the stream slowed enough for me to count accurately: there were twenty-three children sat on the carpet, poring over their paper.

More than five then.

They were quiet and obedient; a little over-awed and unsure. I'd been a teacher for fifteen years though so I'd seen this at least fifteen times before – the Mexican stand-off of the first day of lessons. No-one wants to be the first to pull their gun. The group is waiting to find its rebel, its class clown; the clowns are waiting to see if there's anyone else applying for the position. The teachers, if they have any sense, are standing with whatever dignity they can muster, and appreciating the calm before the storm.

Actually, I wasn't standing anywhere; I was kneeling since the children were all at ground level. And I was trying to convince any one of them to put felt-tip to paper.

'Just draw a picture of your face,' I urged.

The children didn't respond.

Maybe this was too hard? I realised your face is the one thing you can never see.

'OK, draw a picture of your house then?'

Still nothing.

One girl said, 'But I don't know how to draw'.

I'd never met a child who couldn't draw. Mark-making is a basic developmental stage. Two year-olds sit happily 'drawing' and 'writing' for hours, and these children were all at least nine years old.

Then I thought of Hatemja's fruitless search for a pen when I'd needed to borrow one at her house, and about the homes that literacy hadn't touched. And these children weren't two; they were old enough to know what a picture of a person's face should look like and to know that their fine motor skills were inadequate to the task.

'OK,' I said cheerily, 'let's get you copying your names'. We'd forget the pictures, if the children weren't ready to draw – we could just write their names out in big easy capital letters like they would be taught in mainstream schools in Kosovo, and get the kids to copy them.

It was a lot more successful than the drawing activity, and it was probably a more useful life skill too. After all, when you go to the municipality or the bank or the police they don't ask you to draw a picture of your face. Scratching out the letters of their name in purple felt-tip was a good starting point for the children being active citizens of Kosovo.

However, it was still not straightforward. Most of the children didn't know how to write their names, so they were dependent on us to write them for them. Easy enough with 'Afir' where every letter is how it would be written in English; Albanian is phonologically regular, unlike the 'k' and 'f' sounds of 'Christopher' or the other tricks of English. But there are still two ways of writing the sound we'd spell as 'j' and when /Djemeela/ told me her name I didn't know whether it was written 'Xhemile' or 'Gjemile'. For any other word it wouldn't really have mattered, but I was teaching her to write her *name*. I realised that her parents might not know how to spell it either but it just made the responsibility greater for us; this might be the first time that the names had been fixed in letters. Suddenly we had become 'god'parents or sponsors to every kid in the room.

We muddled through and the children were soon absorbed in the laborious letters. I looked around the heads bent silently over their work. People had tried to scare me off these classes, telling me about the 'feral' children I'd be introducing to an activity they were unused to (in one case I was told learning was 'just something they're not able to do').

There were certainly headlice in the bent heads, and cold feet – some of the children had arrived barefoot in slippers through the mud (Hope distributed socks to those who needed them). But these children were my dream class. Calm, desperate to succeed, and smiling every time they caught my eye.

They kept smiling even after the names were finished and stuck up on the powdery walls (N–is–for–*Nuse* had fallen down from my alphabet already). We sang a morning song (another echo from fifteen years of first days in classrooms around London – that the most important thing to establish, along with who's in charge, is what the routines are. I was fierce about the lids on the felt-tips going back on the pens, and I was loud in my singing of an improvised song in Albanian to the tune of Frère Jacques).

'Young' Rob, still dazed from his first encounter with Kosovo, nevertheless came up with a great English session (more singing, and the children learned 'Head, shoulders, knees and toes', or at least hedzshowzneesantows with frenzied pointing). We played a numbers game and Vlora read the story of *Handa's Surprise*. Just as all of our appetites had been whetted with the picture-book images of those 'soft, yellow bananas', 'sweet-smelling guava', 'ripe red mango', we brought out yoghurts and fruit for the children.

They sat back on their haunches and gobbled up the food, licking their lips; never had education seemed to me such a basic way to nurture mind and body. And not just the minds and bodies of the 23 children, but also my own. I looked round, and saw Laura looking at me and we grinned at one another.

But our new clock was showing noon – time for lessons to end. We collected up the yoghurt pots, and then there was an uneasy silence.

We needed a ritual.... We went round the circle of children asking them what they'd most enjoyed today, and then I wished I'd thought of some way to finish off our extraordinary morning. Another song? My mind was blank. I have a terrible singing voice, and I felt like the kids must have done when I'd gaily told them, 'Draw your face'.

'Laura, tell me a simple tune that everyone can learn easily?'

'Er … *We will rock you*?'

It was good enough. And with a bit of tweaking, we could fit the Albanian word for 'goodbye' to the rhythm.

With all the false, bright confidence of the primary school teacher, I started off – in the wrong key, but accompanied by clapping, not least to drown the singing. 'Mir-u, Mir-u, PAFSHIM.'

It means 'goodbye' but literally, 'may we see each other for good'. We reminded the children that there would be more of what we'd done together today, starting at ten am tomorrow.

May we see each other for good.

10 The uncles

They came back.

And they brought their friends. Each day we had more children so that by the end of the first week we had fifty. We realised the extent of the 'godsend' that was Hope and Vlora.

We couldn't fit fifty children into Idriz' mother's former bedroom, so we split them into groups which then swapped between us. Rob and Vlora could work together – he for the English, and she for the Albanian translations – in one room. I took maths in another room. But that still gave us 25 children each, in a space the size of an old lady's bedroom. They weren't ideal learning conditions, and after a week, the class clowns, the behaviour challenges, the differences in ability and prior learning were becoming obvious. Fidan – a boy I'd recognised when he'd turned up at our door, from the traffic lights in town where he strutted up to his captive audience in their smart cars, asking for money in three languages – needed space to learn. Little Emine, eyeing him and the other boys warily as she bent to her work on the carpet, needed to know they weren't going to tread on her laborious drawing as they walked past. Elvira's voice, as huge as her smile, didn't leave enough room for the quieter children to think in our crowded classroom....

Should we be turning children away? Should we divide them between shifts? It would mean longer hours for us – and we knew Vlora couldn't commit to any more time. Maybe children would start to drop out? But was that what we wanted to rely on?

'I heard that your classes in Fushë Kosovë are going well,' my friend Gail said on the phone that evening.

I hesitated before replying with a slightly weary 'yes' and then a more honest, 'I don't know whether we can keep going, though.'

I told Gail about our 'good problem' of too many children wanting to learn at our centre.

'Well, let me share with you another good problem then,' she said, telling me about the uncle of a friend in Kosovo. The uncle was a trained teacher but had left his village and was now raising his family in Prishtina and looking for work.

I was puzzled – 'How is that a good problem?'

'Well, it is if I take the opportunity to pay Uncle Avdil to teach every morning at your centre until September.'

Another trained teacher coming to our team! And a teacher not only trained, but in the ways of the Kosovan school system. I was aware that for all the heart-warming singing and fruit yoghurts, the personalised teaching and bright displays on the walls, the preparation we were giving these children for joining the mainstream Kosovan education system in September was fragile. If that was all they knew, then when they were herded into the echoing, undecorated classrooms set up to hold and control forty pupils at a time, serried in rows with books in front of them and stuff to copy down from the board in silence, the children would be lambs to the slaughter. 'Teacher Avdil' could give them a taste of what they were going to.

I suggested that he should come to see the centre (even a village teacher, used to the improvisations and mud of Kosovan village schools, might baulk at what we had cobbled together here). I checked with Gail – did he know that the children were Ashkali? It was a delicate question ('is he a racist?') but it was worth asking now.

'Oh yes, yes, I've explained it all.'

I thought about the explanations I'd had over all those years I'd lived in Kosovo, reading reports about Ashkali exclusion, education drop-out rates, child labour. It was different when you were here in Neighbourhood 29, but I reckoned Teacher Avdil could find that out for himself. A lamb to the slaughter perhaps.

When he arrived, I realised he was no lamb. Tall, gaunt, greyed and handsome, he was more of a silver fox. He was solemn and serious, but then every so often spat out a sharp hearty laugh. He commanded respect.

Yes, he understood the kind of children we were working with. Yes, he understood what we would need from him. Yes, he was sure he could help.

'But we've no furniture at the moment,' I apologised. In the non-carpeted classrooms we had strewn on the floor old curtains which I'd had at home, as an attempt to create a more comfortable space for the children to sit. It was basic, but after all, most of the children sat on the floor in the homes I'd visited.

Teacher Avdil looked around. 'Well you have some chairs.' It was true – Idriz had left a few in the premises, and Hope had brought some that her landlord had donated to the office. But my experience was that unless you had enough for one for each child, it would be better to offer them to no-one.

'The children can share. It's what Albanians did in the nineties.'

I'd seen pictures of what he was referring to, from the 1990s, when much of Kosovo Albanian language teaching was stopped by the oppressive regime of Slobodan Milošević's Serb-dominated Yugoslavia. The Albanian children who were thus excluded from state education were taught in homes and garages in a parallel education system set up in secret by Kosovo's Albanians. It meant that most Kosovar Albanians in their thirties had learned, like Gjelane and her friends, in flats with no proper resources. I wondered whether they had had centicube substitutes made from beans. More importantly, I wondered whether this experience made what was going on in Fushë Kosovë somehow better or worse. Was this an example of the bullied turned bully – Albanians who had been denied their rights by a Serbian regime now denying rights in their turn to Ashkali children?

If so, it wasn't for want of commitment from Albanians like Teacher Avdil. He waved at the chairs. 'If we have fifty children split into three groups, it's only about seventeen in a group. You have five chairs and a bench and we'll put them together – the children can share.' I didn't dare to argue, and looking at Teacher Avdil's resolute gaze, I didn't think the children would either.

The next day, Teacher Avdil started work. He began at A.

Despite Teacher Avdil's determination, it wasn't easy to manage with so little furniture. And providing a healthy snack every day for fifty children had gobbled up the one hundred euros left from our fundraiser. Luckily, other people had heard about what we were doing and were making donations. A friend had set up a PayPal account for us and was blogging about our project to motivate people to donate; others who had heard slipped me fifty euro notes; we were getting by, but there were certainly no funds for buying big items like furniture.

After mir-u, mir-u, PAFSHIM one day, Arjeta stayed behind.

'My uncle wants to know if you'd like a whiteboard.'

We had been spreading flipchart paper on the floor; yes, a whiteboard would be wonderful.

'How come your uncle has a whiteboard?' I asked. She explained that he had run Koranic classes a few years ago and had been given money by an Islamic organisation to fit out a classroom in a room in his house. Now the classes had stopped but she said he still had some of the stuff in his storeroom.

I wondered whether her uncle knew about the offer she was making. I imagined turning up at the door of a Koranic teacher announcing that I was here to take him up on his offer of a whiteboard.

'Could we go and see him together?'

He was in his shop – a small gloomy space dominated by cabbages a little past their best. I introduced myself.

Bashkim nodded with a smile. He was a short, robust, well-fed man, a Doric column perhaps but certainly giving the impression of being a pillar of his community. Later I learned that he owned other shops in the neighbourhood. If Neighbourhood 29 had had a Chamber of Commerce, Bashkim would have rivalled Idriz for the position of President.

'Yes, yes, Arjeta told me about you. Would you like to borrow that whiteboard?'

I thanked him, assuring him that it would only be until September, but he shrugged.

'If it's for the good of my community I'm happy for you to use it.' He took me round to a storeroom and unlocked the door opening onto a dark space.

'It's somewhere in here,' he said, and as he pushed forward, there were screeching noises and the graunching of lumber against concrete floor. I peered in, trying to see what he was moving through.

It was a forest of table legs and teetering piles of benches.

I licked my lips like the children had when we'd shown them the picture-book fruit in *Handa's Surprise*. I wondered how to start the conversation.

'Er, Haxhi Bashkim,' I began, using the honorific title I gathered Bashkim was entitled to because he had made the Hajj pilgrimage to Mecca.

'Yes?' he turned back to look at me. A decent man. *If it's for the good of my community, I'm happy for you to use it....*

'What are you doing with all these tables and benches?' I blurted.

'Oh these, they're left over from the same classes where we used the whiteboard,' he said, and turned back to brushing dust off the board and levering it out from where it was pinned to the wall by the desks.

'Umm ...'

It suddenly seemed to dawn on him what I was struggling with. 'Would they be useful to you?'

I'm hopeless at asking people for favours.

'Well, maybe you need them?'

The cobwebs were evidence of what a ridiculous suggestion it was.

'It would only be until September,' I reiterated.

He looked doubtful. Had I pushed my luck? 'They'll need cleaning though.'

Together, Haxhi Bashkim, Arjeta and I pulled the tables and benches into the daylight. They did need cleaning, but Arjeta was already on the case. She appeared with a bucket of water.

We bought sponges and detergent from Bashkim's shop, and started to wipe the tables down in the yard by the store. Passers-by stopped to watch and children from our classes began to gather.

'Don't just watch us – you can help if you want,' I told the kids.

By the end we had a dozen or more children being bossed around by Arjeta. They split down gender lines – girls cleaned the tables and benches; boys worked in pairs to carry our new classroom furniture down the street and manoeuvre them awkwardly up the stairs to the flat where they'd be used.

I insisted on writing a formal receipt for Bashkim which set out that the furniture was only on loan until September, and he accepted it in bemusement.

Now we were a learning centre of three classrooms, with enough tables, chairs – and even teachers – for all the children.

More than that, I felt that something special had happened today. We were a centre whose fabric was, slowly, being built by the community we served. This was no longer the whimsical project of outsiders; the children who came tomorrow would sit down at furniture provided by Haxhi Bashkim, and cleaned up and carried in by their classmates.

There was other practical help needed from the community too if this project was to thrive; every day, fifty children tramped through the mud (and worse) to get to us, and spent two hours sharpening their pencils and screwing up bits of paper, and eating yoghurt.... After even one day of trying to do the cleaning up before I set off back to Prishtina, I realised it would be sensible to ask for help.

I went to visit Hatemja.

She invited me into her home, and we sat cross-legged on one of the mattresses and asked the ritual questions.

She wanted to know how Gjelane was doing in lessons, too; it gave us a new round of questions, and a new thing to take shared pride in.

I looked around us and noticed that the room had been smartened up. The furniture had been moved, and the walls repainted. Things were tidier, and I commented on how nice it was looking. Hatemja blushed and seemed pleased that I'd noticed. I thought back to my first visit, six months ago. Now Ramadan's burns were healing; the boys were going to Rrahmon's centre every day; Gjelane was attending our classes … the tidying up didn't seem a coincidence.

It was a good starting point for a conversation.

'Hatemja, would you be willing to work for us as a cleaner?'

It would be her first job — the first time she would ever have earned money from anything other than sitting with her hand out outside the mosque. It would be the first time she'd be required to turn up every day at a certain time; a time not set by the biological rhythms of her children's sleep and hunger, but by the arbitrary timekeeping of a clock.

I realised Hatemja didn't have a clock.

And she had tiny Elhame, and the four others to look after — would she be able to manage a daily task like this with Agron out in the garbage heaps?

She asked the question before I mentioned it, suggesting that she could speak to two of her neighbours who also had children who came to our activities and they could share the work with her, taking turns through the week. She smiled when I left it to her to negotiate with the other women, and when she spoke to thank me for the opportunity she was slightly breathless.

'I'll clean it like it's my own home,' she said.

In fact, she cleaned it to an even higher standard. She or Haxhere or Kumria (the neighbour whose name meant 'turtle dove') would come in after the children had left, while I was marking the work in exercise books, or preparing the children's drawings to go on the walls, and they would trace their own alphabet of mop marks across the bathroom floor, or clean the windows in curlicue 'C's and 'O's. When it came to getting them to sign to confirm they'd received their pay each week I learned that none of them could write. They'd never been to school, and didn't even know the first letter of their names – I wondered whether it was 'too late' for them too. Hatemja would make an imprecise X on the receipt and fold the note she received up small and tuck it away inside her bra – the women here kept their money where they kept their babies; at the breast.

So now we had a newly colonised learning space – the rooms now not only filled with Haxhi Bashkim's furniture and up to sixty local children every day, but fast becoming the territory of three tough women, sweeping and wiping the way to their families' future.

Haxhere and her son

11 Pipes and drums and headaches

Those first weeks were a scrabble of getting the children in,
the teachers to teach them, the chairs for them to sit on, a
box of fruit each morning to feed them, and making sure
the toilet was cleaned. I thought of Maslow's hierarchy of
human needs; we were right down at the bottom – at the
level of food–water–sex–sleep–excretion. What of the abstract
nouns hovering up at the top of Maslow's pyramid diagram;
'achievement'? 'Creativity'? It was time for us to look up.

We delayed mir–u, mir–u, PAFSHIM each day with a new
little ceremony; Teacher Avdil and every volunteer each chose
one child to congratulate for an achievement that day, and
each of those children's names were written up with a star.
Immediately some of the cannier children (the ones who
I'd learned went begging in the streets of Prishtina) saw the
opportunity for a barter economy – 'I'll sit quietly if you'll
give me a star?' I heard Fidan muttering to Vlora one day as
the children settled down for the closing assembly of the day.
Next to him a boy with a lean face echoed him – 'gimme a
star …' in the same slightly menacing wheedling tone you
heard from the pavements outside the mosques, or at the
traffic lights which were considered the best spots for begging.
Was this the only way they knew how to ask for anything? Or
were they just adapting their most finely honed skills to a new
currency; silver coins transformed into silver stars. I wish….

So much for 'achievement' then. What about 'creativity'? One
day at the end of classes, when I was clearing up the rooms,
retrieving and unfolding the tight scrunches of paper which
Jashar would always tear in fury from his book and pitch into

the darkest corner of the class if he made a mistake, there was a knock on the door. A teenager stood there, shifting from one foot to another. He had a dramatic bleached streak in his hair, and despite his obvious nervousness there seemed something bold about him, compounded by the fact that he'd come on his own to see me.

What did he want?

His nervousness made it hard to understand what he was saying, but he was repeating a word I'd not heard before in Kosovo – *sinti*.

The Sinti are a group I'd learned about when I first worked in Hackney and met members of Traveller communities and the education team meeting their needs. They're a Romani people from central Europe, and I'd learned to use their name carefully, trying to navigate the geography and ethnicity of Travellers who don't like to be called Roma, and Roma who don't like to be called Gypsy, and people who explained that 'Gypsy' came from 'Egyptian' derived from the only dark-skinned place the Middle English had heard of. Then there was the group in Kosovo who called themselves 'Egyptian' and who were usually lumped together with the Roma and the group unique to Kosovo, the 'Ashkali'. All three groups traced their heritage back to centuries ago in India, though they believed they'd taken different routes to the Balkans. Their common ancestry was evidenced in their darker skin (an Indian friend working for the UN in Kosovo told me that he had often been taken for Roma, Ashkali or Egyptian here) and the treatment of them as one group was a linguistic as well as sociological phenomenon, where the initials of the three ethnic groups – Roma, Ashkali and Egyptians – were loosely combined to form the word 'RAE' pronounced not like 'ray' as in 'sunshine' but 'rye', like black bread. I'd learned in one of my first conversations with Rrahmon not to use 'RAE', but to spell out the communities individually in eight politically-correct syllables, rather than that one neat acronym. Sometimes, talking to people in England I could take a short cut and call them 'Roma' but it wasn't accurate, and it wasn't polite. Or I could refer to the Ashkalis, since the majority of the kids who were coming to our classes were Ashkali. But I'd discovered that Idriz was Egyptian, as was Haxhi Bashkim.

But who was Sinti?

Eventually the lad with the bleached-streak hair and I disentangled our linguistic confusion. He slowed down and obediently repeated things. He mimed to help me out until I got it: *Sinti* was, it emerged, the Albanian for a synthesiser. And he played the instrument in a small traditional band (I remembered the 'pipes and drums for weddings' sign I'd seen on my first visit here).

'Me and my band could, you know, show the kids who come to your classes. Like teach them how to play?'

Mergim (the name means 'migrant'; I guessed he'd not been born in Kosovo) probably hadn't ever taught anyone before. Certainly, at the first workshop we arranged he had the rookie teacher's hesitant lurch between showing off his skill, and frustration when the children tried – and failed – to reproduce what he'd done.

He stood at the keyboard he'd brought in, and riffed the haunting opening bars of a *tallava* piece, sustaining the last note with the yearning of a saxophone. The children's eyes widened watching him.

Up they came, one by one, to try to echo the melody, with fingers that were too short and made only clumsy parodies. After a couple of goes, he'd nudge them away and replay the piece, but it would be different this time – my Royal Schools of Music Grade 5 training couldn't spot the difference, but I could tell that he was improvising. I wished he'd do with his music what he'd eventually done with the Albanian in our first conversation, repeating and slowing until I could follow.

But he was a talented musician, and he had something else that I didn't have, and nor did Teacher Avdil, or Vlora or Rob or any others of our slowly growing band of volunteers. He was from Neighbourhood 29, one of the people the children saw strolling down the road, hanging out at street corner gatherings, dancing at their weddings, maybe praying in the mosque. Now we had not just the cleaners, and the provider of tables, but the very first teacher *from* the community *of* the community. The room that had been an old lady's bedroom wailed and screeched and throbbed with pipes, drum and *sinti*, and I looked at the kids' faces looking up in hero worship at one of their neighbours sharing his gift, and I got goosebumps.

When we had a donation of money which was enough to cover the snacks for the kids and leave a bit to spare, I thought of the children's hunger for learning beyond our classrooms and decided we would buy a map of Kosovo to hang on the wall of our centre … the children should get ready for a wider world.

All maps are stories, but the neat inked line showing Kosovo's border was a story only just concluded, or possibly a narrative still unravelling. Kosovo used to be part of Yugoslavia and until the 1990s it would have been coloured on our map in the same shade as three of its immediate neighbours; Serbia, Macedonia and Montenegro had all (along with Slovenia, Croatia and Bosnia) also been constituent parts of Yugoslavia. In 1998 the tensions within Yugoslavia which had already boiled over into civil wars and struggles for independence in Slovenia, Bosnia and Croatia, broke out into widespread armed conflict in Kosovo, too. Kosovo did not want to be part of Yugoslavia, or the rump state of Serbia and Montenegro. Kosovo's majority Albanian population wanted independence.

In the face of massacres committed by Serb forces, and remembering what had happened in Bosnia, the international community stepped in, requiring the withdrawal of Slobodan Milošević's Serbian forces from Kosovo, and putting it under international administration with a United Nations Security Council resolution. After nine years of that international administration the Kosovan government assessed that they had enough international support formally to declare independence, and finally to ink that line on the map to show Kosovo as separate from Serbia.

Many governments welcomed this line being drawn, giving formal recognition to Kosovo as a sovereign state. The UK and the US were among the first to officially begin diplomatic relations. A majority of EU countries recognised Kosovo as independent, and a majority of UN members did so too. But Serbia would not. And Russia, a UN Security Council member with an accompanying right of veto, supported Serbia's stance. So Kosovo was still stuck halfway between being a protectorate and a country. Diplomatic negotiations were ongoing and Kosovo's existential crisis wasn't over yet. It had no seat on the UN; it couldn't play FIFA or UEFA matches; it had no international dialling code. So these citizens of Kosovo I was teaching really needed to know what these contested borders looked like; geography is not only history but also current affairs.

We put the map up on the wall and the children practised finding Fushë Kosovë, finding Prishtina. We had the same trouble I've had in every primary school geography lesson I've ever taught of understanding whether Prishtina is in Kosovo or Kosovo is in Prishtina, and the sheer implausibility of being able to put your finger right over Fushë Kosovë – blotting out this very building from the map.

If you're going to rely on education to give you a place in the world you can't rely only on maths, literacy and English.

A few weeks later, a friend from the British Embassy turned up in Fushë Kosovë. Cars with CD numberplates were no longer so rare in Neighbourhood 29 but she was still brought up to me like a trophy.

'You have a guest, Elizabeth,' the nine year-old who had shown Rachel up the stairs said like a miniature butler. He didn't leave the room though, after I'd welcomed her in, his eyes fixed on the briefcase she was carrying.

I was intrigued too, and when Rachel opened the case she showed that it contained a laptop that a friend had been getting rid of. The world had come a little bit closer to Fushë Kosovë.

We wrote out a rota, and sellotaped it to the wall of the office, and every day a few groups of children had a go at typing their name. Idriz installed the internet and we could even show the children how to use their new literacy, logging on to Facebook where they could see the pictures of our classes we'd posted.

The Facebook posting raised our profile, and new people continued to get in touch with us offering help. Now we didn't need carpets and clocks; we were ready for more sophisticated support. An Italian psycho-therapist made regular visits to help identify and support particularly troubled children; a children's author came to the centre bringing several heavy brown boxes from her car. From the boxes she brought out a copy of her book for every child – for most of them the very first they had ever owned.

As well as increasing the quality, we wanted to increase the quantity of the lessons we offered. We had always known that two hours a day wasn't enough, but then what amount of education is? In the UK we're used to a model of education offering about five hours a day (25 hours a week; according to studies just one hour less than the average time the British children I'd taught in London spent in front of the television). In Kosovo, the baseline is different as the flight from the villages to the country's towns after the war ended in 1999 has meant that most schools don't have enough space for their pupils. The result was a system where urban schools ran three shifts a day, each of just three and a half hours. Factoring in that during that time they were taught in groups of up to forty, by undertrained and unmotivated staff, the kids coming to us might have been getting a better deal. But they had some catching up to do and offering them more than two hours would be great.

The problem was that we were at the limit of what was possible with volunteers. One day one had already warned us she wasn't going to be able to come for her regular shift, and two others were taking children for vaccinations. It was going to be a hard day. Then my phone rang; another volunteer calling in sick so there would be just Teacher Avdil and me in the centre. Outside I could hear the playground sounds of children chatting, shouting, giggling – waiting for us to open the door. I did the mathematics of time and space, fantasised about a Victorian prefect-style system for educating silent rows of sixty pupils and looked up at Teacher Avdil. We couldn't do this.

He came down with me and we opened the door and waited till the clutch of learners holding exercise books had fallen silent. I cleared my throat, and then wondered what exactly I was trying to say, running through the euphemisms for 'there's no-one to teach you.' The kids had heard them before, but never from my mouth.

'I'm sorry,' I added, to the faces staring up at me. Some were crumpled in disappointment, others shrugged with practice; people regularly let you down round here, and the children turned their backs and scuffed off down the street to their homes – to tell their parents that today they could go out rubbish picking with dad.

I wrote a big sign to stick on the door – 'Centre closed today; see you tomorrow' with a smiley face. My own face was anything but.

I stopped dreaming of our volunteer team offering more than two hours a day; it would be enough of an achievement if we could be open every morning.

But then Eleanor offered to organise a fundraising dinner for us. She was an American who was in Kosovo because of her husband's work; a deft, petite hostess who'd treated Rob and me to exquisite meals in her home on the diplomats' hill overlooking Prishtina. With her friends she put together a buffet of Thai canapés, Filipino delicacies and other international dishes, as if people from across the world really were contributing each their serving of calories for the hungry and uneducated of Fushë Kosovë. She invited people to buy tickets to come to this feast and the money she raised was enough to pay Teacher Avdil to teach in the afternoons as well as the morning – meaning that our children would have the same number of hours teaching each day as their peers in mainstream school. When we announced to the children that they had the option of coming back to class in the afternoon, they cheered.

They actually cheered. It was the same response you'd get in a London primary school if you announced that the children were going to get the afternoon *off* school.

No-one was making them come here – not the state (who thought they were 'too late' to learn), not their parents (who would otherwise have registered them at the age they should have been registered), not us. It laid bare some of the principles of education which I had never had cause to think about in all my years of teaching. Very few children in the UK actually have a choice about whether they go to primary school, with all the weight of expectation, the requirements for work later on, let alone the social, educational and police systems to track and follow-up with pupils and their parents.

But these children had a choice. And yet they were using it to get themselves up in the morning, to step over sleeping brothers and sisters, to retrieve their grubby exercise books from the plastic bag hanging from the nail in the wall, and to make their way to our centre. How come?

The organisation that Rrahmon worked for, Balkan Sunflowers, recently did some research with the Roma, Ashkali and Egyptian communities of Kosovo. One of the questions they asked the more than two thousand adults in their survey was, 'Why do you think it's important to go to school?' The most common reason given was literacy, followed by the chance of better work in the future. But the community also cited 'being given greater respect' and 'satisfaction'. Maybe this was what got Gjelane sitting outside the centre every morning when I turned up at nine o'clock.

And maybe it's the most delicious proof that children love to learn. We see it and delight in it in three year-olds as they explore and experiment, but somehow by the time a child is nine, and has missed out on school, it comes as a surprise.

Added to all those reasons, I needed to remind myself that hanging out in a room with people of your own age – even if you're required to learn some letters at the same time – is an opportunity that plenty of young people crave. And the alternatives were often just kicking a can through the mud; we had little competition.

Whatever the factors, this was the most rewarding teaching of my career. Everyone – whether child or teacher – was there only because they wanted to be. One of the men from Neighbourhood 29 taught me a saying they had at the mosque – 'leave your troubles with your shoes.' It was a reminder that when you took your outdoor footwear off in order to enter the prayer space you should focus on what you had come for. But as our team of volunteers and I kicked off our shoes at the door of the centre the saying came back to me – this was my place of focus, and once I was padding around the learning space in my slippers I forgot all the other irritations of life beyond Fushë Kosovë – nothing else seemed important.

And the progress we were achieving was tangible, whether in young people learning the fine motor skills to be able to trail their pencils round precise twists and turns to convey meaning (I remembered the first day and the children's hesitation in mark-making of any kind) or in classroom behaviours like putting your hand up to contribute, and saying thank you when resources were distributed. Day by day, I could chart these children getting ready for school.

Which was just as well, since I had given this project six months, and the time was flying past. I was trying to seize all the opportunities available each day – jumping out of bed at half past six in the morning, to be ready to take Azemine through the overlong syllables of her name. I then spent the afternoons meeting with as many organisations and institutions as I could in Prishtina to lobby for the children's acceptance in school in September. There was a new alphabet for me to learn too – the different approaches of OSCE, UNMIK, the EU, MEST, UNICEF ... I was more bewildered than Azemine in decoding some of them. In a bizarre linguistic colonisation, the international community had even renamed the place where we were working. Keen always to use both Albanian and Serbian names for Kosovan places, to show no favouritism, they routinely used names like 'Peja-Peć' or stuttering written forms like 'Janjevo/a'. However, Fushë Kosovë (as the Albanians, or Albanian-speaking Ashkali, would call it) was unique in getting an entirely new name from the international community in Kosovo, apparently designed only to reduce their typing time when producing reports. Presumably wearied by the effort in writing 'Fushë Kosovë/ Kosovo Polje' as they would have had to do in order to reflect both languages' names, they not only reduced the place to initials, but even decided that it was too much effort to repeat the second of these. So I had to learn that in UN circles, Fushë Kosovë was reduced to 'FKP', like a code, a currency or some political party – not like anything that anyone would call home.

All these organisations had different reasons for helping with the issue – or not. In some cases they were simply as outraged as I'd been by the unfairness of children not being allowed into school. In other cases they had particular standards to fulfil – for European integration, for example. But all of them, whether national or international, were large organisations, moving carefully and ponderously, equipped with systems and safeguards to make sure that no-one's outrage carried them too far.

But we needed to move fast. I was haunted by a vision of failing to get the children to school, of folding our project in September, and of returning to visit Gjelane in eight years' time and finding her standing in her yard with a baby at her hip, beating a rug on the line and wistfully saying 'one summer I learned to write my name.' Exhilarating though these weeks and months were, for all of us, I was determined these should not be the best days of the children's lives. They deserved better than a classroom cobbled together above a corner shop.

So I stayed up late, too, blogging and writing emails until two a.m. most nights to bring the children to the attention of all those who could help with their time, skills, money or resources to get these kids successfully into school. Like the children coming to our classes, there was no-one making me do it, so you could ask the same question as to what my motivation was. The answers would probably be similar to how the parents replied in that survey – respect and satisfaction. There was a big dollop of egotism bound up in it too – having set out to get the children into school, and told the world about it I was damned if I was going to let the project fail. And each new person I told was one more potential weapon to fight on behalf of the kids ... and one more member of an audience I felt watching me and increasing the stakes if this all went wrong.

But, perhaps for the first time in my life, I nevertheless discovered a limit to my stamina. I started to feel sick. First in a way that just made me squint a little as if trying to readjust for being in a moving vehicle, or out at sea, but after the first day the feeling got more acute, and I started holding my head to steady it when I was sitting down, putting my hand to my face to support myself when I was talking. I went to visit Hatemja and sat in her dark room holding my head as I gave her a message.

'And what's new with you?' I asked politely.

'Oh, you know,' she shrugged, gesturing around her at the unchanging chaos of her home. But then, as if something had just occurred to her, 'I'm going to have another baby.' Her hand went instinctively to her tiny belly.

'Oh, Hatemja ...' I began. I tried to pack into my voice all that I could of rejoicing for a new life, and of commiseration about the increased poverty the baby would bring. I looked at her face, trying to see what she was thinking, but I couldn't read it. She was shyly proud, but perhaps officially disapproving. I decided it was more tactful to go with my first reaction.

'Congratulations!'

But she looked angry at me – or perhaps at herself, and her fate.

'Why congratulations? Another baby here?'

She was right of course, and I shook my head. I remembered the traditional Albanian blessing for a baby,

'May he have a long life together with his parents.'

She knew the traditional response too, and thanked me and we said no more of the things that couldn't be said.

I was worried about her, but she seemed more concerned about my headache and gestured me to lie down among the old blankets on her floor. It was tempting, but I decided it would be better for me just to go home early today. I looked round and saw Gjelane staring up at me with a frown. She slipped her hand into mine and squeezed.

'Go with her, Gjelane,' said her mum, so I was escorted out, and back to the centre, with my hand in hers and helped all the way.

Even gulping maximum doses of ibuprofen when I got home, the pain filled my head. I went to the centre the next day and we held our morning meeting of volunteers, but as soon as it was over I rushed to the bathroom and threw up. I was not going to be able to continue teaching today.

I ate hardly anything during those days, and although the pain eased eventually, for eight weeks it was a constant companion. I had lost weight from not having eaten properly for so long, and people remarked on how different I looked. My family were worrying and told me that nothing I was doing could be worth it.... This could clearly not go on for much longer; the children needed to be in school by September.

12 Not singing hallelujah

I was trying to summarise the exhilaration and the exhaustion in response to the question of how things were going in Fushë Kosovë. I'd had a call from Rand, the founder of Balkan Sunflowers. But how was he? Was there a reason why he'd called?

Rand's a wise and thoughtful guy, a little Honest Abe in his rhetorical style.

'You know,' he said, 'a few weeks after we started our learning centre in one municipality in Kosovo we heard that a rumour was going round that we were teaching black magic.' I laughed politely and in slight mystification. I think I said something clever about the black magic of education.

'And I'm telling you this,' Rand went on, 'to show that people will easily misunderstand and misrepresent things, and that you can't believe rumours. But I wanted to let you know that there's a rumour in Fushë Kosovë that you are teaching religion at your centre.'

I took a breath, confused. I thought about Haxhi Bashkim and his desks and chairs. I thought about the Agape Foundation. I thought about my own lack of any faith.

'Er, do you know which religion we're supposed to be teaching?'

'Oh yes,' Rand confirmed. 'They say you're teaching Christianity.'

I didn't know what to say – to him, or to whomever was the source of the rumours. I thanked him for the heads up and ended the call.

From whom had the rumours come? Who else had heard them? Was there any basis in them? I didn't know what would be more unfair – if they were malicious or if they were misunderstandings. But it was a time when our energies were already stretched and I sank into a chair feeling suddenly exhausted. When Rob came home from work I asked for a long hug.

The next day I went down to the shop to find Idriz. I made an oblique reference to what Rand had said, and watched for recognition in Idriz' face. He looked uncomfortable. Yes, he knew what I was talking about.

Did he have any suggestions for how I should convince people of what we were really trying to do? How could I share with the community some information about what went on in our lessons?

'Would people come to a meeting if I called one at the centre?'

'I believe so,' he said, which meant he wanted to believe so.

'Would you be willing to come?' I asked, thinking of the comfort it would be to have a familiar face and the benefit of the doubt if accusations were thrown.

'I will,' said Idriz, with a sincere bob of his head. That was a lot better than 'I believe I will'.

In a whipping wind I taped up a notice outside the centre, announcing a meeting at five o'clock the following day. 'Come and learn about our work with the children here. All are welcome,' it said. I added a jaunty exclamation mark.

I spoke to Teacher Avdil whom I knew was not only an observant Muslim but had even been attending the mosque in Fushë Kosovë after his lessons on Fridays, so must be at least a familiar figure in their worship; I asked him if he'd be willing to stay. Jeta, our Albanian volunteer who was also an observant Muslim said she'd be with us. Hope and her husband from the Agape Foundation, together with Vlora, said they'd come; the stakeholders were lining up for our unexpected inter-faith dialogue session

I channelled all my jitters into energy for cleaning the centre and setting out some drinks. I sorted through bags of donations we'd been given recently, which were cluttering the office, and found there some sets of Hilton hotel guest slippers still in their cellophane wrapping. I decided they could be arrayed at the door for visitors who would take their shoes off before entering.

By five o'clock the centre looked its best: clean and professional – and secular – with children's work displayed on the walls, and a rainbow of soft drinks awaiting any member of the community willing to be our guest. Teacher Avdil and Hope and her husband were having a polite conversation, translated by Vlora. We all kept looking toward the door.

There was a knock.

I went to open it and found a group of three men whom I didn't recognise. They each had one feature in common – a big beard that seemed thrust out provocatively at me.

I put on a big smile to parry right back at them. 'Welcome,' I said and ushered them in. They started to take their shoes off and with satisfaction I waved at the new pile of guest footwear I had just unpacked. They each slipped on a pair of Hilton branded slippers, and their beards seemed a little less confrontational as they shuffled through to the room where I'd set out the drinks.

I introduced them to our team and started to pour drinks. While I was doing so, more men were coming in. I turned to greet them and held out my hand. A young man behind me hissed, 'they won't shake your hand,' and I saved myself (or them) just in time, turning the palm to my heart in the accepted greeting I'd learned when travelling elsewhere in the Muslim world. It was the first time in Kosovo that I'd come across reluctance to make such formal physical contact between the sexes.

I had no time to think about it then; in the end about ten people had come to the meeting; all men, and apart from Idriz – who had kept his promise – none were people I knew.

They sat in a silent row resisting any attempt to make this feel cosy. So I took a deep breath and stood up in front of them.

'Greetings, gentlemen, and thank you for coming.' I explained that we wanted to tell the community what we were doing, since we had heard a rumour that people had misunderstood our purpose.

They all nodded; yes, they had heard the rumour. They understood that I had previously worked in a Christian organisation in the community of Gadime, 45 minutes away. They were worried that I was going to do the same work in Fushë Kosovë.

I felt as disoriented as I had done when Rand had first told me about the rumour. I had been to Gadime a total of three times in my life, and never to the Roma community there. I'm not a Christian ... I tried to say these things as calmly as I could, not to appear defensive.

The men were mainly courteous and some seemed genuinely interested in understanding what we were doing.

'We've heard you're teaching songs though? Presumably they're Christian songs?'

'No, no,' I assured them. 'We have two songs – a good morning song and a goodbye song.'

'But do they have 'hallelujah' in them?' asked one of the men.

'Listen …' I heard myself beginning.

And so it was that I found myself singing the lame lyrics we'd composed for our morning song to the tune of Frère Jacques to a dubious audience (some of whom had the decency to grin gently into their beards).

I sensed something changed after that.

'Look, our door is open at any time. You can drop by without warning if you want to see what we're really doing. You know, you could even come and help …'

There was an exchange of glances between the visitors, and one of them pushed himself off his chair. The formal part was over, and I think we'd passed some kind of test.

Conversation went on after that. I had explained that our staff and volunteers included some Muslims – nodding at Teacher Avdil and Jeta – some Christians, pointing at the Agape Foundation group, and people like me who were of no faith. The men were interested in talking to the Agape Foundation, and things were soon getting a little too theological for my liking. I wondered whether Hope and her husband with their evangelical Christian faith actually had more in common with the devout Muslims sitting opposite us than either of them did with me. I was bemused, listening to them talk.

Then one of our visitors turned to me.

'You say that you're of no faith?' he queried. I nodded.

'So why are you doing this then if there's no religion involved?'

I stumbled over formulating a clear answer. It wasn't simply a case of telling him what I didn't believe in (and I was wary of laying myself open to conversion attempts either from Agape or the local mosque) – I wanted to explain what did motivate me. Listening to Agape talking about the importance of the Bible for them, and looking at the alphabets and literacy aids around the room, I tried to say something about myself as a person of the book. Not a holy book, but any book – that I was a believer in the power of literacy to change people's lives and life-chances.

It wasn't an answer that could match eternity, but the longer I spent here, the more evangelical I felt about it.

13 Hatemja bakes baklava

This brush with the community had made me wary. Was there such scope for misunderstanding between different cultures and religions? It was a relief to go round to Hatemja's house; from Gjelane's hand in mine when I was feeling so ill, to Hatemja's welcoming smile always inviting me into her home, and Agron's loyal championing of me to anyone he spoke to, I was newly grateful for the family's friendship.

It was an odd friendship of course – they out-numbered me; I out-educated them. I had more money; they had more time. But we had a particular situation and aspiration in common, and a growing community in common too – the children who came to the centre, and Hatemja's neighbours. When I went round to see Hatemja, one or other of us usually had a bit of news of someone to share. Her children seemed to have got used to me and would rush up to greet me and snuggle into my side. I'd hold them tight, though seeming always to find their prominent ribs with my fingers. A cuddle from a child suffering from malnutrition has none of the rounded edges I was used to from my friends' children in England.

One day when I arrived, I found Gjelane outside the house chopping wood.

'Wow!' I said, 'I've never done that.' She couldn't believe me, and allowed me to watch her splitting logs, making clean white wounds in the wood with each stroke. Then we went inside together and when she was playing with my pen, inking her hands, I showed her how to make biro-ed heart-shaped tattoos that you could press from your hand onto the hand of your friend. It was a poor exchange of skills, but by the time I left, I and all the children too had imprints of stars and hearts on hands and cheeks.

As we got to know each other better on my frequent visits to her home, it seemed natural that one day Hatemja should come to my house. I hoped that she would come round for tea, that we'd sit on my sofa passing on some surprising fact, checking on the narratives of each other's lives, in the way we'd got used to in her home. But how would she get to me? With no transport or money of her own to pay for it I'd have to pay for a taxi to bring her, and money turned fragile friendships into prostitution.

In the end, it was the launch of my first book which gave us an opportunity to meet on my home ground, though not the way I planned. I was going to hold a party for the book, and amid the expats and volunteers, and the friends and colleagues whom I wanted to celebrate with, I imagined seeing Hatemja. I was going to have to make a speech at the party and I imagined looking out over the crowd of heads who'd be gathered at the Ethnological Museum; seeing Hatemja's encouraging smile would be just what I'd need.

We were sitting in her book-less home when I told her about the recent publication. I paused but she said nothing about the achievement – perhaps for a woman who couldn't write her name, the production even of a signature was a phenomenon no less significant than writing a whole book.

'It would be great if you and Agron could come and join me at the party,' I added.

For a second she still said nothing. And then she shook her head, 'I couldn't come.'

Why? Was there something immodest about coming to a foreigner's social event? The guys with beards had made me nervous about getting it wrong.

'I'd like you there, as my friend,' I said. 'And it would be fun.'

Would it? Or would it be a social torture, a room full of people Hatemja had never spoken to before, and had nothing to say to? A thought struck me – 'you'd know some of the people there – Zsofia and Jeta are invited too.'

Still she was shaking her head, at the impossibility. And then she spread her hands out, palms up, over her stained skirt.

'I don't have anything to wear.'

'What you wear doesn't matter,' I said, with uncertainty shaking my voice even as I said it. It was true, it didn't matter to me – not to the bohemian who'd had a washing machine at her disposal every day of her life.

'It does matter,' Hatemja said firmly, like it was a fact, not an opinion. 'I'm not going to let down' – the Albanian phrase literally translated as 'take the face of' – 'my friend.'

It was an impasse. For a moment a fairy godmother instinct tempted me to offer to buy her an outfit, but the fear of pimping came back to me. And what if this was just an excuse not to come – if I bought the outfit I'd be leaving Hatemja with no dignified way out. Again, I felt the euros in my purse weighing down this delicate new relationship.

'Well, think about it,' I said as I left. But I knew she wouldn't come.

In the end the fairy godmother flew the other way; the day before the party the need for Hatemja's support came back to me with new urgency. The book I was launching was about my early experiences in Kosovo, including what I'd learned as a beekeeper, and given the honey connection of the book

I wanted to make appropriate honeyed desserts for my guests. The Queen 'B' of Kosovan honey desserts is baklava so I planned to bake several trays of the flaky syruped pastry.

But when? Baklava is time-consuming to prepare and as I scanned the 24 hours ahead of me I couldn't see when I could fit it in. If only there was someone reliable, competent, flexible….

I went round to Hatemja's house again.

'You know that tomorrow I have this party,' I began. I saw her stiffen, as if she thought I was going to push her into parading her dirty skirt in front of my friends. 'Hatemja, I need your help – would you come to my house and work with me for the afternoon before the party to prepare the food? Of course I'll pay you …'

She smiled proudly at the suggestion and then she was frowning.

What was it? Was this too awkward? Would Agron not allow her to come? Could her children spare her? Did she have the energy as she thickened at the waist with the new baby?

'Yes, I'll come but … but … I've never made baklava before.'

I stared at her. Baklava is made by every Kosovan housewife I'd met, for celebrations of all kinds – Independence Day, New Year, religious festivals, weddings….

'Well, that's no problem – I know so I can show you.'

In my kitchen I set out the walnuts, the filo pastry, the butter, lemon juice, cinnamon and honey for us to start cooking. The first step is to melt the butter, and I set a small *xhezve* – the tiny long-handled stove-top pots for making Turkish coffee, which are just the right size for this task – on the hob.

'When I've shown you today, you can make baklava for the children when it's Bajram,' I smiled at Hatemja. She didn't reply at first, but when I then showed her how to pound the walnuts for the baklava filling and made a comment about how her sons would like this, she finally spoke, quietly and with a wriggle in her shoulders as if she was trying to dodge an uncomfortable truth. She gestured at the sunspots of lemons on the kitchen counter, the gleam of honey in its jar.

'But Elizabeth, we could never afford to buy this kind of stuff.'

Now it was me who didn't speak, even more embarrassed than she had been. Despite my days working with the community in Fushë Kosovë I realised I was being depressingly slow to learn what living on the breadline – not the baklava line – was really like.

But Hatemja was a quick learner, and she moved the conversation on to questions about the pastry. She was absorbing the new ways of working in a kitchen of melamine and worktops (three feet higher than the food preparation she was used to on the floor, in her home without a table) and where you could turn up heat with a twist of a knob, and no need to go outside to the woodpile.

Once the butter was melted and had cooled a little, we dipped our fingers in it and slathered the fat over the pastry sheets. We worked across a square of filo together, our hands glistening and dripping with an abundance of dairy products. We built up a rhythm together, as if to prove that we could overcome my stupid comments. I watched her skinny, cinnamon-coloured hands working alongside the pastry-coloured flesh of mine. The butter was blood temperature now, and about the same density as the sub-cutaneous layers that had, calorie by calorie, thickened my wrists and arms. It felt cruel to watch it slipping from Hatemja's slim fingers, like the possibility of nutrition that instead she was preparing for my well-fed friends.

We laid another sheet on top, and smoothed the butter across it, the illiterate woman and the foreigner carefully working together at a pastry parchment with our fingers as if we were reading Braille.

'I can do the next one by myself,' Hatemja said, deftly taking another paper-thin filo layer from the pile, and anointing it with butter. I thought of her tending to Ramadan's burns every morning and evening, eking out the cream I brought her across the tight skin of her son, and about the different ways that women learn competence – Hatemja's daily care of her injured boy in a dark, damp room in Fushë Kosovë, while plumper women like myself worked with golden fats and imported spices to prepare sweetmeats for guests to eat when they weren't even hungry.

Thinking about the guests and all the other things we needed for the party, I wondered whether I could leave Hatemja to work on the food preparation while I went to buy the drinks that we needed for the evening.

'Would you be OK in the house on your own?' Hatemja was probably never alone – she wouldn't go out without Agron or a female neighbour, and she had five children in and out of her home, at the breast or on the hip, being scooped up or sent away.

I set off for the shop, leaving Hatemja at work. When I came back she had finished the baklava and prepared all the vegetables for the crudités dip I had planned. Julienne strips were lined up neatly at one end of the chopping board, and a pile of vegetable remains at the other.

'You can throw those away,' I gestured.

'But I didn't know where,' she said. 'I went outside but I couldn't see a place for rubbish.'

I was busy unpacking the things I'd bought, and I was brisk.

'It's just there,' I pointed at the kitchen bin.

'But that's ... inside the house,' Hatemja faltered. I stopped my sorting of the packets and bottles I'd brought back with me, and looked round my room. Recipe books, the laptop I'd left playing music while we worked, white goods, fruit and biscuits; tea and coffee. And sitting right in the middle of it all on the floor – a metal container filled with discarded food going slightly rotten ... I thought back to Hatemja's home, dank and riddled with children, but I had never seen any food or rubbish piled inside. The outside yard – fetid with the overflow from the toilet, rusting with awkward angles of metal that Agron had grubbed up from the city's skips; that was the place for the discards of your cooking.

I looked out from my kitchen, across the hall to the bathroom, and thought that Hatemja must think even less of me for pooing in the house.

Although Hatemja had never offered me food at her home, I would have been squeamish about eating it, and I wondered whether my approach to hygiene turned her stomach in the same way. But I wanted to help somehow with the nutrition of her slim hungry body, and especially its incongruous bulge of the new baby. Hatemja left with a jar I'd brought back from the shops with me for her – a litre of concentrated sugars in the form of a pot of honey. It was just one gilded drop in the ocean of Hatemja's poverty, but maybe it would make her children sticky-fingered and give them the chance to lick up a little taste of baklava luxury. She held the crock of gold like it was a precious novelty, but we both knew that it wouldn't change anything for her really. Looking around my funny home, with its inside garbage and its inside toilet, it was for me that things were changing.

THE RUBBISH-PICKER'S WIFE

14 Banana milkshakes and bottle tops

On other occasions I asked others of the women I met in Fushë Kosovë to come and help me in my house, though it made for awkwardness with Hatemja. I didn't want to wreck a fragile friendship by having her clean for me, but then if I was a real friend wouldn't I have chosen her to be paid? (If she were a real friend, wouldn't she do it for free? I could feel how money makes prostitutes and pimps of us all).

The women were fast, ruthless cleaners, impatient with me standing next to them in the bathroom or kitchen squeamishly pointing out the slicks of dirt I needed their help for. My gentle hinting Socratic method might have worked better in the classroom than the mothers' brusque slapping away of ignorance or insolence, but when it came to dealing with dirt, they made me realise I was ineffectually polite. With their dousings of bleach and sloshing of cold water until their hands were red, the enamel gleamed.

Sometimes I'd catch them standing at a kitchen cupboard, holding a packet or a tin and staring at it with a frown. There wasn't much packaging in Fushë Kosovë kitchens where even eggs would be bought singly or in the exact numbers they were needed, then carried back in an artificial amnion of a plastic bag. My kitchen shelves were filled with imported food that had travelled all the way to shops in Prishtina from England, Germany, Italy or beyond, but had never made it to Fushë Kosovë.

And not only the products but my way of using them was alien, and perhaps revolting for women used to eking out too few calories between too many children. Seeing a hungry woman picking up food from my fridge that now needed to be thrown away because it had mouldered, uneaten, turned my own stomach.

One day a woman called Afërdita was clearing out my fridge and removing such food past its best. I sat at my computer while she worked.

'What about these?' she asked, bringing out some cartons of yoghurt.

'I don't know whether they're still good to eat,' I explained. 'Have a look at the date on the lids.'

She looked blankly at me, 'But I've not been to school,' she explained, with panic in her voice.

The connection wasn't immediately obvious, between an education and the woman doing basic housekeeping. But then I realised her meaning. She'd not even been to school enough to understand the date that would stop her eating food that had gone bad.

I thought about the children I'd been working with that morning on their numbers. I'd been worrying about getting them to school, but even if they didn't get there at least these were now sixty more consumers in Fushë Kosovë who wouldn't be eating mouldy yoghurt out of ignorance.

Afërdita pulled another item from the fridge. It was pickled garlic and she hadn't seen such a thing before.

'Can I try some?' she asked and went for a taste.

'Very nice!' she approved. 'How much did it cost?'

My turn to look blank. I possibly hadn't even looked at the price in the shop, confident in the padding insulation that my little purse of euros gave me against hunger. I had known I could afford any item in the small Kosovan supermarket where I'd bought the garlic, locked in my own pampered form of innumeracy. 'I'm sorry, I don't know,' I said.

Afërdita laughed at me and got on with clearing out the excess of appetite from my food stores.

I was now spending a high percentage of my waking hours in Fushë Kosovë and the boundaries were blurring between two worlds I'd thought of as miles, and centuries, apart. When I'd spent an afternoon in homes that smelled, as Laura put it, 'of unwashed hair', I could smell the same thing on my clothes. This was now a part of me, mediated in the headlice that jumped from warm nesting places behind the children's ears into scratchy homes in the warm places on my own scalp, and the colds the children shared with me, in small wriggling viruses which swam through me before leaping onwards from me to other children; I had become part of this ecosystem.

I was starting to blend better with my environment too; there was a skirt that I saw hanging in a shop in the neighbourhood when I was walking to the taxi stop one night. It was in the panelled 'gypsy' style popular that summer, with little beads sewn into it. At eight euros it was a bargain and I proudly wore it to teach the next day. The aunt of one of the girls who was attending our classes came to meet her at the end of lessons and grinned to see me wearing the exact same skirt that sat around her slim hips. We shared a brief moment of sisterhood and I reflected on how I was being colonised by this place.

It worked both ways. The children were learning my English, and my English habits (my insistence on *faleminderit* or thank you, which is so un-Kosovan; here, thank yous are saved only for something that you're really grateful for, and many people

I'd met in Kosovo had laughed at the nervous tic of the polite foreigner in a restaurant, thanking for the food, thanking for the bill, thanking for the change being brought). The children were also changing their style of dress as we gathered more and more shoes and clothes from foreigners in Kosovo or friends who collected for me in England, so that the shoes kicked off at the entrance to our centre had posh English names inked inside them from their first owners. Just as I was learning to walk in Hatemja's shoes, Gjelane was quite literally walking in Harriet's.

The work here was changing me on the inside, too. I was learning new vocabulary – the unique mixture of Turkish, Serbian and Albanian spoken in the roads (not the Albanian *rrugë*, but the Turkish legacy *sokak*) here gave me words for 'pen', for 'shoes', for 'dirty', 'to visit', 'to shout', which were all new to my vocabulary of formal Albanian – half-breeds born of the voices that had miscegenated here for generations. Some of the Albanian was turned on its head; when the first child said 'zavitue' instead of 'vizatue' for 'to draw', I thought it was a chance spoonerism. When I came across it again, from adults as well as children, I realised I was hearing a genuine local dialect, shared by perhaps six hundred isolated and largely illiterate families – the beginning of what could become a whole new oral language. Even what I had thought of as the international language of mathematics had to be translated – I learned that Kosovan children were taught to multiply with a dot and not with an x. The way I wrote the number 9 confused the children, until my lollipops were finally changed into single quotation marks so that they could understand.

Sometimes the Elizabeth I saw working in Fushë Kosovë seemed a different person from the woman who set out each morning from her home in the centre of Prishtina. I would sit with a child labouring at writing something, watching his fingers with dirt under the nails, from the rubbish-picking he'd done before arriving in class, and I'd catch the scent of the smart face-cream which I'd put on that morning at my mirror, and would wonder how these two worlds could co-exist. Was there some deep hypocrisy in me spending money on that face cream and then coming to try to help the children who'd be later grubbing up the discarded packaging as part of their quest for an income for their family?

One Saturday there was another small invasion of our Prishtina by the community who were taking me in. Rob had gone out shopping and when I heard his key turn in the lock and went to the door to welcome him home I discovered he was not alone, and it was a shock, the idea of an unannounced visitor at our house in Prishtina. This was our place, our refuge, and for all that I'd learned in Kosovo about your home as belonging 'to God and the guest' and for all our friends and people who'd come to stay or to eat with us here, ours was a negotiated hospitality, dependent on the issuing of invitations, careful timing of visits, the special preparation of food. There was no-one in Prishtina who made what my neighbour called 'Albanian visits' – without warning – to us. So who was this?

Nine year-old Labinot was one of the boys who came occasionally to our classes, sharing his name with Hatemja's son. I knew the reason he was with us only occasionally because I saw him with his brothers in Prishtina at the traffic lights in the centre of town. In one hand he'd hold an old Coke bottle filled with washing up liquid mixed with water, and when the cars drew up at the lights he'd douse their windscreens and swab down the glass whether the drivers wanted it or not. I'd seen him wooing them with a cheeky grin, swearing at them and their mothers, scooping copper glints of danger money into his pocket; I'd seen how he'd move on to the next car with a swagger which he never had in class where I'd watch him struggling through pages blotted with unfamiliar little black letters as unintelligible as flies caught at speed against car windows. I knew the eldest boy went out through the rubbish dumps too, all of them working lads with little time for luxuries like literacy.

Apparently Labinot had been soaping down a car window when he'd recognised Rob, asked him where he was going and whether I was at home, and had downed his tools to pay a social call. Now he stood there on my doorstep.

I welcomed him in, offering him some slippers in the traditional way as he kicked his shoes off at the door. It was a dizzying shift in our relationship – not just that he was here, literally on my home territory, but that he was the guest. In the Kosovan tradition that it's the guest who does their host the honour, I was now there to serve him. As a woman, that meant I should offer drinks, ideally accompanied by homemade sweetmeats…. I managed to find a bottle of fizzy orange. I realised that every minute he sat there was costing him in missed customers at the traffic lights and I searched – in vain – for some biscuits to serve too. Labinot sat watching me as I moved around our small kitchen.

He was looking around with interest; reading – more carefully than he had ever done with the storybooks we had at our centre – the evidence about my life in this house. I followed his gaze flickering across our drifts of papers, and the landlord's mismatched 1980s furniture.

But it seemed he wasn't interested in my material wealth.

'Do you have people round?' he asked, looking at the table. I guess the place seemed quiet to him.

He asked about the other rooms so I showed him the bathroom (where we poo in the house) and the bedroom and the spare room where I have my exercise bike. Labinot spends his days in traffic, judging time and distance, so within minutes and with a quick readjustment of the seat height, he'd hopped up on the saddle and was pedalling nowhere fast. I explained how the numbers went up to show the speed, and his skinny brown legs became a blur while the digital display told him the numbers he called out to me, like an impromptu maths lesson, between increasingly ragged breaths.

Eventually with a gasp he kicked his feet free and let the pedals spin on without him. I suggested he was ready for more fizzy orange so we went back to the sitting room and made more awkward conversation for a few minutes while he gulped down some liquid. Then he politely asked if he might leave, and I politely said that it had been a pleasure having him. He grinned at me.

'I'll come back. I might bring my brother.'

It was the very next day that there was a knock at the door. Labinot and his larger, stockier thirteen year-old brother. I recognised him from our classes, but he'd been less patient than Labinot, more aware of the discrepancy between his age, his size, his aspirations to manhood and the simple texts we'd tried to decode together. He'd start at it, with darting, inaccurate guesses, and then he'd swipe at the page as if it was a passing car and his squeegee could get the job done with one wave of his hand. Then he'd dismiss it with his favourite word, *palidhje*. You'd translate what he was calling it as 'stupid' but it literally meant 'unconnected.'

So here was Ebubakir the Unconnected at my house. He looked a little sheepish but I welcomed the boys in. Labinot showed his big brother the way with a confident stride and it was with him that I checked 'another drink?' as if he was the host of this impromptu party.

But I realised I didn't have any of the disgusting fizzy orange left. I ran through the contents of my fridge rather desperately, and asked them if they'd like me to make them a banana milkshake. Labinot found the blender almost as exciting as the exercise bike and then I poured them out a glass each and they sat slurping enthusiastically until the glasses were empty and each of them had a cream moustache.

Ebubakir nodded approvingly at the milkshake. Labinot pointed out features of my sitting room and kitchen area. My washing machine – another nod – and the bag of bottle tops which had intrigued him. There was an initiative to collect plastic bottle tops which were then sold on for recycling and the money raised bought wheelchairs for those in need. I'd explained it to Labinot and he faithfully repeated it to Ebubakir who nodded with some interest. Turning trash into treasure was one of their family's areas of specialism.

This was all very well but....

'Could I show him the bike?' Labinot asked politely. So the three of us trouped into the back room and Labinot jumped into the saddle again, and showed how to make the numbers go up. His brother smiled as he watched him – a smile of expectation of victory. He took his own turn, pistoning his legs and watching the display while his smile got bigger in pace with the numbers until at last the figures shown there were even higher than Labinot had pushed them, and he gave up with a jubilant final gasp.

'It's good here, isn't it?' asked Labinot enthusiastically.

'Yeah, but she doesn't have children. Without children it's … *palidhje*,' Ebubakir philosophised.

The boys left soon after and the house felt quiet.

The next afternoon when I was home I wondered whether there might be another knock on the door. I'd made sure I had some spare bananas just in case. But no-one had come by the time I had to leave and I locked the house up a little regretfully.

When I got back home it was dark. I turned the porch light on to see to unlock the door, and spotted a lumpy plastic bag leaning against the wall. It was a present for me to pass on for the wheelchair project; the bag was full of sticky plastic bottle tops, grubbed up from the bins and the dumps where Ebubakir spent his days when he wasn't learning his alphabet.

15 Emine spells her name out for the big black book

Muscles were building – mental muscle of stamina and practice as well as Ebubakir and the other bigger boys bulking out with hard manual labour. There were also the little muscles – fine motor skills in fingertips being trained each day as the children learned their way around their letters, and how to match the salmon leaps of the tongue in the mouth with a flick of the wrist and the pen to capture a sound and lay it out to dry on paper.

But we still didn't know what it was exactly that they needed to learn in order to be accepted into school. There was no syllabus and no standardisation for the test; there was no set date on which the test should be held. I met again with the Ministry, and with the school. The EU office in Prishtina got involved, and Unicef. The Organisation for Security and Co-operation in Europe offered legal help to understand the law; the Ministry for European Integration said they saw it as an issue for proving the EU-ready credentials of the Kosovan system. Yet with each meeting I had, and each email I exchanged, the process became less clear and the arguments more circular. Sometimes I tried to engage with the issues – the way the law was written, the Ministry's by-laws, the schools' registration processes (which they maintained were so inflexible that it was this above all which prevented children who hadn't been signed off as attending the first grade from ever entering second grade). Sometimes I simply ignored these Byzantine discussions and sat quietly, repeating my first, thunderingly obvious point, as set out in the Kosovan constitution and every international charter: these children have a right to education. So what was their state offering them?

Despite the confusion, there was one rule which everyone agreed on, even though we were never to find it written down anywhere. This rule allegedly specified, as Gjelane had told me at that very first meeting with her, that after the age of nine a child could not be admitted to school unless they passed the mythical test. The corollary seemed also to be believed – that up to the age of nine, no test was necessary. And as we got talking to some of the children and families we were working with, we realised that this did in fact offer a way in.

Ages in Kosovo are sometimes given not by how many years have been lived by the individual, as is standard in English, but by how many years you will have completed on your next birthday (I had the same problem with telling the time in Fushë Kosovë, where rather than a standard Albanian way of telling you how many minutes past an hour it was, people said how many minutes yet to go until the next. As in Serbian and German, 'half past seven' was 'half to eight'). It was an aspirational, forward-looking approach to measurement, and it had led little Emine and Shkurte, for example, to be included in our classes for nine year-olds because they had told me quite truthfully that they were 'on the way to nine'.

When I found out, I was frustrated with myself for not having understood this subtlety, but what was poor news for my language proficiency was great for Emine and Shkurte's chances of an education. By the school's own rules, they would have to accept the girls to start class at the beginning of the next term. No test, no quibbling. I was assured that it was just a case of a parent or carer taking the child and their birth certificate to the school and registering the name with the school. I spoke to Emine's father and we agreed a time to go to the school together after lessons the next day. A young woman from Rrahmon's team said she'd come with us as she'd registered children from her community before.

I wondered if Emine's dad would remember. After all, this was a father who had not quite got round to registering his child when she was six or seven; what would be different now she was eight ('for nine').

When the classroom door opened that morning for the children to take their places, I understood what would be different this time. Emine bounced into class. 'Teacher, you're going with my dad to register me at school today.' I smiled at her,

'Yes, I know, Emine.'

When the children had settled to their work, Emine put her hand up, so I went to her side. She was bent over the letters of her name. E with its one, two, three horizontal strokes. M for 'mali' (the mountain mnemonic worked in Albanian too), down–up–down–up–down. A dashed off vertical line for I, and now she was paused.

'What do you need help with, Emine?'

But she'd sorted it out and was triumphantly tracing a half-mountain (down–up–down–up). The top bar of the E that followed lifted into the air like an arm raised in jubilation. She smiled at me. 'And will you be ready as soon as lessons finish?' I assured her I would.

When she left my class to go to the next lesson, she sneaked up and hugged me. 'I'm so excited about registering for school.' She mentioned it again before her father and I finally met at the end of classes and headed to the school. As we walked, with Emine chattering between us, I realised I hadn't given Emine – and her friends – enough credit. I had been worrying about how I, or Unicef, or the Ministry for European Integration could become better advocates for them but I'd paid no attention to what good advocates they were for themselves.

Emine's bounce lasted all the way to school. It lasted up the stairs to the Deputy Director's office as our footsteps echoed in the stark stairwell. By the time we had reached the door of the office, I saw Emine's little hand creep into her father's big one. We knocked and went in. The Deputy Director was sitting at a huge black-bound ledger, like something out of Dickens. She looked up and I smiled at her; she did not smile back.

With an artificial brightness in my voice, partly for Emine's benefit, I explained why we were there. I made it sound easy – like an administrative procedure which we were all anticipating would go smoothly.

The Deputy Director came out fighting at the very beginning. She was a small, compact woman and she reminded me of the way small compact dogs yap and snarl when someone comes into their territory. And this, she was quite clear, was her territory. It was certainly not mine – I conceded that – but I had hoped it could belong to Ferdona, the colleague of Rrahmon's, or, most importantly, to Emine. Emine's hand was now squeezing her father's and her chatter had stopped completely.

The first thing the Deputy Director said to us (without even the introduction of 'hello') was 'you've registered her before.'

No, Emine's father replied, he had not.

'Yes, you have!' the Deputy Director all but shrieked.

I saw Emine turn her head from one to the other.

'I know what you're like, all of you,' shouted the Deputy Director. 'You just want the books. You register your children to get the free books and then the child drops out and you sell the books in your market.'

Emine's father looked bemused, and admirably calm. Meanwhile, I was trying to work out the economics of what the Deputy Director was suggesting. The textbooks she was talking about were given out free by the government to every child in school. So even if Emine's father did do what she was suggesting, who would be buying? Anyone in school would already be getting them for free. And anyone not in school would surely not want them.

I looked at the woman, tried to understand where her rage was coming from. If only she could understand what life was like for the families we were working with; then she'd see what a fragile miracle it was to have got this girl, this father here in this school. Surely then she would work to nurture the miracle. If only she knew what their conditions were like....

I looked at her again and had a sudden startling understanding. I could have been completely wrong, but there was something in the woman's snarl; something in her dentistry perhaps; this woman did know. She'd been poor herself. Perhaps grindingly poor. Perhaps so poor that you were taunted for it; a poverty that could turn you against your family and make you ashamed of who you were. And now she wasn't poor. Of course, by the standards of any British civil servant, her salary was a scandal, but in the Kosovan system she was just about OK. She had enough to eat and clothe herself and her family respectably. She had good shoes.

Perhaps more importantly, she had a black book. And she wanted to forget the time when those things had not been true. She didn't want to help poor families scrabbling for an education; they made her mad.

The Deputy Director was repeating her allegations, leafing angrily through the ledger to try to find Emine's name as a previous registration, try to prove that the father was wrong, wrong – and that he and his community could not be trusted. She had an unreasonably loud voice as she berated him, and he was starting to get angry now himself.

'I've come to register my child,' he shouted.

'Don't shout at me,' she yelled.

I leant down and squeezed Emine's shoulder while Ferdona tried to get the two other adults to lower their voices. I repeated what the father had said,

'We've come to register Emine. Here's her birth certificate.'

The Deputy Director was shaking with the after-effects of her rage, but she took the paper and thumped the huge pages of the ledger over and over until she found the first blank page and started to write Emine's details.

'Right- or left-handed?' she snapped. I looked blank; I couldn't remember. Emine wasn't really strong on which was left and which was right, so the Deputy Director passed her a piece of paper. 'Write something,' she barked.

Emine's face lit up – this was her showtime! When she'd first come to our classes she hadn't known even the first E – let alone the last one – in her name. With her tongue sticking out just a little bit beyond her teeth she picked up the pen and began.

'Right-handed,' the Deputy Director concluded, and moved on with filling in the columns in the ledger. She wanted Emine's address, date of birth, father's name ... and Emine's father gave the information. Below their conversation, Emine scratched on at the table, finally coming to the end of the word she'd been practising every day ... practising so that she could come to just this building – the place I'd been promising the children was theirs by right, and was their ticket to the future. She looked a little bemused, and I felt my eyes prickling.

Emine picked up the paper and passed it to the Deputy Director with a proud grin. The woman frowned and swatted it away. It had just been a way of finding out which hand Emine wrote with; it had served its purpose and she had no interest in reading what the girl had painstakingly scratched out with her right hand; there was no column for that in the ledger.

I gave Emine's shoulder another squeeze and mouthed 'bravo', and the girl put the paper down confused.

'That's it,' the Deputy Director said as she filled in the final column of the ledger. She didn't say 'congratulations'. I mumbled an insincere thank you and the four of us left the room.

So, one of the children was registered for school: the first tangible achievement of what we'd set out to do. Hopefully Shkurte would be next – and then it might be Gjelane. But I hardly felt like celebrating.

'You were great,' I said out in the corridor with the most enthusiasm I could summon, and Emine smiled distractedly, looking around her at the scary halls, the doors behind which children were shouted at, their parents insulted by school staff, where they were taunted with unfounded allegations of criminality. I looked at her father to see whether he was as angry as I was about the way we'd been treated. But he seemed untouched by it.

I realised that it was possible that my life as an educated woman living and working largely in places where I was in the majority had not prepared me properly for the educational experience which was awaiting the kids we were working with. I thought of Hatemja's responses to conflict, with officials' scorn at the hospital, or when her new neighbour had shouted at her for what he alleged was her rubbish left outside his door. I'd been furious on Hatemja's behalf then, and I called back at the raging neighbour – 'It's not her fault; it's the municipality's fault that they haven't come to collect it. Will you come with us to complain?' The man had sneered at me – 'I'll come and leave it outside your house next time,' – and as I felt bubbles of indignation rise inside me at this, Hatemja had just laughed, like she had outside the doctor's office.

'*Lejë, lejë,*' she'd said (the words mean 'leave it' but are pronounced, 'lay', and as she'd said them, she'd flung her hand out exactly as if gesturing to those of us with soaring blood pressure that we should lie down). Maybe the secret of avoiding an early heart attack in Fushë Kosovë was *lejë, lejë*.

I was pleased that Emine didn't seem as close to tears as I was, but as we set off for her home I started to have doubts; what was I leading these children to? In insisting in my smug educated-white-woman way on their 'right' to education, was I actually putting them in harm's way? For the first time in my sanctimonious child-rights-based mission I had doubts about whether I was doing the right thing.

As we walked back, I asked Ferdona what could be done, whether it was normal, how this deputy director could

Emine

continue behaving like that with the children. She shared my outrage, but not my surprise.

'She was worse today because you were there – she was trying to show you that they wouldn't co-operate.'

I had never considered it might work like that – I had presumed the staff would be on best behaviour with an NGO present.

So Emine and her father had been insulted because of me. The thought was uncomfortable if it was true. Should I not come on the other days – just suggest to parents that they took their children alone? After all, Emine's father would have been able to complete the process, and it hadn't needed me. But what if a parent didn't; what if the situation for the children aged eight was the same as it had been when they were seven, and parents didn't quite get round to it; the urgent priorities of health and food overtaking the administrative tasks like registering for school. It would mean another lost year.

Whether it was control-freakery or children's rights, I couldn't decide. But I knew the next day I'd go back to register our other eight year-old – Shkurte.

Shkurte's name means 'short' and although she is in fact a slim little child, that's not the reason she's called this. The name is traditionally given to a girl born to a family who wants boys, as an imprecation that the line of girls they've had so far will be cut short.

If you meet a girl called Shkurte she's unlikely to have an older brother, and it was indeed one of Shkurte's three older sisters, who came with us when we returned to the school to try the registration process once more.

The sister, Samire, was only twelve herself but old for her years – bright, mature and enquiring. She came from an observant Muslim family and she and her two next youngest sisters – but not Shkurte – all wore headscarves. En route to the school, Samire chatted to me about what we were seeing, things she'd heard about, ideas she wanted my opinion on. She'd learned the song, 'We are the world,' on some organised camp the previous year, and sang it happily as we walked, but then confessed that she didn't know the meaning of what she was singing ('we are the ones who mayer berra werr so let's start giving'). We translated it together and then fell quiet – we were at the school gates.

In we went, and up the echoing stairs and to the Director's office. It was locked, and I sighed. That meant the Deputy Director again.

Turning to her office we knocked and went in. Maybe she had thought about the shouting match yesterday; maybe she'd be embarrassed and conciliatory?

The first thing she said was, 'Why are you wearing that in here?'

She was talking to Samire about her headscarf.

Samire's a good girl. She stayed calm, 'It's my choice to wear it,' she said simply.

'Not in here,' said the Deputy Director, with her voice rising. 'It's against the law in a school.'

Though I'd heard about that law, it was the first time I had even thought about this issue. It was only a minority of our pupils who wore headscarves, but even so, did it mean that what we were encouraging them to do would force them to choose between their religion and their education? I filed the question away; for now, surely, it was irrelevant.

'But it's not Samire who's coming to register – she's here as carer for her younger sister.'

The Deputy Director snarled back. 'Well she needs to know that if she comes to register herself, she'll have to take it off –' she made a snatching motion with her hand as if she'd like to rip the scarf off Samire's head right away.

We moved on – the ledger was opened and the columns had to be filled. We established that Shkurte was right-handed, we passed on her address and her date of birth, the final column was completed, and the Deputy Director gave the grunt I was getting used to in place of a welcome to the school. Shkurte was registered.

Two down. Could I do this more than sixty times over?

16 The angels versus the Mother Book

'Imagine I'm the Minister for Education …' I began. The children were looking blank. I was attempting to build a class of advocates – kids who were self-confident and knew their rights and had some of the skills needed to assert them.

'What do you say to me?' I asked the children who were being encouraged into this little role-play.

They'd obviously heard this rhetorical question before. One of them remembered what worked last time.

'Faleminderit,' chirruped Anita.

Ah yes, they had lovely manners now. They knew that when I handed out the yoghurts in the morning I expected a *faleminderit* ('thank you'). They'd say it when they were given a pen, too. They'd all written thank you letters with *'faleminderit'* in big capitals to the donors who had made these classes happen.

But it wasn't the right answer this time.

'What are you saying *faleminderit* for?' I grumbled. 'Save that for when he's given you your place at school.'

The letters we were writing were to the Minister of Education. It was June and after a series of frustrating meetings with the Ministry representative, still no sign of the promised action plan for how these children were to be integrated into state-funded education, and a dwindling amount of time before school started in September, I wasn't feeling minded to say *'faleminderit'*. I was fretting that the possibility of the children being admitted to school for the beginning of the new term was fragile. I needed to do more; we needed to do more.

So I went over it again with the children. It's a child's right to go to school – 'Whether you're in Africa, in America, in England or in Kosovo,' I said.

'Or in Belgium,' added Astrit.

Yes, in Belgium too.

And they wanted to go to school, right? So now they had to tell the Minister why.

I didn't prep or prompt them, I just wrote down what they said (and when the top group had their lesson, they wrote it themselves without help). The letters they wrote were heart-breaking in what they showed that these kids knew about the things they were missing.

'Dear Minister, I want to go to school because without school you look stupid.'

'I want to go to school because when I go to the pharmacy I want to know what the tablets are for.'

'If you don't know how to write then when you go to register your birth certificate you can't sign it.'

'If you don't know how to read or write then people cheat you.'

'I want to become a doctor.'

'If you don't know how to read then when a letter comes from the electricity company you have to go to your neighbour to ask them to read it for you.'

'When you know how to read and write you can get a job.'

In the bottom group they copied out a sentence each. I collected the papers in, planning to present them to the

Ministry. At the bottom of Anita's it seemed she couldn't stop herself. With a little heart she had doodled the word, *Faleminderit.*

If the Minister could give a commitment to these children to them being educated by his institutions by the beginning of September, I would send him a letter myself, and I would doodle more than one heart around the word *faleminderit.*

The process was stalling – our first step had been to look for the law which the director of the school had told me about, and the woman at the Ministry had been so sure of – the one that they used as a reason not to accept children over nine years old without them passing a test. I'm no legal expert, but I'd looked through all the laws and by-laws on the Ministry's website, and couldn't see any reference to this provision. I had met with the Organisation for Security and Co-operation in Europe, who had responsibility for rule of law initiatives in Kosovo, and spoke to the people there who actually were legal experts, and they in turn went through all of Kosovo's laws and by-laws.

The good news was that there was no such law.

The bad news was that there was no such law.

If there had been a law, we would have been able to challenge it, and no doubt, with the Kosovan constitution on our side, to have it changed. With a stroke of someone's pen, or the delete key on a Ministry keyboard, Hatemja's daughter would have had her right to school.

But if there was no written law, it meant that the barrier to Gjelane's education was in people's heads, where it is a lot harder to find the 'delete' key. There was no clear way to tackle the problem, so we resorted to making as much noise as possible about it, asking for advice from whomever we could, hoping to build a consensus that this was a problem, not only for Gjelane and her friends, and for her community, but for Kosovo's society and beyond – that 'injustice anywhere is a threat to justice everywhere,' as Martin Luther King put it.

We were lucky to have some good friends. The EU office in Kosovo had given recognition to the issue and said they would mention it in the annual 'progress report' the European Union issues for countries seeking to join the Union. They convened a meeting for us with the Ministry and the municipality, the Prime Minister's Advisor for Human Rights and Unicef to try to find a way that the school would be prepared to accept the children.

The meeting was tinged with tiredness and racism, and frustration on all sides. The Ministry explained – patiently, and repeatedly – that children had to be recorded in the ledger that translates as the 'Mother Book' as they passed through each class. If a child wasn't recorded in the school's Mother Book for grade one, then the child couldn't pass to second grade. The children in our classes weren't registered in the Mother Book so there was no way that they could go into any class but grade one. And – they explained just as patiently – the children were too big for grade one. They wouldn't fit the furniture, for example....

I and the representative from Unicef mentioned the Convention on the Rights of the Child, and it produced the Pavlovian reaction of much nodding by the Ministry and Municipal officials. Oh yes, no-one was disagreeing with the right of the child to education. But the problem was the Mother Book....

Could they see that the Mother Book was effectively taking away these children's right to education?

They looked shocked and a little hurt. You should never insult someone's Mother Book.

We left it that Unicef would work with the Ministry and the Municipality on an action plan for how to include these children in school. A deadline was set.

The deadline passed.

We sent an email asking when we could expect the action plan. The cc list read like a list of the Kosovan cabinet.

We received no reply … and it was then that we decided the children might succeed as advocates where we had so far failed.

In fact, things moved on before the letters could even be sent. It's not the story I want to tell here, because I'd love to narrate that Anita's felt-tip heart was the secret to a change in the policy of educating a whole community. But what actually happened, almost as the felt-tip was drying on Anita's letter, was that I went to have a cup of tea with some friends. They are one of Kosovo's power couples – she is a respected Kosovan journalist and he is a British diplomat. They had been following what we were doing in Fushë Kosovë and asked for an update. I told them that I was the closest I had ever been to giving up; that I now really didn't believe that the kids were going to get to school in September. And that I wasn't sure whether I could lock the door of our centre on 31 August and walk away, saying that I had done my bit … a brave attempt … that it had to be in the hands of Kosovo's institutions from now on. I could feel my eyes brimming with tears as I talked to them.

'Sorry …' I tried turning the conversation onto other subjects.

But Elida was angry now – partly on my behalf, but also, I sensed, with her country.

'It's ridiculous!' she stormed. Ruairi was frowning too and they held a quick muttered conversation.

'Hang on …' Elida said. She got up from the table and left the café, and Rob and Ruairi were left sitting rather awkwardly staring at a tear-stained teacher at the end of her tether. We didn't quite know what to say to each other, and I swirled my tea with a spoon, and felt pathetic.

It was a relief when Elida came back. 'Well, I've spoken to Vlora. She's going to see what she can do,' she said. Vlora Çitaku was the Minister for European Integration and a dynamic young Minister who did seem able to get things done. I looked up from the swirling tea. It was very good news. Who knew whether it would make a difference, but it was a step in the right direction.

I knew that it had indeed made a difference when I got a phone call a few days later. It was Minister Vlora Çitaku. And she said she had just come from a meeting with the Prime Minister. She quoted him as having told her to 'do whatever it takes to get those children in Fushë Kosovë to school. They should have their constitutional right'.

So now the Prime Minister, Anita, me, and glamorous Vlora Çitaku – a strange team – were all on the side of the angels. The angels vs the Mother Book … it sounded like a scene from Harry Potter.

And the Mother Book lost. I knew that on the day that the school Director called me to set a date for the assessment of the children. He said that a Commission was being convened and that each child would be assessed individually and orally by the Commission.

I wondered how the children would respond to the news – whether they'd be scared by the prospect, or whether I'd need to explain more about its significance. When they were all sitting down at the beginning of lessons, I told them.

There was instant and enthusiastic applause, kids turning to look at each other with big grins on their faces and wide eyes. Someone whistled.

These kids were ready.

The school had given us three days to submit the details of all the children to be assessed for registration and were asking not only for name and date of birth but also the form of ID we had seen, which we had never recorded. It meant that we had to make repeat home visits to all the children who were to be registered at school. I divided the work with a new volunteer called Kaltrina – an inspirational young woman from Kosovo who was currently studying in Canada, but had come back for the summer and for an internship with us. She and I knocked at doors, called into empty hallways, bumped into people in the street, even interrupted a wedding, until we had a neat spreadsheet showing the details of seventy children who hadn't registered in the first two years of school, but whose parents said they wanted them to go to school. We watched seventy birth certificates being unfolded from careful storage. In most cases the mothers (it was usually mothers who reached for the carrier bag filled with documents hung on a nail on the wall) handed us a sheaf of birth certificates and asked whether we could help tell them apart because they didn't know how to read their children's names.

In a few cases parents, even of those who had attended our classes very regularly, said they wouldn't allow their children to start at the 'big' school. The reasons were varied, mainly unfounded, and we had gentle debates before leaving those houses. Was it really true that the Albanian kids would beat their children up? Were they sure it was too far to walk?

Plenty of children manage it every day. Yes, Nerxhivane has an eye infection, but that shouldn't stop her going to school. If Lume needs to help his dad with scrap metal collection, couldn't he fit it round a few hours of going to classes every day?

The next afternoon Nerxhivane's mum came to our centre. She'd brought her daughter's birth certificate. 'I'd like her to register on Friday,' she said. We chalked up one small victory, and submitted her name with the others.

After that we had three days to prepare ourselves. Avdil spoke to all the children about how they should present themselves when they went to school. He'd told me once about his own children – five of them with American educations. 'A good teacher is a good parent,' he'd said, and his advice to his pupils now was fatherly. 'Clean faces, clean clothes, nails neatly trimmed,' he ordered them. 'And you should bring a tissue with you so that if you need to blow your nose you don't use your sleeve.'

The next morning Fidan greeted me by patting his pocket ostentatiously.

'What have you got there, Fidan?' I asked.

I'd seen Fidan in Prishtina at the weekend, cleaning car windscreens at the traffic lights. I guessed it was some of the money he'd earned there that he used to buy himself a pack of tissues so that when he was to turn up at big school at the end of the week no-one could judge him because of the way he wiped his nose. I almost needed to borrow one out of the pack myself.

Would they all come on Friday? It was mosque (= begging) day, when our numbers were always down. By then it was summer and state school holidays, and wedding season had started; some children would be caught up in family celebrations. And some would be sick and others would discover they were needed at home or to go and help their dads, and maybe some would get cold feet about this state system that had been readied for them. They were going to have to walk a mile out of the *mahalla*, and into a large echoing state institution; I wondered how many of them really had the stomach for it.

A squad of volunteers were with me that morning and ready to knock on all the children's doors an hour before we were due to set off for the Commission, to leave the children no excuse that they forgot or overslept. Agron said he would come with Gjelane. I knew Fidan would be there with his newly blown nose; Afir wouldn't miss an outing; Gazmend couldn't wait to tell someone his times tables; Besmire wanted to be a doctor when she grew up. Those are the things that get children to school all over the world, and now the system in Kosovo had adapted so that those were the things that could get a crowd of children here to school for the first time too. Was it enough?

I was literally on the edge of the car seat as our taxi drove into Fushë Kosovë that Friday. It was as if I was readying myself to jump out, into action. I had an egotistical belief that what happened today would somehow depend on me.

It was reassuring to see children waiting outside the centre as the taxi turned the corner. But there weren't seventy of them…. Our volunteers sprang out and set off to the roads they'd been allocated in our plan. We'd divided the area into the streets where the children lived and each volunteer was responsible for checking on ten children, making sure they were awake and getting ready for the Commission.

Meanwhile, the children waiting at the centre were greeting me, jittery with adrenaline. Florinda was wearing a startling flowery dress I'd not seen before. The sisters Mirjeta and Arjeta were wearing new matching pink T-shirts with sequin designs. Everyone had blown their noses (Astrit showed me two packets of tissues in his pocket, and Fidan stood by looking rather crestfallen).

I checked against the list I'd been allocated and saw that Elvira wasn't yet there, so I set off down the alley that led to her house. I found her washing her face at the standpipe in her yard. 'I'm cleaning myself up – I don't want anyone at that big school to say that the kids from Elizabeth's school are *palidhje*', she reassured me. *Palidhje* struck me as a good metaphor for today, when the kids from 'Elizabeth's school' were being *connected* up to the mainstream system for assessment.

Once Elvira was ready we returned to join the other volunteers and compared notes. Now we had 62 children. Where were the other eight? I wanted to go back to those houses, start the conversations about the future, about rights, about responsibilities…. But it was time to go, so we set off – a straggling, giggling line of children strung out across the *mahalla*. Agron was the only parent who'd come with us, but he helped marshal the children and keep them in line. Gjelane walked solemnly beside him. The children greeted the adults we passed in the road,

'I'm going to register at the school!' Old men murmured ritual blessings and prayers for good luck, which contributed to the tone set by Florinda's dress that this was a special day, a particular rite we were on our way to; something between a wedding and a war.

Just outside the school gates I regrouped the children, hushed them, reminded them about manners, about being quiet. The gates are big enough that they would probably have done that job for me, and the children slowed to a wary walk as they entered the playground. At the door of the school we found not only the school Director but also the Director of Education for the municipality, who greeted us carefully. Later, staff from Unicef and from the Ministry came too. It wasn't just the kids who knew this was a big day.

The children were led to wait in a classroom (sat in a classroom! As I watched them taking their place at the desks I thought how many of these children came from families who knew something about squatters' rights. They'd each made a part of that school their own now, and I reckoned they'd be back) and I was taken to be introduced to the Commission in another classroom down the corridor.

The Commission was made up of three kindly teachers from the school, plus the Deputy Director and a community representative. I was dispatched to collect each child in turn from the waiting room and bring them to the Commission. On the way they skipped down the huge corridors, and only the occasional one snuck their hand into mine for a brief moment of reassurance. That's what struck me most about the day – their self-confidence, in their learning and in the rightfulness of taking their place in this school. As I walked Astrit to the room for the assessment, I said to him, 'Don't worry – they'll just ask you what you know of your letters and numbers.'

'I know up to one hundred, he said. 'Will they want me to count it in fives or tens?'

Agron came in with Gjelane and watched almost in wonder as his daughter squeaked and screeched the chalk across the board to spell out her name and the stupid sentences the Commission dictated to her.

It took three and a half hours until all the children had shown off their counting and their letters, and the commission conscientiously took notes on each child. When they had finished, I was called in to the Director's office.

I was less brave than Astrit as I walked the corridor. I wondered what trick questions the Director might ask me.

When I entered his office I found him sat at his desk stamping a document. His hand shook on the stamp as he forced the ink down onto the paper.

He looked up.

'This is for you,' he said grimly, and handed me the piece of paper. It had 62 names on it, and next to each one was a class number; the kids were to be accepted in school in September. The bottom right hand corner was daubed in the mauve stamping ink. So it was official.

I wanted to hug someone, but the only person to hand was the Director and I wasn't quite ready to hug him. I felt adrenaline quivering in my voice as I thanked him, and a release of tension ripple down my body till my legs shook on my way out to tell the children.

17 Fair interviews

On the wall of my classroom in Fushë Kosovë I started a countdown – 'how many days until we start at the big school?' My first job of the day, before sharpening pencils, setting books out on desks, writing the lesson aim up on the board, while I was still alone in the quiet of the classroom, with only that clock ticking like a gentle reminder, was to wipe clean the number I'd written the day before. The first thing I did with the children once we'd sung the 'good morning, did you sleep well?' song and while they were tucking into their yoghurt and fruit juice, was to see who could read the new number. It started at 50.

Fifty more renditions of the song. Fifty more lesson plans. Fifty more trips to buy yoghurt at the minimarket…. Rubbing away at the marker pen each morning (why does wipe-clean never wipe quite as clean as they claim?) there was a sense of liberation – from having to come here every morning, having to make sure there were volunteers for each class, and that the cleaners had come, and all the spoons for the yoghurt had been washed, and liberation from the responsibility of overseeing the learning and welfare of all the minds and bodies that rushed and wriggled their way into our centre each morning. A sense of pride, too – that we had done it; that the children whom I'd been told were unteachable had been taught; that families whom I'd been told would never send their kids to school had registered them all the same. A sense of relief that nothing had gone wrong. But when I rubbed out the number '1' and there were no more days left of our activities here, no more need for our strange cobbled-together curriculum and motley crew of a staff, what would I do? Who would I be? Who would need me any more? This building and the miracle taking place in it had defined me for six months. What was there to take its place?

I remembered swirling my tea when I'd met with Elida and Ruairi, and how my voice had wobbled when I'd told them that I wasn't sure that I could lock the door on the centre and walk away. That had been because I had thought I would have been leaving the children without a teacher. But now they had the best teachers the Kosovan state could provide, and yet I felt that I still couldn't lock the door of the centre and leave. Perhaps I was more concerned about the teacher being without the children than about the children being without a teacher.

Along with my vanity and my need to be needed was a more rational call for me not to throw away the key. It was voiced by our volunteer, Rob Williams, who suggested that he and I could meet for a coffee (these drinks that punctuate decision-making processes in Kosovo! No wonder reading the coffee grounds is seen as a way to know the future here – you can tip up one of the tiny Turkish coffee cups and see the shapes of what will come, because without the cup of coffee, nothing will ever be decided and there will be no future). We met in a bookshop café, the home of the autodidact, with shelves of learning towering above us like a vision of what we had been trying to achieve together over these six months.

'They're not going to stay in that school,' he said, shaking his head sadly. 'Not without some extra help. They'll be eaten alive.'

It was not what I wanted to hear.

'We've done all that we can do,' I said. Which was true – he and I had both given more than we'd thought we could, in daily lessons, in keeping spirits high, in finding money to keep our classes going. 'It's up to Kosovo's institutions now,' I said; this was how it should be.

'Yes. And the kids are not going to stay in that school,' Young Rob repeated. And with a sigh and a queasy feeling in my stomach, I acknowledged that it was true. Some of them would – the ones who'd picked up their alphabet quickly, who had self-confidence, who had missed only two years of school; the ones who would be put in the classes of the smiling teachers who'd been on the Commission. But would Fidan really make it to that big building every day when his parents had been used to him going out begging and bringing back money for food? Would Anita, so quick to tears? I thought of the way the Deputy Director had talked to Emine. Would Anita stand up to kids in class calling her racist names, or teachers with inaccurate ideas about what this community was like?

Even Gjelane, who I knew wanted to go to school ... would her drive to learn survive the morning chaos of a family trying to get five children up and dressed and fed? With all those competing demands for childcare, who would be there to get her to school on time every day?

'OK. But what can we do?' I asked Rob. And inside my head was a voice saying, 'Please don't ask me to keep this up. I can't. I can't do it.' And it wasn't just the voice that was in my head, but that familiar pain which had started up about a month into our classes and had never fully left me. I winced.

But Rob was being practical; he wasn't asking for sacrifice and heroism.

'We could do activities on Saturdays, so we see the children once a week. We could check whether they're actually going to school, and we could give them extra teaching to make sure they're not too far behind the other kids. Maybe it would give them a sense of solidarity to see each other again, since they'll all be in different classes after next month.'

It was a great idea. And it led to another; while I had been conscientiously narrating our countdown, our volunteer, Aurélie had been counting in the other direction – thinking about sustainability and scaling up and where we should go from here.

Another hot drink (always chamomile tea for Aurélie, as if she permanently needed calming down from the buzz of ideas and energy she brought with her; for me fruits of the forest, with two sugars, until it tasted like boiled sweets) and Aurélie told me her idea. She thought we could apply for some funding (she suggested ten thousand euros, and the amount seemed obscenely huge) and we could use it to employ someone – our first member of staff from the community – whose job would be to keep in constant contact with the families and teachers of our precious 62 children, to check whether they were going to school, or whether there was anything they needed to help keep them there. We could apply for money to give them all a school bag, and a pair of shoes to start the new school year....

Aurélie wrote the ideas into a funding proposal and we sent off our request to the Austrian Development Agency, ADA. As if it was all so easy, we heard back shortly afterwards that our application had been accepted.

Ten thousand euros! In my mind I imagined the lanes and homes of the community in Fushë Kosovë – the mud brown and the concrete greys. I imagined ten thousand euro coins, or a hundred thousand glittering ten-cent pieces raining down onto the families, among the giggling children, into the work-calloused hands of their fathers … I tried to imagine the transformations that could be made with ten thousand euros. It was a new, but wonderful Midas-like responsibility, that almost overwhelmed me.

'But can we spend that much?' I asked Aurélie. I was thinking of the 1300 euros we had raised at that very first fundraiser at Zsofia's house.

'Well, how much has this project cost so far?' she asked.

It was a reasonable question, and I didn't immediately have an answer. (Old) Rob and I had been keeping a careful box in our bedroom of receipts for everything we'd spent, and an accompanying spreadsheet. We had a file which showed the money we'd received in donations, from that initial 1300 euros, through the PayPal account a friend had set up for us, and in envelopes of crumpled fifties or twenties that people had donated, as well as the bigger contributions from the fundraising efforts of people like Eleanor. We'd had one thousand euros worth of materials including tables and chairs, textbooks and a fridge to keep leftover yoghurts fresh, from the United Nations Volunteers through UNDP. So I knew that we'd spent more than the 1300 euros we'd raised at the beginning, but how much more?

When I finally went through the spreadsheet and totalled the numbers up it was a shock. Shock at the price of education, even when it's a patched-up process run by volunteers in a flat above a minimarket. And shock at my naiveté in having thought that that 1300 euros would be anything like enough to have funded the six months of classes we'd run. The six months had cost us seven thousand euros. Thank goodness for Aurélie's wisdom. And thank goodness for the Austrians.

In fact, very little of the ten thousand euros we'd received from ADA would be needed for the position we wanted to recruit. Salaries in Kosovo are pitifully low, given those teachers with university degrees who only get three hundred euros per month. We weren't requiring anyone with a university degree (in fact, in the circumstances we decided we didn't even need candidates to have finished high school though we required basic literacy) so we advertised the position at 250 euros per month.

'Advertising' was a different process from previous recruitment drives I'd been part of, too. There were no websites that could reach the pool of candidates we wanted to attract; but sellotape and a photocopier helped. With a sheaf of duplicated information sheets I set about making sure that every telegraph pole in Neighbourhood 29 had information about the position. We copied the information for each child to take home with them too. And I had a conversation with Agron.

'Are you going to apply for the job, Agron?' I asked.

'Of course,' he said, with a little smile.

That was good news. But ...

'You know that we'll choose the best person who comes for the interview, don't you, Agron. That might be you, but it might not be.'

Agron looked genuinely confused.

'But Elizabeth ... You've known me for six months. You know I'm good. I've worked so hard to help you and the children. And we have a baby on the way ...' It was all true.

'You know you can trust us. Hatemja's been to your house ...' In the Kosovan job market (a market with official unemployment around 40%, where most jobs would have more than one hundred applicants, and many of them would be perfectly qualified, if not over-qualified) what Agron thought he had was a dead cert. He'd already done competent work for us like the job for which we were offering a salary.

He knew I liked him; he knew I wanted to help. And his wife had been to my house. In Kosovo that meant that the job was his.

I could see him trying to understand what lay behind my ambivalence.

'Do you not think I'm good? I'm an honest man; you've always trusted me.' Yes, I would trust Agron with my life.

'Is there someone else you think should have the job?' No, there was no-one else I knew of who was better qualified, no-one whose wife had visited me at home more often than Hatemja…. But maybe there was someone better – our recruitment process would find that out.

'We'll ask everyone the same questions at the interview and the person who answers them the best will get the job.'

Agron sighed as if he thought it was a pretty poor way to judge long-term suitability for a post, and I hoped that these interviews would be easy – for him and for me.

From the 37 applicants for the job we shortlisted ten for interview; Agron was one of them. Others were men I'd seen before in the street, or parents of children who'd come to our classes. Avdil and Aurélie and I sat behind a desk and politely asked the questions we'd prepared to each one.

'What would you do if a child we'd registered for school told you that they didn't want to go any more?' we asked.

'I'd shout at them.'

'I'd tell Elizabeth.'

'What can you do? If they don't want to go then there's no point trying to change their mind.'

One man, the father of Shkurte, and Samire who wears a headscarf, went for none of those options.

'I'd talk to the child,' he said, 'but softly, because you need to be gentle if you want a child to tell you the truth. And I'd find out the reason, and then we could deal with it. That's what I do with my own children – you have to know the reason why they're behaving the way they do.' I could see Avdil and Aurélie both scribbling enthusiastic notes on their interview forms.

Agron's answers to all the questions were fine, as I had known they would be. But they didn't show the skills of working with children that Hysni had shown. We compared notes at the end of the interviews, and we all agreed – Hysni was the best candidate.

We phoned him to offer him the job, which he accepted with careful thanks. And then I went to break the news to Agron.

It was horrible.

'But you know me, Elizabeth,' he kept repeating. So I kept telling him about our points system at interview, about the panel – that it wasn't just my decision, how fair we were….

'I really needed that job,' he said, with his voice rising. 'Look around you. LOOK!' he was shouting now, in his tiny, dark, dirty one-room home, and Hatemja was at his back, partly trying to calm him down, partly engaged in a reproachful stare at me.

'How am I supposed to keep these children with no job?' he asked rhetorically.

'I'm sorry,' I mumbled, wondering what I'd done. All I had set out to do was to help this family and now they were shouting at me.

'You see, Hatemja, there's no work for me. I'm no use to you or the kids,' Agron said dramatically. I closed my eyes.

'I might as well be dead,' Agron went on.

'Don't say that, Agron,' I began … it was time to go. Time to run away and wish I had never got involved in any of this. Agron was hurt, and now I was hurt.

'You have to find me a job,' he said.

And I flipped. My own voice was rising, in pitch as well as in volume. My Albanian was stumbling, verbs losing their endings, none of the nouns agreeing with their adjectives.

'No, I don't, Agron. I don't *have* to do anything,' I was telling myself as much as him. 'I'm trying to help – I'm trying to do the right thing; for you and for your children and your community. We had fair interviews …' I stopped myself from trumpeting once more my perfect HR procedures that Agron wasn't really in a position to appreciate.

'I'm going now, Agron,' I said, and levered myself up from the dingy mattress on the floor where I'd been sitting, waved a grim goodbye to Hatemja and the confused Gjelane who'd been listening to all this; and I walked off down the street in tears.

18 Shaking hands with Hysni

Our team meeting the next week was Hysni's first. He seemed a bit overwhelmed by the gathering, and looking along the faces huddled round two tables at our usual café, I could see that the phenomenon of what we'd become might be baffling. From that early team of Zsofia, Jeta, Laura and I, we'd been joined by volunteers from abroad like Kaltrina and Rob, by expats in Prishtina like Aurélie and Elena, who'd been coming every week to help children one-to-one where necessary, and also by helpers from within Fushë Kosovë. Around the table, it wasn't just one conversation now and it wasn't just in one language either. Hysni turned his head from one to another, listening as Elena told us about the operation she'd secured for a little boy with a hernia, or Aurélie updated us about the application for funds she'd submitted. She told me there was a visit I'd have to make which I might not enjoy.

So soon I was back at the school in the Director's office – the same place where I had sat six months earlier and been told that it was too late for Hatemja's daughter to be educated. We both knew that what I'd been told then had turned out not to be true; the Director frowned when I came in.

I tried to see the situation from his point of view – children's rights champion, turned bad guy. His school had one of the largest intakes of Roma, Ashkali and Egyptian children in Kosovo. I knew it had been used as an example of inclusive education in the past.... And then we'd come along and made a very audible fuss about the fact that although there were many children from the community who did go to his school, he was in fact not allowing in the huge group of kids we had worked with who wanted to come.

And now he had to explain to his teachers working in already overcrowded classes, that they were going to be accepting an additional 62 children – two classes' worth – but with no additional space or staff. And that these children had had less schooling than the other kids, and would need more help … I could understand the frown.

I had come with an olive branch. Part of Aurélie's clever planning of our grant application to ADA had been to include some resources for the school – a recognition that their resources were going to be stretched by these new kids, and a small contribution to supporting the new needs they had. So I began,

'It's good news that the children have their right to education now – thank you for all your support to them.'

The Director was looking at me with brows that were still bunched.

'We wanted to be able to help the school, so we've applied for money for resources for you, and I just wanted to know what would be most useful for you. Do you need footballs, science equipment, a projector…?'

The Director had a new look now – a wary smile.

'What do you have for me, Elizabeth?'

'Well, whatever you think the school needs most. Is it sports equipment? Furniture for the classrooms?'

'No, but for *me* …' the Director insisted. 'I did all that work to get the children registered. That's not my job, so what do you have for me?'

For a few furious, confused seconds I didn't speak at all. Finally I found a tactfully oblique form of words. 'I'll pay you exactly what I'm getting paid to do this …' The director's eyes lit up as he started to calculate, and then he glowered as he realised my meaning.

I felt revolted by the conversation, and also scared: had I made it clear enough that there was no money for the Director? Did I need to say more? Should I have said less? I wondered about walking out right then.

But we had promised our donor that some money would go to the school. And it was destined for the school's pupils – any and all of the pupils.

My voice was bright and false.

'So, is it footballs or a projector you'd like for the children?'

In the end we agreed on repainting the walls of two classrooms. The Austrian grant would pay for the materials and the labour, and while the countdown to Day 1 at school continued in our little classroom above the corner shop, the rooms in the Big School were readied for the new arrivals. I went to see the finished paintwork during one of the hot days of August; the rooms smelt reassuringly fresh and we fixed a sign on them proudly bearing the names of the 'Austrian Development Agency' and of our charity, 'The Ideas Partnership'. I imagined the children from our centre filing into the new spaces along with their new classmates, feeling bewildered, and then seeing our familiar logo and maybe being comforted that we were somehow here. And then I remembered what the Director had said, and wondered whether I wanted anyone ever to think we had been linked to this place in any way at all.

While the school was preparing itself we were getting into the routines we hoped would help to keep the 62 children there. Hysni's new role was an unfamiliar experience for both of us – before he was employed by us, he had been earning money as a manual labourer, going through the bins when there wasn't any other work. And now we needed him to write things down, attend meetings, account for his time…. And just as he was getting into these new ways of working, I was having to learn that The Ideas Partnership was no longer a carefree band of volunteers; we had to learn about tax laws, and contracts, and work out where we recorded leave arrangements (though Hysni seemed bemused by the idea that he had a right to leave – a right to leisure. He only ever used his leave for religious holidays and when his brother-in-law came from Sweden to visit. He tried to use it when he was sick, too, but we explained that having paid time off when you were sick was a right as well).

I liked him – for his smile, for the fact that he squatted down to talk to the children at their level, and learned their names. This was unusual – Avdil, and most Kosovan teachers, would still call out 'O, girl' with a jabbing finger if he wanted to get the attention of a child. The people in the community I heard in the streets calling out to children would amend it to, 'Hey you … Ahmet's girl' or 'Jashar's boy,' so that children didn't have an identity beyond that of their father. When I used the children's names in conversations with other adults from the community they seemed to see it as a quirk that I knew individual kids by name, like one of those people who can remember phone numbers or post codes. Presumably having your name learned was something that only happened in adulthood, so that people could refer to your own children by using it.

And I liked having an adult from the community to guide me here. My attempts so far at formal dialogue in Fushë Kosovë had come to an end with the final note of my rendition of

Frère Jacques at that meeting, but now we had Hysni with us there was the chance of something more meaningful.

I had thought that it would be a good thing to try to get in touch with the *hoxha* at the community mosque. Perhaps a meeting now would be better than waiting until issues came to a crisis about the girls in headscarves, for example. And I wanted the *hoxha* to know that I was willing to support girls wearing headscarves, that our priority was education; certainly that we wouldn't be putting any pressure on girls who chose to wear a scarf. One Friday I dressed carefully in my longest skirt and went round to the mosque. It had only been built a few years before – a modest building painted in the green that is Islam's sacred colour. I waited outside in a well-swept courtyard, by the taps for ritual washing and the shelves for worshippers' shoes; loitering with the dirt of the world and the mud of the street, unwilling to trespass on the holy space inside. Eventually an elderly man came out from the prayer room and bent to put on his shoes at the door. His movements were slow and meditative and I recognised the state of calm and mindfulness I sometimes managed on my yoga mat.

I approached him hesitantly, sorry to interrupt, asking whether the *hoxha* was available. I gave my name and said I'd like to set a meeting. The old man nodded silently and held up a finger for 'one minute' and then stooped again to his shoes, unlacing them so he could go back inside. I stood in the sunshine, wondering what conversation was going on in the cool dark interior I could glimpse through the door.

It was clearly something of a debate as it took some time. Albanian speakers would call his 'one minute' *a baker's minute* – the time you have to wait for the buns to come out of the oven. Like our own *baker's dozen*, it is more than you expect.

Eventually, after a number of *hoxha*'s minutes the old man came out with the message that the *hoxha* was busy and I should come back on another day. I tried the following week, waiting self-consciously once more in the courtyard until someone came out from prayer. This time I was told the *hoxha* had just gone.

Next I tried through Hysni, asking him to pass a message to the *hoxha* asking for a meeting. He looked uncomfortable, but said he would take the message. The next day I asked what the reply had been, and Hysni said the *hoxha* had agreed to a meeting the following day. I checked my skirt length again that morning, and my sleeves. I was as demure as I could be without covering my head, and I waited for the *hoxha*'s arrival.

He never showed.

I decided he must despise me – as a non-Muslim, perhaps as a woman? As someone coming and interfering in his community? He didn't value my work, and he didn't want to be seen to be meeting with me? So many theories.

I asked Hysni, 'Why won't he meet me?' and waited to see how Hysni could answer tactfully.

But his response wasn't what I expected at all.

'He's scared of you, Elizabeth.'

I never fully understood why, but I didn't want to compromise Hysni any further, and the *hoxha* and I never did manage to meet. It only made me more curious about Hysni's faith community.

One day in the week before Big School began, Hysni and I stayed after lessons to organise 62 sets of bookbags and school materials. It wasn't easy as the requirements for exercise books were different depending on what class you were in, and we had children starting in classes from one to five. We'd bought boxes and boxes of exercise books with the Austrian money, and laid out book bags in rows on the desk, and were walking between them setting out the right books (thin lines/ fat lines/ squares) in the right quantities on each. It was mechanical work and a good place to talk. I ventured a question to Hysni about the Muslim men who'd come to the meeting early on in our teaching. I was still wondering about the man who wouldn't shake my hand. I knew that Hysni went to mosque; he had a proud beard, and daughters wearing the headscarf, yet he shook my hand whenever we greeted each other in the mornings, just like the others in the team. I wondered what the difference was between him and the guys who'd come to that early meeting who'd swiped their hands away and resisted shaking mine.

Haltingly, I opened the discussion. Maybe he'd heard about that meeting, even though he hadn't attended himself? Yes, he had been told about it.

So I mentioned the people from his mosque who hadn't been willing to shake my hand, as a woman. 'Yet you always greet me with a handshake. What's the reason?'

'Well in fact, Elizabeth ...' Hysni mumbled, and I saw him look awkward.

Maybe we didn't know each other well enough for this conversation. I stopped him, 'You don't have to talk about this if it's not a good conversation to have – I'm sorry. I'm just trying to understand.'

'No, it's not a problem, and I'm happy to talk about my faith. And I'm pleased you respect Islam – I thought that when I applied for the job I wouldn't get it because I'm, you know, a Muslim.'

'Oh no … of course that doesn't make any difference,' said the infidel, realising as I said it that of course it makes a world – this world and the next – of difference for a believer.

'And in fact, since you ask about shaking hands, the day you first greeted me it was the first time I had shaken hands with any woman who wasn't in my family.'

I was speechless. Not that Hysni was following the traditions of the others that we'd met, but that he'd broken them for us. I couldn't imagine how he must have felt, that first time. I wondered what he'd thought of us, the hussies or the gauche Westerners, extending our feminine hands to him and requiring him to touch us. I thought of the sticky feeling in my palms from when the children in Fushë Kosovë slipped theirs into mine, and how I would make sure not to put my fingers in my mouth, or eat anything, until I'd managed to wash somewhere, or squirt on some hand sanitiser. It must have been a similar feeling – and one he couldn't remove with sanitiser – for Hysni every morning and every afternoon when I clumsily grasped his hand.

'I'm so, so sorry, Hysni,' I said, and was once more grateful for his humility, in metaphorically squatting down to my level as an ignorant Westerner, just as he spoke gently to the children.

Hysni just smiled, and passed me a pile of books to be allocated to the top classes.

On another day we were out together walking the paths and middens of the neighbourhood on our way to making some house calls for children who had stopped coming to classes. We were on the far side of the railway tracks, in a neighbourhood with a different feel from where Hatemja lived. There was still poverty, but there was space. The sewage trickles which in Hatemja's part of town pooled right outside people's homes here gurgled like rustic becks into the field

Hysni

opposite. In Hatemja's part of town barefoot toddlers padded across your path; here it was dogs, drawn by the garbage piles that collected here, where no municipal vehicle could reach. The roads were almost all mud, and as Hysni and I picked our way along them, I realised how little I'd understood mud until now. It had always seemed an incidental detail – a grey splash spoiling your car's paintwork on a rainy day, or something within the creosote lines of a sports field to be banged off your hockey boots when you came home. Fushë Kosovë mud was, instead, a fifth element. It clogged up any spaces in the tread on your soles, and then formed further clumps and clags under your feet, squashing into great unsteady plates extending either side of your shoe, so that you walked with something pulling at you with every step. Mud here was a feature of the landscape requiring particular techniques for navigation in the same way that a river or a mountain does. It made you slip and fall, it pulled you down and it spun you round. It flicked and slicked across your skin so that you found it silting up your shower when you washed at night. Hatemja's tin trough for washing the children's clothes was a sludge of mud as their trousers and socks sat steeping in the grey-brown stew.

It delayed Hysni and I as we made our way to the children's homes, making us take illogical routes to avoid the worst patches, or pick gingerly using stepping stones of garbage – a shattered desktop computer casing, sodden half-submerged car seat squab – to lift ourselves above it. We were later than planned, and then from a distance – from the other side of the settlement – we heard the call to prayer. I paused in my conversation as I'd learned to do from the children and volunteers who would stop and pray, whether silently or out loud, at this point.

'Do you need to go to mosque?' I asked Hysni apologetically, knowing that it had been my idea that we should make this final call. I remembered his reluctance, and had attributed it to wanting some lunch. Now I realised his mind had been on something higher.

'No, it's too late now,' he explained. 'You have to have finished your washing and be ready to pray by the time the muezzin calls.'

'Will it be a problem?' I asked, wondering whether what kind of problem I was referring to – a problem with his fellow worshippers? With the *hoxha*? With Allah himself?

'Not as long as I make up the prayer before the next specified prayer time,' Hysni explained. He had just less than three hours then – and the next prayer time still fell in working hours.

'And what will happen if you don't pray by then?' I pushed.

Hysni looked sorrowful. 'It will lose me 44 000 years in Paradise.'

Later I heard different arithmetic – another of our volunteers said it would cost you seventy years of hell, and another person said seven hundred years. Someone else pointed out that we can't be sure what penalty Allah will give on the Day of Judgement – and that Allah is merciful. Even so, my light suggestion that we could do just one more home visit, and indeed all my time management, suddenly acquired dizzyingly higher stakes. Hysni and I might seem to be doing the same thing – checking our watches for example – but while I did the mathematics of time and motion, Hysni had visions dancing in front of him of angels and demons and his immortal soul.

I wasn't sure how much Koranic basis there was for this or the other rules and reasonings I learned in Fushë Kosovë, but it didn't really matter – the people who told me about them believed that these were the requirements of their faith. If they were unorthodox traditions then it just made them harder to predict.

'Let's eat now before we go,' I had said to the team once when we'd grabbed some snacks from Idriz' shop, in a rush to get everything done. We were standing in the office and one of the team shook his head regretfully.

'It's against our religion to eat standing up. We should sit down, or we should eat on the move.' I had the same sense I had with speaking Albanian, that as I blundered through these foreign structures, although I could generally make myself understood I must be causing sensitive listeners to flinch repeatedly as I got things wrong, broke rules, and transgressed in ways I wasn't even aware of.

It wasn't just me, though. One of our volunteers from the community, who would describe himself as a Muslim, organised a popular dance class one evening a week for the older children. I went to watch them sometimes – girls who slipped quietly into the centre, hanging round in small nervous groups while Faik prepared the room. And then the music came on and the dancers took up position, tossed their heads and long dark hair, and became haughty as hell, stepping nimbly and confidently through the moves he'd taught them. When they'd rehearsed enough, they arranged a show at the municipal Cultural Centre and they put up posters to advertise it. The day before the show I found Faik deflated. Normally full of energy, from the hip-wiggling dancing he could do to any music – Kosovan or Western – to his enthusiastic attempts to speak English which came out peppered with the German and Swedish he'd learned during two sojourns as a refugee, today he was slumped. 'They've taken the posters down – the guys from the mosques. They say it's *haram*.'

The same word was used one summer day when one of the male British volunteers wore a short-sleeved T-shirt revealing his tattoos. I hadn't known that body art was prohibited by Islam, and although we prepared our volunteers with guidelines about obvious ways to avoid offence in their dress and behaviour I'd done nothing to prepare the boy for being followed round Fushë Kosovë by an admiring crowd of pre-adolescents, as revolted and intrigued by the snake coiled round his bicep as if it had been a real reptile.

The community itself was changing in its understanding of these rules and mores. Towards the end of April, as the day was getting nearer, I had asked Agron about the traditional Roma festival of *Shëngjergj*, 'St George's Day'. This is officially an Orthodox festival, but also particularly marked – as *Hederlezi* – by the Roma community, as well as by others in Kosovo, even if they are Muslim by religion or Albanian in ethnicity. I'd heard about animals being killed that day and their blood used to daub the foreheads of children for good luck and good health. Agron had shaken his head, 'No, we don't celebrate,' he said briefly.

But a few days later Hatemja had come to me.

'I don't know if you know, but *Shëngjergj* is coming up,' she had said. 'I want to kill a lamb for Ramadan; could you give me the money for it?'

'But I thought you didn't celebrate,' I said and she had shrugged. She wasn't going to get the money from this vegetarian anyway, so we hadn't discussed it further. But on the way home I had realised another reason for her reluctance to go into more detail. On the door of one of the shops was a printed poster incorporating a large picture of a lamb with a cross through it, clear enough for the illiterate to understand. The Albanian text beneath it read, 'Don't kill a lamb or even sell one. This is not our festival, it's not Muslim and it's *haram*. When the Day of Judgement comes don't say you didn't know.'

A little way off I spotted a small ragtaggle herd of goats optimistically crunching the varied crop of Neighbourhood 29's litter-riddled grass. I wondered whether they were refugees from the infidel parts of town where the upcoming celebrations could soon get bloody.

As the festival approached I had asked others whether they'd be celebrating. I had gone to visit Hikmete, a woman whose kids came to our classes. Hikmete wore a headscarf, and when I'd visited her with (Old) Rob one day she'd greeted us demurely with '*Salam aleikum*'.

Rob had replied respectfully, '*Aleikum essalam*,' and since then, and taking as additional evidence his beard and the fact that he had not shaken her hand, she had been convinced that he was Muslim, despite my assurances to the contrary.

I had come to see her now to discuss a problem with one of the children. I opened with small talk, and had admired the repainting of the walls that was in progress. I'd learned about house painting from Hatemja; like a fruit ripening, the walls of her home would change between my visits from green one week, to yellow or pink, depending on the half-pot of paint Agron had found in the rubbish or was given at the end of a building job. Often the colour didn't stretch to the whole space, leaving patches in corners sometimes going back several painting generations, to show how it had been. Hatemja told me that painting was better than cleaning for disinfecting from bugs.

'Is the painting for *Shëngjergj*?' I asked, though remembering the *Salam aleikum*, I wondered whether it would seem offensive to ask whether she was celebrating the festival. *This is not our festival, it's not Muslim and it's* haram. *When the day of judgement comes don't say you didn't know.*

'Yes,' she confirmed.

'So what will you do to celebrate?' I asked.

'Oh we used to celebrate,' she said with eyes shining beneath her headscarf. 'Four years ago we'd go down to the river –' she used the Serbian word. Everything was being relabelled now – 'and everyone would wear their wedding clothes and it would be wonderful.' Her words were accelerating as she spoke, with remembered excitement. And then she stopped, as if collecting herself.

'But now we pray,' she said, eyes looking down and voice calm. 'And the celebrations are *haram*.'

The next day was the day before *Shëngjergj* and one of our volunteers came to see me. He was a young man who wore shades and proudly displayed a wristband saying Couchsurfing which he'd been given by an American who'd visited Kosovo. His Facebook profile was peppered with flattering selfies, and his Friends list included a disproportionate number of long-haired smiling girls. He had come to apologise for having to leave our activities early. Well, it was spring; I guessed one of the long-haired girls had something to do with it.

'You know, I've got to go and collect the nettles,' he explained. 'To flick water at people with in the morning for *Shëngjergj*.' I let him bounce away with springtime in his step – just like Hikmete would have done four years ago.

The battle for the souls of Fushë Kosovë's inhabitants (whether with four legs or two) was a public and ongoing redefinition of customs and beliefs. While the newspapers in Britain ached over the meanings, opportunities and threats of Islam, here in Neighbourhood 29 every day girls were deciding whether or not to pull on their headscarves, mothers were having to choose whether to sacrifice a lamb for their son's health, or to obey the posters in the shop windows; men were learning new arithmetic for paradise.

We had one volunteer at our activities who was a gifted educator, telling stories that had the children wide-eyed and silent as he spoke. He came once a week and I'd always be pleased to see him, and would greet him, along with all his colleagues. After months of working with us, he came in one day and with an enthusiastic smile I said good morning and extended my hand. With a charming smile as his hand swooped away from mine to touch his chest he said, 'I respect you very much Elizabeth; maybe you understand.'

I didn't understand; I felt like I'd been slapped. I was suddenly aware of myself both as a woman and as somehow dirty as a result. I'm old enough to be this guy's mother, and I started wondering whether there could honestly be a belief that I could lead him into sexual trespass. It made me furious – and also somehow afraid – watching a person, and maybe a community, change from week to week. I felt a hot flame of frustration and anger in my chest – right at the point where my colleague's hand had been held to his heart. I resolved that whenever I felt it burn I would take it as a reminder to myself of the importance of offering literacy, making connections with a wider world, teaching critical thinking, and creating a sense of belonging beyond a faith community. That could be my small part of the fight against fundamentalism.

I had to learn quickly. One Sunday we went out to the park outside Prishtina for a volunteers' outing. Lounging on the grass together, passing cartons of orange juice around (you see, I was so culturally sensitive – I knew not to bring beer or bacon sandwiches to these multi-faith gatherings) we were chatting about a documentary that had been on television the previous evening. We were a mixed group from Fushë Kosovë and beyond and were wondering together at some of the discoveries of scientists that had been on the documentary; it felt like safe, shared ground.

'But not evolution,' said one of our team from Fushë Kosovë, who had a beard and a sharp, enquiring mind and the varied appetite of the autodidact.

'That's just offensive. Offensive to human beings, to say they came from monkeys,' he went on, tutting into his beard.

I found myself without argument. I'd read Dawkins, and sentences formed in my mind, studded with words like 'fossil record', but I discovered I was actually ill-prepared to justify one of the fundamental principles of modern science, at a multicultural picnic. Partly it was because I hadn't expected to need it here – perhaps if I'd been visiting a religious group in Arkansas I would have done some background reading. But I'd assumed … I had assumed that the almost one hundred per cent mapping of my beliefs with Jashar's when it came to the right to schooling; the fact that we responded in exactly the same way when a child was misbehaving, or when a mother came to the office close to tears, that we shared a sense of humour and irony – I had assumed that these things meant that there were other fundamental similarities in our world-view. I navigated the world around the assumption that Islam existed within it but not with the assumption of evolution deniers; with a shock I realised that I had just met my very first. Shock was followed by disappointment with myself that I had nothing to say to him, which made my own proud belief in evolution – a mark of my intelligent, science-based engagement with the world – seem a little hollow.

Nevertheless, it made such engagement seem all the more important. Later, in discussion about the bears which still lived wild in Kosovo's mountains. I discovered that the guy who drove the van for us when we travelled between Prishtina and Fushë Kosovë – a man who'd completed secondary school – hadn't ever heard of hibernation. Maybe it didn't matter whether you knew that some animals slept all winter, but if there was a connection between that information and your approach to evolution it mattered more. I wanted every potential scientist in Fushë Kosovë to have the tools to make up their own mind.

The time when we talked most about such issues was the month offering the biggest test for the Muslims with whom I worked – the holy month of Ramadan. It was noticeable across Kosovo where even for people who otherwise ignored the requirements of Islam, there was evidence of movements coming slower, breath more sour, tempers more fragile. During this month the observant abstain for taking in anything – food, drink, cigarette smoke – during the hours of daylight, so the marking of nightfall by the call to prayer – for most of the year just an exotic soundtrack to Prishtina's café culture – is suddenly attended to with care. As the month is part of the lunar Islamic calendar, it doesn't fall on a regular date within the Western calendar and this shifting gives the month a different flavour every year, and there are widely considered to be tough Ramadans and easy Ramadans. This year it was in August – with long days and hot temperatures, making it particularly difficult to go without liquids. I was tempted to try it, partly out of the curiosity of the spiritual tourist, partly to show solidarity with our team in Fushë Kosovë. But it was only when I received an invitation to *iftar*, the evening meal with which the fast is broken during Ramadan, that I committed to trying one day – just one – of the fast. I felt that if I was to sit down at 20.15 with a room full of people who had starved themselves all day, and then share with them the experience of eating and drinking, it would be somehow deceitful if I had been gorging myself on chocolate and iced drinks just an hour before. If you accept an *iftar* invitation, I felt you should accept the fast which it concludes.

Hatemja helped me understand the rules. I had to wake up at half past two in the morning and eat the last meal I'd be able to consume for over seventeen hours. Traditionally this is a meal of meat, and another friend suggested that a good vegetarian alternative could be based on peanut butter. When it came to it, however, I couldn't face the cloying saltiness of peanut butter and I ate nothing but a tin of peaches; most of all I was focused on hydration. I knocked back all of a large bottle of water at my strange solitary midnight feast, thinking of Hatemja and Hysni and all the others I knew in Fushë Kosovë preparing for their testing day, and went to bed with a feeling of queasy dread.

I was right to have been apprehensive – when I woke up after a warm night, I was already thirsty. An early morning trip to the toilet presumably offset all the benefits of my night-time hydration, and looking at my watch I realised I still had twelve hours of sunshine to go. I wondered at the six hundred million people who were joining me worldwide in this deliberate deprivation.

During that day I thought less about Islam than about hunger, and about need. I knew that many Muslims take the opportunity in Ramadan to give to the poor, to dole out the food they haven't eaten — or its cash equivalent — to those in need. I realised that my symptoms of hunger and thirst, curious and unfamiliar to me — almost thrilling in their dizzying of me — were daily life for many of the families I'd got to know, for whom this discomfort in the gut was not a quaint tourist experience but a daily threat. Just as when I'd started learning about poverty I'd discovered as much about religion, I now found that in setting out to learn about religion, the insights I gained were into poverty.

19 A crocodile crawling out of the *mahalla*

Among the drab colours of many-times-washed, many-times-dirtied hand-me-down clothes, the new rucksacks dominated, their colours blurring as the children outside our centre jostled one another. I'd been looking forward to this day with the anticipation of a grand finale – the choral piece at the end of a long and complicated musical. All the parts would be on stage and well rehearsed for a Barnum and Bailey-style education extravaganza.

Hope was there and a volunteer from the Agape Foundation had the responsibility of taking a photograph of each child with their book bag, ready for their first day at school. We were going to print out the photos and give a copy to each of them; I wanted them to have an image of themselves as learners propped up somewhere in their overcrowded homes.

Some of the girls who wore headscarves had come along too. There were five of them in total and their heads were still covered. We knew the law – in theory they wouldn't be allowed into class in a headscarf but I wondered what the school would actually do about it today. Should I say anything? In the end I decided we would take our chances.

Hysni was calling names off a list to check that everyone had arrived, counting heads, and dispatching volunteers or by-standers to go and get children from home if they hadn't yet turned up. This was an inspiring group of people about to set off gamely to claim their right; they'd come a long way in six months, and so had I. I thought back to our first days together; the children seemed bigger now. And I guess they were – six months of growth (fuelled in part by fruit juice and yoghurt in the mornings in our centre) had made a difference. But it was also those bookbags they were each wearing on their backs – garish pink and green things which jutted out above their heads, and bulked out their fine shoulder blades like African babies carried in brightly-coloured bundles. The bookbags were practically empty at the moment, apart from the exercise books and pencils that Hysni and I had sorted out into a pile for each child, and which I could hear whumping from side to side whenever a child darted past me. But they were waiting to be filled – with the prescribed curriculum of Kosovan state education, its free textbooks, offered as a right to every child, its History and Geography and Citizenship Education – subjects we'd not had the time or the expertise to cover in our makeshift classrooms. The children really were setting off on a journey.

'Are we ready, Hysni?' I asked. He was still frowning over his list, and trying to count the milling heads around us.

'I think so … Hang on,' he said. I checked my watch; we were cutting it fine now, to be at the school on time. These children were all already two years late; we didn't want to make it two years and fifteen minutes.

'Let's go,' I said – and we started walking together out of the *mahalla*.

I was at the front, and Hysni at the back of our loose crocodile on the pavement, with other volunteers running along the sides, checking the roads for traffic, looking over their shoulders to make sure the children were staying out of the road, slow-jogging alongside them like bodyguards for our VIPs. Suddenly I heard my name being called by Hysni. His voice was urgent and I could tell we had a problem. I turned, with images of disaster, vomiting or traffic accidents flashing before me. Hysni called out one word,

'Gjelane.'

No, she hadn't been hit by a car, or done anything to disgrace herself or us…. In fact, I realised as soon as Hysni said the name – she wasn't here at all.

How could I not have noticed? It seemed incredible, but in all the ticking of lists and the children coming asking questions, somehow I hadn't realised.

'I sent one of the volunteers to get her, and I thought they'd brought her back,' said Hysni, mournfully. 'I'm so sorry, Elizabeth.'

I cut him short. It didn't matter how it had happened, but it did matter – very, very much, to me and hopefully to Hatemja and her daughter – that we got her into this crocodile immediately. If it hadn't been for Gjelane none of us would have been here today; if she'd not brought me face-to-face with the real issues of children out of school, and if she'd not skipped round her friends' houses to share the news about the classes we were starting, these 61 children would today be at home, or at work, learning from their parents and their older siblings about a life lived outside the alphabet and outside the system. But … I knew I needed to be with the 61 other children now; I needed a Jesus for this lost sheep.

Aurélie had overheard the conversation. She understood – not just the significance of a lost sheep, but the importance to me that day of getting Gjelane to school.

'I'll go,' she said. Hatemja's house wasn't far from where the crocodile had paused, and she hurried off.

The rest of us walked on a little faster to try to make up time, and I wondered what was happening with Gjelane. She had missed a few days of our classes in the last weeks of teaching, and of course I wondered about Agron and his fury and hurt at not having been selected for the job that Hysni was doing. We hadn't seen each other since that hard conversation. Would he really try punishing me through Gjelane? I believed that he cared about education; about her education. So why was she not here today? Had I got it so badly wrong?

One of the girls at the front was waiting for my answer to the latest in a series of nervous questions that she'd been asking all morning. 'Will we have homework?'

I grinned bravely at her, 'Oh yes – this is big school now!' and she grinned bravely back.

When we got there we found the school bubbling over with new pupils and their parents who filled the corridors, blocked the entrance ways, huddled round a few ripped and poorly photocopied lists sellotaped to the wall. No-one seemed to know what class they should be in, and when they gave up jostling at the lists on the wall, parents were trailing new children into each of the seven first grade rooms and hopefully calling out their child's name to harassed teachers who would check a list before shouting back, 'No, try next door,' or 'Yes, hurry up and sit down.' Some children were wailing. Mothers looked like they were close to tears.

I was all smiles though; bright artificial smiles that I beamed on everyone – anyone – who could help us. Even at the Deputy Director who was shouting and the Director who was standing with his arms half extended from his sides, like some sustained shrug denying responsibility in the midst of the tumult.

More than anything I was beaming at the children whose jubilation had evaporated in the hubbub. Like using a magnifying glass to start a flickering flame on paper I was focusing all my bravest, most positive energy on each of the faces, willing them to break into a small tentative fire of courageous smiling recognition.

I wasn't having much luck; I saw that some of them had grabbed each other's hands. No-one was jostling or giggling now; they were standing in silence and staring. As the angry tones of the Deputy Director's voice yelling at a father who'd asked for help echoed down the stairwell the children looked terrified. Their eyes darted around trying to take it all in. They flickered over me; they had trusted me when I told them that this was where they should come; that this was the way to a future. Again, the phrase came to me, 'lambs to the slaughter.'

What had we done?

'Stay there,' I motioned to the children, though they weren't going anywhere. And I planted myself in front of the Director. I beamed.

'So, *Zotëni Drejtor*' – Mr Director (it was the correct form of address in Albanian. It also seemed a helpful reminder of his position – that he should be, well, directing things) … 'Where should the children be now?'

He wasn't able to answer.

'Wait,' he said, 'and I'll bring the teachers.'

I didn't understand what he meant, but soon the auction he was proposing became clear. The first teacher bustled through to our group. She had a big hair-do and lots of lipstick on lips that were pursed shut. She surveyed our ragtag group grimly and pointed to two of the more well-dressed children.

'You, boy, and you, girl. Come with me.'

The Director spoke to her, not bothering to modulate his volume.

'You have to take more than two. Everyone does.'

'I don't want any of the others,' she said loud enough for everyone to hear.

It was evacuees in 1940s Britain. It was the slave markets of nineteenth century Liverpool. It was inhumane and humiliating, and here in my professional home – a primary school – I found myself one of the powerless.

At last I stuttered, 'Please don't speak like that in front of the children,' but the bouffant hair-do was wheeling away and back to her classroom, with the chosen two in her wake. I heard a sniff next to me and saw that Besmire was weeping quietly.

The process repeated with each of the other teachers. They didn't open up the children's mouths to check the quality of their teeth, but they might as well have done. At the end, there were still a few children left unclaimed, and the Director grabbed them by the arm and took them back to the classrooms for a second round of auctioning.

I turned to Hysni, 'and what about the girls in headscarves?' He was shaking his head, and he pointed. I looked through the glass of the door and saw four girls huddled in the playground.

'She said they had to take the scarves off, and they refused.'

'What about Shefkije?' I asked as I couldn't see her outside with the others.

'She took hers off and put it in her pocket,' Hysni said. I couldn't tell whether he approved or not – we both wanted as many kids as possible into school, but ignoring what you believed God had told you to do in order to get there?

'Let's go,' I said. And the four girls and Hysni and I trailed miserably back down the road to the centre. Halfway there my phone chirruped at me; a message from Aurélie. Yes, she'd successfully brought Hatemja's daughter to school and Gjelane was in class now.

For today that would have to be enough.

Hysni and the children registered for school

20 Headscarves

As Hysni and I and the four girls in headscarves got nearer
to Neighbourhood 29 we started passing people we knew.
At that point in the community's gender geography it was
all men – this was the outer edge of the settlement, where
exchange could be done with others, but also where conflicts
with the majority community could arise. The women were
snuggled much deeper into the residential parts of the *mahalla*.

First we passed the gathering of men standing at the corner
opposite the station. They were hoping to be hired for
physical labour – loading up lorries, or pulling up potatoes.
They were the vanguard, offering themselves for trade with
the Albanians. They're tough, with compact bodies bulked
up by hauling sacks from pallets or roots from cold earth.
They watched us pass and one of them asked why the girls
were returning so soon from school. I explained what had
happened, shaking my head and tutting at the school's policy.
The men tutted back; it was a scandal. Something should be
done. I agreed with them.

One of them asked me, 'If we write a letter, will you sign it?'

'Of course,' I said – I'd be happy to agitate for the girls to be
in class, and happier still to help their own community get
them there.

As we got nearer to the centre we passed a new demographic
– the internal traders in the mean little market usually selling
secondhand clothes and secondhand vegetables; broccoli and
peppers as grey as old jumpers. Everything in this market was
fuscous and beige – dull potatoes, the colour of clod, the shoes
browned with wear and mud, even the computer peripherals,

yellowed with age and use, sitting like old fruit on a blanket. In brown palms, the coins that clinked were the dirty bronze of small change.

The guys standing there looked up as the group of headscarved girls processed through with me. 'What happened; why aren't they at school?'

I explained the law. It wasn't the fault of the municipality, I pointed out – this was the law of Kosovo. The men shook their heads over their wares.

By the next day the wider Muslim community across Kosovo was shaking. Frustration at the perceived injustice of the law had spread and the observant community had mobilised. No-one ever did give me a letter to sign but a rally was organised outside the government building in Prishtina, and I got a phone call from Ardi, the co-founder of our charity. He's a Kosovar from a Muslim family, though I'd never known him observe any part of the faith other than family celebrations for the big festivals, just like I celebrate Christmas. He had seen Hysni on television at the rally and we agreed that it would be good to talk.

Ardi and I agreed on many things; he had lived in London for a time, and had a dry, 'British' sense of humour. He was well-read and bright, knowledgeable about an extraordinary range of areas of Kosovan life, having worked as a journalist in Kosovo before the war, and as a fixer for foreign journalists during the war. His English was idiomatic and fluent, and his perspective on many things was shared with mine; indeed many of my opinions about Kosovo were what Ardi had taught me, or had grown out of experiences he had made possible. We disagreed about London (he loved it) but agreed about the need to protect Kosovo's cultural heritage; he couldn't understand my almost indiscriminate love of local food when I was in Prishtina but we had the same taste in pasta, and it was he who taught me about putting wine into the water when you cook spaghetti.

But it seemed that now we had found something significant that we disagreed on. The strange thing about debates on girls wearing the headscarf – whether the discussions take place in Turkey or Australia, France or the UK or Kosovo – is that anyone arguing from a non-religious point of view always seems to start from the same premise yet it seems that you can launch from there to completely opposite conclusions. Ardi and I were both passionate about human rights. Neither of us wanted fundamentalist religion to dominate public life in Kosovo. And yet from this shared starting point we reached diametrically opposing positions.

Ardi agreed with the Kosovan law which said that no religious signifiers (no crosses, no headscarves) should be worn in schools. He wanted schools to be places of reason, not of superstition or religion. He worried that doing nothing to disincentivise girls wearing headscarves would lead to an increase in girls covering their heads, and a growth in fundamentalism.

I also didn't want religion to get in the way of education, but for me that meant allowing girls to access teaching whatever they were wearing on their heads, or round their necks. For me, there was no surer way to breed a nation of dangerous fundamentalists than to ensure that anyone coming from a tradition of this kind was denied an education, and the skills that would enable them to question what they were told by religious leaders.

Other friends assured me, 'It's not the girls who choose to wear the headscarf anyway; it's their fathers who make them.' When I told them that I had spoken to girls like Samire wearing scarves who had given me well-argued reasons for their choices as a sign of their faith, not as a denial of their sexuality, and assured me it had been their decision, my friends would snort, 'Well, of course they think it's their decision, but it's deep, suspicious cultural forces at work.'

But when I'd stood in the maelstrom of the school lobby waiting to find the classes for the children, the girls in headscarves had not been the only ones who had been victims of deep, suspicious cultural forces. One pre-pubescent girl had walked in wearing a tight top and miniskirt with the stars and stripes picked out in sequins. She was showing her identity, and it was an identity I would rather she hadn't selected. She no doubt believed that she herself had made the choice for it; I would contend that it was more the result of deep suspicious cultural forces at work. There did seem to be a pattern in the debate and usually when I was talking to men – whether in Prishtina or London – it was assumed that that if a girl covered her head men had made her do it, but if she expressed her sexuality through the clothes she wore, it was assumed that it was her own free choice. Where do these assumptions come from of what women want?

In the end, I concluded that it was the particular choice of identity adopted by these four girls which upset Ardi most. Like many Kosovars, he saw the form of Islam which required girls to cover their heads to be an 'imported' Islam (no matter that I contended that all Islam was 'imported' in Kosovo; and all Christianity, too, just as the two religions were not native to the UK or anywhere other than Saudi Arabia and the Holy Land). It seemed that what he found most distressing was that the girls in headscarves were allying themselves with Arabs – not to say with Al Qaeda – against the vision of a European future for Kosovo. For me, the number of girls wearing headscarves was merely bringing Prishtina a little closer to what was normal on the streets of the European capital I had called home for fifteen years, and whether Rasime covered her head or not made no difference to Kosovo's foreign policy. I'd tried explaining to some Kosovan friends (no need to do so to Ardi, who from his studies and his work knew more about international relations than I ever would) that indeed the Anglo-American-led intervention in Kosovo in 1999 to support the Albanians against the (Christian) Serbs had in fact gained much of its significance for Blair and Clinton precisely because the people on whose behalf we were intervening were Muslims; after letting down the Muslims of Bosnia so badly, Blair had seemed to want to be able to demonstrate that he was not a religious partisan.

Ardi and I were never going to agree on this but we did both share one important view – that education was essential for all of Kosovo's citizens, and we should do what we could to offer the girls a chance to learn. We started classes (carefully scheduled outside school hours so there could be no suggestion that we were encouraging the girls to come to our classes instead of to school) teaching the basics – literacy, maths and English – to girls who wore headscarves.

We never discussed the reasons for headscarves with the Muslims among our volunteers – those who wore headscarves themselves, or whose wives and daughters did. We never discussed it with the girls either. And when one of our volunteers posted on Facebook a pro-hijab graphic showing two lollipops, one hygienically wrapped, the other left open, half-licked and glistening in a quasi-clitoral state, with flies stuck to it, and the slogan, 'Which one will you choose?' I said nothing. Neither Facebook nor an NGO seemed to be the right place to explore publically whether a sucking sweet was really an appropriate metaphor for 50% of the population and all the skills and insights they had to offer society.

Samire's sister Shkurte still had her head uncovered and was attending the proper school. I was waiting for that to change – I'd already seen some of the girls who'd started our classes bare-headed now coming in scarves. Even Gjelane one day had worn a headscarf, though that turned out to have been just to cover up headlice. I had overheard some of the girls talking one day when Shefkije had come to the centre wearing a headscarf for the first time. Liridona commented to her friend that she'd asked her mum about wearing a headscarf, 'But my mum said I need to go to classes, finish school and then put on the headscarf.'

I breathed out, but still couldn't stop fretting about the headscarves lying in store for each of these double X chromosomed bodies; a timebomb ready to be triggered once a certain hormone saturation had been reached.

And for those girls, volunteer-run classes in the rooms above the minimarket were all we could offer. Samire learned an eclectic syllabus, pulled together by Rob, teaching once a week after work, and our retired US Air Force colonel, Marilyn, and additional volunteers who passed through. One day, however, she explained that she wouldn't be able to come the following week as her cousin was visiting. She invited me round to her house to meet the cousin.

It wasn't the first time I'd been to Hysni's family's home but it was always a treat to be there. It was an older house – I guessed built in the 1950s, which made it something quite unusual in Fushë Kosovë where, as across Kosovo in general, about half the homes were destroyed in the conflict from 1998 to 1999. It was set in a yard with chickens and children and washing, none particularly clean but the children were always smiling and the chickens were always clucking while the washing flapped and snapped in the wind. Hysni's large and cheerful wife (without whom there would have been none of these things) made you feel like you had made her day just by turning up. On wet days she would take my boots and set them to warm by the fire. On cold days she made tea in the double *xhugym* shaped like her – a small round pot on top and a bigger one bellying out below. In summer it was a relief just to go into the cool dark of her sitting room and if it was hot one of the daughters would be sent out to get us a bottle of fizzy drink which would be poured for me and for the children like an impromptu party.

I'd taken Hysni's wife to the doctor one day when she needed help, and we'd taken the opportunity to share some girly one-to-one confidences as we weren't able to in the public arena which is a sitting room in Kosovo, with children in and out, and a television chattering in the corner. She'd told me then that she and Hysni had been introduced through a *mësit,* meaning that the first time she had met him was to decide whether she would accept him (and he, her) as a spouse. She had been a teenager at the time. How could such significant decisions be made in this way? I knew I was in the minority – probably in the world today, certainly during all human history – as a woman who had had free choice in whom (or whether) I would marry, but it still seemed a crazy, risky approach to human happiness to have your marriage decided by others, with only the fragile power of a brief meeting when you could veto suggestions made by your uncle. How could one meeting give you enough information about the person on whom your economic, social, sexual, emotional and family well-being would depend for a lifetime. But then I thought about my own meeting with Hysni – the interview questions and our certainty that Hysni was right for the job. All Western recruitment processes are predicated on the idea that some external sponsors (referees) and a short interview (like Hasime's cup of coffee with the bachelor Hysni) are enough to identify the best person with whom to spend your working life and on whom you'll depend for economic success. Indeed, wasn't this broadly the process I had been trumpeting to Agron as so effective when he had been telling me that it would be better to know someone properly, have hosted them as a guest at your house – have a long and multifaceted courtship....

However they had managed it, there was no doubt that Hysni's and Hasime's was a happy home, with beautiful and well-behaved children (and chickens). The only time Hysni had ever talked about marriage was when he and I were discussing another family in the community, where it was known that there was domestic violence, and Hysni told me thoughtfully, 'You know, Elizabeth, it doesn't matter how poor you are; you can survive poverty if you have a partner [there are two words for this in Albanian – one is the same as the word for 'friend', the other translates loosely as 'the person with whom you share the lottery'] who understands you. You can face your problems together and feel like you're united. If you don't have that, it doesn't matter what else you have, because you have nothing.'

So it was a pleasure to go to Hasime and Hysni's home on this invitation to meet the family back from Sweden. I banged on the corrugated iron panel that worked as a gate to their yard, and called out until one of the children in the yard heard me and came to twist the nail which kept the gate in place. Hasime had gathered what was up, and came out cooing and smiling to greet me. I was helped off with my shoes – an awkward business where I tried to negotiate the mud and stink of dirty footwear while I stood on one leg to undo Velcro or zips, and one of Hysni's daughters wrestled me, 'No, no, teacher, let me do it,' and I finally stopped wobbling and allowed little fingers to pull at the fastenings and show their care and respect to me as a guest by undressing me.

Then I was tugged into the busy sitting room; today busier than ever because Hysni's sister and brother-in-law were there with their children. The long large sofas around the sides of the room were full, and I was introduced, greeted and kissed in turn. Off to my right sat a version of Samire – a girl just a little older but with the same dimples and thoughtful intelligent gaze. She, too, had her head covered in a scarf though hers was worn more like a medieval wimple. I couldn't work out the way the material was structured but there was something more elaborate than Samire's usual tight band around her forehead; there were more pins, and it was very elegant.

She was called Aisha, and she was as articulate and forthcoming as her cousin. The girls chatted to me, nudging each other occasionally at private jokes. Yes, Aisha had been born in Kosovo, but she'd left for Sweden during the war. And yes, she was at school in Sweden. But what about her headscarf? Ah but in Sweden you could wear your scarf to school.

'Here,' said Samire, 'it's only when you get to university.'

Did Aisha want to go to university? Oh yes, to study biology – the specificity left me in no doubt that she would get there. This was a young woman quite sure of her place in the world. Samire looked wistful. I knew that she, too, said she wanted to go to university. But the odds were against her. She'd need to study enough in our brief, volunteer-led sessions above the minimarket, to be able to pass her diploma. And then she'd have to do the same with the high school curriculum. If she could keep her motivation (if we could keep our volunteers' motivation) for that long, then she could get to the dubious delights of the Kosovo higher education system. I tried to imagine the two girls in the war – just a year old as the paramilitary bands roamed in non-Serb neighbourhoods with tanks of petrol to throw at houses along with a lighted match, as the NATO warplanes droned overhead, as the refugee columns thickened along the roads out of Kosovo. And little Aisha, wrapped up tight in a blanket, not then in a headscarf, wailing along with her parents hurrying to a future for her in Sweden, while little Samire stayed in Fushë Kosovë. The girls growing up, starting to cover their heads, Aisha off to school every morning, and Samire left with the chickens. Their trajectories were taking them further away from one another with every day of Aisha's schooling, moving onwards and outwards from this conversation, beyond university into careers, life choices and their own children, money and health … I wondered how long it would be before Aisha's life, and that of her country, was unrecognisable to Samire in Kosovo.

At the end of the summer Aisha went back to Sweden, to start the new school term there. She asked to become my Facebook friend and occasionally I would have an electronic chat with her about how things were going. And the next time I saw Samire, I noticed that she'd done the same clever thing with her headscarf, wearing it just like her sophisticated cousin, fixing the material with complicated pleats and twists around her head. It formed an elegant shape covering her hair in exactly the way that would stop her being allowed into school.

21 Plums and orange juice; the sharp edges and soft spots of rubbish-picking

'Hey Agron,' I called his name with a slightly forced smile as we passed in the street. The chance meeting offered the first opportunity to move on after our hard conversation the day of the job interviews.

I tensed as I waited to see his response. Did he still see me as the woman who'd stolen his family's livelihood unfairly? Had he had time to understand what I had been trying to say? Would he blank me?

He looked up from his wheelbarrow and saw who it was. And his face broke into his familiar lopsided smile. I felt myself relax.

'How are you?' I asked. 'How's the family?'

'Good, thank you Mrs Elizabeth,' he said. I'd never been 'Mrs Elizabeth' before. 'And how are you?'

I breathed out and gave the routine answers. It felt great to have Agron talking to me as if he didn't blame me or hate me or feel let down by me. Maybe those feelings were still there, but even talking normally to each other was a step forward after his angry, hurt haranguing of me last time.

I saw Hatemja at our centre when she came to clean, showing her pregnancy now in a proud bulge against her slim, underweight body. We talked as if things were back to normal too, and of course I saw Gjelane, going to school every day. Eventually it felt like it would be OK to pop round to the house like I had done in the past. And I had something I wanted to ask Agron, anyway.

'Can I go out with you one day with your wheelbarrow, Agron?'

He didn't seem to have understood what I was asking. I wondered whether I'd once again muddled up the word for wheelchair or shopping trolley with the word for wheelbarrow? I mimed ... 'You know, when you collect the rubbish to sell on for recycling.'

'It's not good for you to come,' Agron said.

'Because it's dirty?' I asked.

'Yes,' said Hatemja.

'Yes, Mrs Elizabeth,' said Agron, as if he was making a point.

'Will I be in your way if I come?' I asked.

'No, no.'

'Well, I don't mind getting dirty,' I said. 'And you've seen where I work; I want to see where you work.'

When I followed up by suggesting a time I could come round on Saturday Agron shrugged and gave a brief nod.

I made sure I took some rubber gloves with me, and wore my oldest clothes. When I turned up at the house Gjelane was outside. Her eyes rounded, 'Wow! Trousers!'

It was true that I didn't often wear trousers. I smiled shyly and tried to stand up straighter. Then Agron came out and shook my hand. He was stifling a grin.

'Why are you smiling?' I asked. Surely Agron wouldn't laugh at me in trousers.

'The gloves, Mrs Elizabeth,' he said. 'You don't need those.'

'So what do you pick the rubbish up with?' Maybe there was a traditional tool or technique.

'Nothing – just my hands.'

Well he could laugh at me, but I wasn't going to grub around in bags of discarded sanitary towels and rotten vegetables without gloves on.

'I'm coming to help!' sang Gjelane and I looked at Agron. She was a child; everything I had tried to work for here had been for the rights of children to a childhood, not to be working illegally; shinnying into garbage skips surely counted as heavy labour. I really didn't want Gjelane coming – not on my watch.

But Agron was nodding, and it wasn't my watch. As we got the wheelbarrow ready, with some strapping wrapped round the handles, and a piece of hardboard laid over the hole where it had rusted through, a couple of the neighbours came over and stared and I realised that Gjelane might have another function. Perhaps in this conservative community, a chaperone for Agron and a foreign woman would be a way of guarding him against gossip…. It wasn't my watch.

The three of us set off, and when we reached the main drag of Fushë Kosovë I could see a minimarket up ahead.

'We'll need black bags, right? I'll buy them.' I had the enthusiasm of apprentices everywhere, happy to be able to contribute something, and knowing that despite my unfamiliar trousers and the laughable rubber gloves, I had something that Agron did not: in my bumbag was a clean fold of notes from the cashpoint that would enable me to solve this problem.

Agron was unimpressed by my offer, 'We don't buy bags,' he said, pityingly; 'we'll *find* the bags.'

We turned one block back from the main road, behind the shops, and into residential streets. Our first stop was the large skip behind a block of flats. It was filled with plump black bags of domestic refuse and Agron climbed up to get among them – closely followed by Gjelane. He started untying the black sacks and emptying the contents. She sifted through them, holding up anything made of recyclable material – plastic bottles or aluminium cans – like a trophy. Agron passed the empty bags down to me and Gjelane handed me the plastic bottles to squash and put inside. Even through the material of my gloves things were sticky from the skip and edges were sharp. I wondered about Agron's exposed skin, Gjelane's small fingers; about tetanus and hepatitis.

Most of the items Gjelane had passed down were plastic bottles and Agron assessed the haul.

'It will be plastic today,' he said.

As we walked on along the lanes between houses – established homes with disposable incomes, and incomes for disposables – we spotted bottles lying in grass on the verges and added them to our collection. In the sunshine and with Gjelane's enthusiasm it felt almost like a game. She asked me the English word for what we were collecting and called out happily, '*Bottull, bottull*,' whenever she spotted one. It could have been an Easter egg hunt – if it wasn't for the hepatitis and the tetanus.

We reached a neighbourhood of small houses, each in their own garden. There the rubbish was collected in individual dustbins, inside the gates. Agron explained that we mustn't take things from these bins without permission, and went through the first gate and up the path to ring on the bell. I stiffened, wondering what an Albanian householder would say to find on his doorstep a dirty Ashkali with a swagbag on his back. The door opened and the woman who came out smiled to see Agron. She looked down to Gjelane waiting with me at the gate and waved to her. Gjelane called back.

Agron came back to join us and told us we could take what we wanted from this bin. At the next house the same scenario repeated, and I turned to Agron, 'I thought they'd be angry.'

'But they know me,' Agron said, straightening as he explained. 'I've been doing this since I was fourteen years old, and my dad used to do it before that.'

Sure enough, at the next house where we stopped, the man who answered the door called Gjelane over. She came back with her T-shirt stretched out to make a shallow basket for the clutch of plums she'd been given, and we stopped for a break, standing in the sunshine while she sucked enthusiastically at them, licking the juice off dirty fingers.

At another house she got seventy cents, and later on a woman called Agron inside and he came out with a smart leather jacket which he laid carefully on top of the bags in our wheelbarrow. We walked on, continuing to pick from the street and from the bins where people were at home to give permission (no-one refused) and I thought about the public service that Agron – and his dad before him (but please, not Gjelane after him) – did in cleaning the streets; Kosovo's unofficial recyclers.

Finally we had filled the wheelbarrow to capacity (the purpose of the strapping now became clear as Agron used it to secure the precarious load, with the leather jacket still stretched out on top, where it wouldn't get crushed or dribbled on from the bottles). In addition, we each had a bag on our backs and one hung from each of the wheelbarrow handles. It had been three hours of walking, much of it at a strange angle to match the odd lurch of the wheelbarrow; I had sunburn and my back was aching, so I was glad when Agron said we should take our load to the depot now. I asked him how much we might have earned today, thinking rather proudly of our effort – three working hours of two people and a small and nimble child. It was hard to translate Agron's answer into likely profit, but he said that plastic bottles were seventeen cents per kilo. For aluminium you got more; for paper as little as eight cents per kilo. Best of all, he said, were car batteries, at 75 cents a kilo – 'and they weigh a lot'.

The depot was a monument to greed, a compound constructed of our guilty, dirty secrets. The ores we had dug up from the earth's core for bottles just so we could take a sugared drink with us on a journey; the vehicles we'd tired of and left to rust when we moved on to newer shinier gewgaws; the plastic we'd smashed and cracked, forgotten or over-engineered; the self-important piles of papers which in the end would mulch to a grey smudge. Cars were butchered here, sawn into pieces, their bodywork stripped of leather interior skins so the metal was exposed – the comfort of a well-upholstered seat revealed in all its spiteful springs of steel. The bonnet sections lay lined up in front of us, eyeing us with a glassy stare like fish-heads left to one side while the fine meat is filleted.

On the left the metal that had just been received was heaped in a snarl of jagged edges and rust. Two cars were heaped at the back, not yet sawn up, and doing it doggy style while they awaited their destruction.

Picking our way through the stour of the rubbish-pickers who had come before us, we approached the weighing station. They took the loads off the wheelbarrow and I tried to multiply by seventeen. The operator counted out coins into Agron's hand …

Two euros and eighteen cents.

I stared at it, learning what my time was worth in this new economy; Agron shrugged.

I was tired and hot and smeared with residues I couldn't identify; I said goodbye to Agron and Gjelane. I was running late to meet a friend for a drink so I went straight to the café, heading for the bathroom for a long wash of my hands – and my face and neck. Then I sat down heavily and ordered a cool freshly-squeezed orange juice. The menu listed the price as two euros and fifty cents. I'd lived in Kosovo long enough to stop translating prices into pounds sterling, but now I had a new currency to convert into. I sipped miserably at the orange juice that cost more than nine man-(and child)-hours of work gathering garbage, and played with the straw wondering about the patched together shreds of plastic it had come from, and the wheelbarrow where it would end up.

22 Soap

Thinking about the chink of the copper coins in Agron's dirty palm at the end of our morning with the garbage, I was convinced just how fragile the economy of these families was; their complaints of poverty were not fabricated or exaggerated. But I was also convinced that the money brought in by working children's contribution to the family economy was easily replaceable. If a morning when a child like Gjelane was out of school to work with her father contributed only a part of 2.18 euros, then it was a sum that could relatively easily be found from another source.

Surely I could find a way for Hatemja's family to earn an additional income, on condition that the children went to school. Something that Hatemja could do for short periods of time, in between feeding a baby.

'Can you sew, Hatemja?' I asked. I had an old linen skirt that was ripped beyond repair, but I liked the material, and needed a new cushion cover. I gave Hatemja the dimensions and asked whether she could make the cover for me from the old skirt if I paid her.

The cushion came back a few days later and I put it proudly on the sofa in my living room. It was a little bit of Hatemja's home in mine.

The problem if I wanted to scale this up was that the cushion was rather too reminiscent of Hatemja's home in mine. I was sure Hatemja would have worked on it in that tiny space, filled with babies and cooking; the cushion had certainly come back marinated in the odours of babies and cooking.

For me, in my childless sitting room as we ate our takeaway pizza, the cushion was evocative and maybe even homely – but it would be a hard sell on the open market.

I tried a scent-based market scan of potential business ideas for Hatemja and her neighbours. I ruled out food-based products and textiles, even items made of wood that could absorb an aroma … and then I turned the question around and considered what could come out of Hatemja's home that might leave her living space more fragrant than before. I searched on YouTube for how to make soap.

It seemed like the kind of process that Hatemja and other women without a formal education could do beautifully. I knew she could make baklava, and the techniques for this were no different – oil and soda and water with mixing bowls and whisks; the same transformational process as pouring together eggs and flour and butter and producing a cake. This was like making a cake that you could wash with.

Zsofia did some research, too, and we made a soap-making date at my house. When she arrived we put on some music and got out what we'd learned from the internet. We followed the instructions carefully, weighing out the soda on the scales, and zeroing them before adding the oil. We whisked and poured, winced at the idea of boiling oil, learned how the lye stung if you inhaled, and watched the alchemy of blending oil and soda and water until it formed a sludge and suddenly became soap. We lined a makeshift Tupperware pot mould with greaseproof paper and left our magical creation to set.

Yes, we thought Hatemja would be able to do this well. And the ingredients were relatively cheap so we thought we could get a decent mark-up on the product. Hopefully once people had tried the soap once, they would come back for more – after all, everyone needs soap; the more our customers liked it, the more they'd use and the more they'd buy. This was capitalism and consumerism at its cleanest.

And if the soaps didn't sell, then we'd be able to do something with the surplus — we bought soap every week for the bathroom at the centre, and the beekeeper in me was happy at the idea of moving to self-sufficiency. And beyond our centre were families who'd be grateful for any leftovers; just the previous week I'd taken a little boy to the doctor for treatment for a terrible scalp infection. The initial infection had been made worse by him scratching, and the scratches getting infected, until the whole surface of his head was either oozing pus or encrusted where sores had dried. His glands stuck out in his neck like Brussels sprouts on a stem and it was difficult to know what was cause and what effect in this beleaguered organism. The doctor prescribed vitamins and antibiotics and cleaned up the boy's scalp with iodine, and asked his older sister who'd come with us, 'Do you have soap at home?'

Maybe children brought up in homes like Bajram's learn to say 'no' to any question about what they have; certainly if they're asked about an inventory of their bleak home, where I'd seen them eating a meagre dinner of bread set down on the bare floorboards, 'no' is likely to be the true answer more often than not. But maybe it was in fact the case that the meagre dinner would have been prioritised over a bar of soap and Bajram's parents really had nothing with which they could keep these sores clean. At least Hatemja and her colleagues could provide for their neighbours this way if we couldn't find anyone who would buy their produce.

The next time the children left our classes they each took home a photocopied notice explaining that their mothers or sisters or grandmothers were invited to come and be part of a project to earn some money. They would have training and then all the profits from sales would be divided equally among the women. The only condition was that the children in their family had to continue to go to school.

A group of volunteers got everything ready for training, with five sets of scales, and five camping stoves and electric blenders and bowls. We bought olive oil and essential oil for fragrance, and a big bag of lye from a pharmacy near the hospital. I translated the YouTube instructions into Albanian and added pictures, and copied them five times.

The women who turned up were self-conscious and silent. They concentrated carefully on what we told them about the project, and their eyes widened at the gleaming new kitchen equipment set out on the tables. Only one of them – Vjollca – had been to school at all, and the others said this was the first formal training of any kind that they had ever had. Hatemja was one of them, determined despite the baby coming, to have a chance at this new project. Haxhere, her neighbour who shared the cleaning with her, and was the community's birth attendant, came too. The mother of Elvira (who'd washed her face on the day of the school registration 'so that the Albanians couldn't say that the children Elizabeth taught were *palidhje*') came, and so did little Emine's mum. Another of the group was the older sister of a girl we'd registered for school.

We explained the process to them and oversaw them pouring out the oil. They were neat and careful and conscientious. No drips.

'It's like making *çorba*,' one of them said, and indeed the non-native English speakers in our group of volunteers kept confusing *soup* and *soap*. We giggled at the idea of a bubbly broth, peppery with lye.

Next they had to use the scales. 'So we zero the scales,' I said, fiddling with the dial of the set I was showing as a model. The women looked blank.

I had thought that zeroing the scales would be easier for them than trying to do the arithmetic of adding one weight to another. But if they weren't familiar with zeroing then I tried explaining the addition.

Still blank.

'So how do you use scales at home?' I asked.

'We don't use them,' explained Haxhere quietly.

'I can't read the numbers,' said Hatemja.

Who was stupid now? The women who'd found workarounds to ensure that they knew the right quantities of the materials they needed in their lives, or the eager university-educated (well yes, and in this case YouTube-educated) Englishwoman who had gone out and bought five sets of useless measuring devices whose strange calibrations and printed symbols carried no meaning for the people intended to use them.

'I'm really sorry,' I said. 'So how do you measure?'

'By spoons and teaglasses and cups,' said the efficient homemakers in front of me.

Sometimes translating has nothing to do with words; we took away the instructions we'd written up from the internet and did a useful translation ('one teaglass and two spoons' worth') to explain how much of each ingredient was needed for the perfect soap.

The following week we invited the women to see the first batch once it had set. It was cream in colour and smooth. The women and I fingered it in wonder, like a newborn, conceived by a miracle.

We had visualised selling it in slices so we worked together at cutting it. It wasn't easy – sometimes it shattered, and we ended up with as much in waste pieces as we did in marketable lumps. Teacher Avdil had been teaching some classes at the same time as the women were working and watched with interest.

'You can still use the leftover pieces,' he said. 'Like we did in the Yugoslav army, in our socks.' I didn't understand him at first, but he demonstrated how you could take shavings of soap and bundle them together into an old sock, and then wet it and wash with the suds which came out through the weave. We all looked at grave Teacher Avdil with new respect.

The women were as proud as Zsofia and I were of the pieces of soap they had produced, and I talked about our ideas for selling; how we could package them in little cloth bags (classier than Avdil's socks), and advertise them through Facebook; how I'd buy some for all my friends for Christmas. I suggested a reasonable price was two euros, but the women looked sceptical. They couldn't believe that anyone would pay so much for a bar of soap – they pointed out that the mauve soaps in Idriz' shop downstairs sold for thirty cents. I remembered again the coins in Agron's hand and could understand their scepticism – who would part with nearly six hours of labour for this home-made sliver in a little bag. I told them about Lush. 'You know, people buy it as a present.'

No, they didn't know. Gift-buying was not a part of social life in Fushë Kosovë. Even for big events, such as weddings, guests would turn up bringing only bottles of Coca Cola to contribute to the festivities. Those who didn't consider celebrating birthdays to be *haram* might indulge a child with sweets, and for the Bajram celebration at the end of Ramadan, children would get coins or new clothes. For a special treat women would part with something that belonged to them – a skirt or a top would be passed on, sometimes still warm from the body of the woman who was giving it away. But there were never any circumstances when someone would go to a gift shop and buy a chi-chi bar of soap.

Well, it didn't matter if the members of the community wouldn't buy; they just needed to believe that there were enough customers out there. Zsofia and I decided that the women needed a trip to Lush.

The Lush stores seem to exhale essential oils; perhaps they do literally have an extractor fan to make sure that the fabulous fragrances of their soaps and creams are shared with passers-by to entice them in, in the same way that the bakery section of the supermarket spreads the aroma of fresh bread across the aisles to tempt shoppers. Just walking past feels like a dip into a spa; it would be a treat for me – and hopefully for our group of women – to do some product research there. Incongruously, Lush had just opened a concession in a mall about twenty minutes from Fushë Kosovë so we organised a works outing.

The six women in our project wandered through the store like a jewellery shop, wondering at the bright gem colours of the Lush bars, reaching out to touch and sniff as if they were in a garden. I thought of Hatemja's dark cramped house, and the babies and the cooking, and the funky 'bath bomb' she held in her hand seemed to glow, not just with the rose oils and mango and scents she had probably never had in her home, but also with the vision of a place you could wash yourself with products like these. Not a standpipe in the yard, but a large white enamel tub; brass taps; leisure time.

As much as at the scents, the women marvelled at the prices. There was something slightly revolting about revealing how much 'people' (me, my friends) would spend on these luxuries, when I knew the income in these women's homes. But it was a market to which we were offering them access – a market where their own products could compete, and where the profits from sales would bubble and steam back to their families. They were convinced, and the next time we met for our weekly soap-making session there was a new seriousness in their work. Albanian – tellingly – has no word for a businesswoman, but the feminine ending on the transliteration of 'businessman' was enough for this group – each of them was now inspired to be a *biznesmenja*.

We refined our recipe, learning precision with the measurements of tea glasses and spoons. We experimented with additions to the soap: mixing in lavender buds or chamomile flowers – which left nasty brown stains in the mixture; we tried to colour what the women called the 'batter', still using my cake analogy, with fruit tea, which turned from red to green under the intense alkali of the lye. We mixed in different essential oils, tried honey, orange peel, and oats, and the women even one day stirred in some vitamin powder to make a lurid orange 'vitamin soap'. The visit to Lush had inspired creativity.

The training in soap-making was almost complete, but there was one more element of the production cycle I wanted the women to have experience of. We had gone ahead with the idea of little cloth bags to package the soaps, and since The Ideas Partnership had been working in another village in Kosovo some hours away from Neighbourhood 29, where women had been trained in sewing, we asked them to produce a batch of cute drawstring bags that could hold the soaps. These women were also Roma, Ashkali and Egyptian and we thought that they would be interested in meeting the producers of the products they would be packaging, and that the Fushë Kosovë women might like to be introduced to them and see how their project was running. And it would be a day out for everyone.

We organised a minibus to drive the Fushë Kosovë women to the village near Istog, out near the mountains of the north-west. On the way we were able to chat. Fitore wasn't with us as her husband had just left her, and, wide-eyed, the women pooled the information they had about what had happened. One said that the husband had left for a woman in Montenegro, another that he had met the woman on the internet; it wasn't clear which was further away – and thinking back to Fitore's sparsely-furnished home, where there wasn't always a pen to be found, let alone a computer, the internet seemed unlikely. But friends had phones with 3G; there were internet cafes – it was possible. Perhaps it was more likely that the sparsely-furnished home, and the five children to support in it were the reason. But now that her husband had left, Fitore and her children were left without a home that belonged to them; the frisson in the women's voices today wasn't just a thrill at marital gossip, but a tremble of fear.

With these oblique references to sexual appetite, another conversation started, about headscarves. Haxhere and Hatemja wore scarves; Refiqe, out today in a tight T-shirt with sequins, and Vjollca – often dressed in bright colours like her name, which meant 'Violet', and always in lipstick – did not.

'It's *haram* – forbidden – not to wear one,' said the demure Haxhere quietly. 'What about paradise?'

'What about this life?' retorted Vjollca, 'As long as I'm beautiful, I'm not going to wear a headscarf.'

When we arrived at the little village of Srbobran, the women from Fushë Kosovë looked around in wonder and undisguised envy. 'They've had all this built for them?'

The houses were far from luxurious but they were neat and fresh; a miniature new town of seventeen homes all the same design. Each had a generous garden front and back and – far from the power plant that polluted Fushë Kosovë and Prishtina – the air was fresh off the mountains. In the middle of the settlement was a community centre, where the women The Ideas Partnership supported in the village were trained, and a small playpark. It was a long way from Fushë Kosovë's mud streets and rubbish heaps hugger-mugger with the shacks.

Srbobran, and the many communities like it, were a political necessity which made many people in Kosovo uncomfortable – and others very comfortable indeed. This was a 'returnee' community built for minorities (in this case Roma, but others were often Serb) from Kosovo who had left during the war when their homes were destroyed. The majority Albanian government was under pressure from the international community to prove a commitment to assertions of a multi-ethnic Kosovo by encouraging these refugees back to their homes – and under just as much pressure from the countries where the refugees were living, whether that was neighbouring states of the former Yugoslavia, or EU countries like the UK. The result was an international effort to make it attractive for people to come back to Kosovo. Families' homes were rebuilt, usually with a mixture of donor agencies' money and local government contributions, and the returnees were offered some money for furniture and food and firewood while they re-established themselves in Kosovo. The families also received some start-up funding for small businesses, maybe a trailer for transporting goods, or training in a new skill. It was a humane process that made complete sense – to the individuals returning, to the foreign governments supporting their return, to the Kosovan government showing the welcome they were extending to their multi-ethnic country. It made complete sense to everyone except Hatemja, and the thousands like her, whether Roma/ Ashkali/ Egyptian, or Albanian, who had stayed in Kosovo – not fled like Aisha's family, to the warm Swedish embrace of welcoming EU states, and not been returned, like these women we were about to visit, to the forced smile of the Kosovan government. Hatemja had stayed for most of the war of 1998 and 1999, finally leaving for Montenegro through the NATO bombing but returning at her own expense to her father's tiny home in Mitrovica. I guessed Agron had gone out with his wheelbarrow grubbing for something to eat or to sell; even during the darkest of those days people had still been generating rubbish. And for Hatemja, the housework, the endless struggle to keep the dirt floor of her home clean, to keep shitting children clean, to make a sack of flour last for as many meals as possible – those things were unchanged whether as daughter or wife, in Serbian or Albanian, as part of Yugoslavia or Kosovo under United Nations Security Council Resolution 1244, or the independent Republic of Kosovo. Agron and Hatemja had endured and worked and stayed in Kosovo … and no-one had built them a new house.

One of the houses I'd visited in Fushë Kosovë had a family who were newly returned from Germany. They had gone as refugees, overstayed on the expiration of their leave to remain, and had had a dawn knock on their door, the police taking them to the airport with no time to pack, no time for children born there to say goodbye to their friends, no time to gather school certificates. By that afternoon they were back in Fushë Kosovë, staying with a resentful sister-in-law whose nieces and nephews didn't understand her because they had grown up speaking German. The trauma of their experience was obvious in the face and the bowed, taut posture of the woman who kneeled, pouring detergent over a vat of clothes in grey water.

'I used to have a washing machine,' she said to me, as if she saw me as someone who would understand the life and the pride of a suburban housewife in Dortmund. I ached for her, and her confused, resentful children.

But Hatemja had never had a washing machine. Her children had never had the benefits of a German kindergarten. Was it better to have had those opportunities and had to lose them, or never to have known them?

The women from Fushë Kosovë admiring the little houses arranged in front of them seemed to know what they would have preferred. They were happy to have the outing, but there was an edge of hostility towards this group I was bringing them to meet. I was suddenly wary of how things would go when the two groups of women came together.

We got out of the van by the community centre where a small gaggle of the Srbobran women were waiting. I went ahead and greeted the women and their elegant Albanian trainer, Zyrafete, who was helping co-ordinate their work. I turned to introduce the women from Fushë Kosovë who were hanging back shyly or sullenly.

'This is Zyrafete,' and they smiled politely.

'And this …' I gestured at the group, to start introducing them one by one, beginning with Trashe, who stood nearest me. But I hadn't even finished my sentence when shy Haxhere from Fushë Kosovë broke free from her group and rushed across me to Trashe.

'It's you!' She flung her arms around her and I saw that Trashe was crying.

The two women were cooing and rocking each other in their embrace while the rest of us stood back confused. Eventually Haxhere let Trashe go.

'I haven't seen her since the war,' she said. 'We were refugees together. She used to look after my son when he was a baby.'

'And it was Haxhere who held my mother as she died,' said Trashe, welling up again.

They explained that when Haxhere had come back to Kosovo, they had lost touch. Neither had mobile phones; neither could read or write … the world had seemed a big place. And yet for all these weeks, Trashe had been sewing bags to package the soaps that Haxhere had been making on the other side of Kosovo. We all had goosebumps witnessing the reunion, of a soap and a bag to put it in.

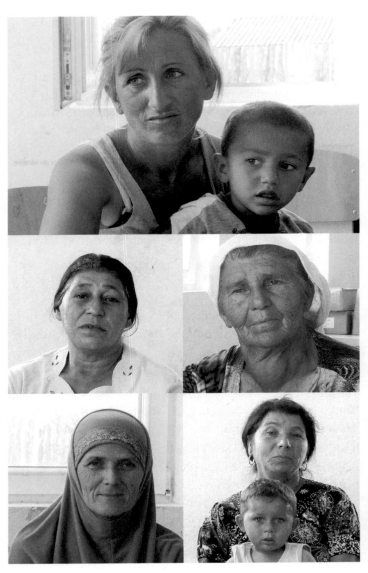

Some of the women in the sewing project

23 A time of gifts

'Are you ready to be famous, Hatemja?' I asked. I'd come round to her house before we went into Prishtina together with Vjollca. The soaps had been on sale for a while now, and the women had stood at freezing stalls during craft fairs, and orders had been placed on Facebook and through friends; they had had their first payment of profits. Now the women had been invited on a Kosovan radio station to talk about the project. They had nominated Vjollca – the only one with any formal education, who knew how to write her name (but, as she said, wasn't certain about which way round the 'J' went) – and Hatemja to represent them and we were going to travel in together.

I sat on the mattresses teaching little Elhame a clapping game while Hatemja got things ready for the family for the hours she'd be away in Prishtina, moving slowly now as she neared the end of her pregnancy. She told Agron what needed to be done in her absence and he nodded at each instruction. I wondered what he felt about his wife the *biznesmenja*. Perhaps a full stomach at night compensated for any wounded pride. And he was a doting father, so time spent with his kids wasn't something he'd complain about – I watched him playing with Ramadan while Hatemja fetched nappies from the cupboard stuffed with the children's clothes.

Looking around the room I noticed some fancy slippers by the door. They were in faux silk – blue with silver thread and pointy Ottoman toes. They gleamed in the dark room and I gestured at them to Hatemja.

'Wow! The slippers are gorgeous! Where did you get them?'

She blushed. 'Agron gave them to me. They're for when the baby comes. He found them.' I imagined Agron stumbling on them like diamonds in the dust, or sapphires in the trash, brushing them off and putting them carefully away from the squashed drinks cans in his wheelbarrow, and then coming home and presenting them to his bride for her special day.

'Oh, how lovely!' I said with genuine enthusiasm for the little romance, smiling up at Agron the swain, who grinned goofily back.

Hatemja looked proud to have impressed me.

'Have them!' she said.

I presumed I hadn't heard correctly.

'What?'

'Take them! I want you to have them!'

'No, no, no,' I insisted, laughing at the spontaneous generosity. 'They're yours Hatemja – for when the baby comes.'

'But you like them,' (oh, I wished I hadn't mentioned them), 'and I want you to have them,' she reiterated, now banging the slippers on my hands as if they were dancing to me.

I was almost angry now, and quite determined that I wasn't going to take them. But Hatemja was just as determined. Her voice was rising,

'I want to give you something. *I* want to give something to *you*,' she said, staring full into my eyes. With a sigh I stopped the slippers' dancing, and held them.

'They're beautiful,' I said again, though Hatemja knew they were. That's why she'd given them to me.

'Thank you,' I murmured and I hugged her, feeling inadequate and unworthy. She held me tight, as if she understood how I was feeling.

We met up with Vjollca and drove towards the centre of Prishtina and the radio station. It was clear as soon as we arrived, and the interviewer's eyes travelled across the dark faces of his guests, that he hadn't expected them to be Ashkali women and he struggled with the best way to share this extraordinary fact with his listeners, who wouldn't be able to tell from the voices. 'But you're ...' he started. 'You're the first....' He never finished his sentences. Nevertheless, he was courteous, and the women were less shy than I'd feared. Their voices became stronger as they talked about the project and how they made the soap. They presented the host with a free sample and he described on air the drawstring bag packaging, and the consistency of the soap inside.

Afterwards I took Vjollca and Hatemja to celebrate with some *burek* meat pie. But then it was time for some direct sales. We had had the idea that in order to generate bulk sales we needed to try to get hotels to buy guest soaps for their rooms so we set off with a bag of samples to try to woo the managers of some of Prishtina's biggest hotels. We started at the largest, the Yugoslav era 'Grand Hotel'. Walking in, even the garrulous Vjollca stopped talking and looked around in awe at the vast lobby.

The receptionist took us up to the manager who listened politely and accepted our sample but didn't offer us much hope. We thanked her, shook hands, and left. Outside, I shrugged. 'Ah well ...' But Hatemja was still wide-eyed.

'Did you see how big it was! And the carpet...!'

To be honest, I hadn't noticed the carpet. But from what Hatemja was describing, it was a fitted carpet rather than rugs. That would fit with the 1970s look of the place.

'Nice!' I said, without much enthusiasm. But I don't think Hatemja had seen a fitted carpet before. I thought about the floor of her house, with blankets spread over concrete and I realised there was in fact something quite wonderful about a fitted carpet.

We had a few more hotels to visit, and then our plan was to try taking the samples of soap into cafes and bars to sell to customers. I was feeling protective of Hatemja, and even of the cocky Vjollca – unfamiliar with Prishtina and the ways of the big city, the big carpet. I realised I would have to show them where to go, and take them under my wing.

After the last hotel (another sample given out; another polite brush-off) I pointed out the café I suggested we should try for the first of our direct sales.

'They won't let us in there,' said Hatemja. I smiled at her temerity, her naïve fears in the capital.

'Yes, yes they will,' I assured her, with all the confidence of a well-travelled foreigner who had lived in the town a few years.

'They won't. We'd be better trying that one,' she pointed next door.

'Why do you say that?' I asked

'Because that's where I used to go when I was begging.'

And then I understood that for all her ignorance of Axminster and underlay, Hatemja's knowledge of Prishtina was detailed, and practical. For what we wanted to achieve right now, selling the soaps her group had produced, I would be better to shut up and let her guide.

They didn't sell much, but they sold more than we'd managed in our negotiations with the Grand Hotel. I wondered how their takings compared with the money Hatemja would have got if she'd brought Elhame with her, begging. The brand name we had come up with for the products was 'Sa-Punë', which played on the Albanian word for soap, *sapun* but had a literal meaning of 'what a lot of work'. Hatemja's peddling of her handmade soaps around the cafes where she used to beg was what it meant to emphasise work, not charity.

But it was a new education project; the easy bit was teaching Hatemja and her colleagues how to measure out olive oil in spoonfuls. Beyond that, we had to explain about keeping back some of the profits each month to buy olive oil for the next batch. And even that was nothing to having to educate our customers. The idea of Fair Trade, or even of ethical consumerism, was new – in a country where consumerism itself was less than a generation old. And even our supporters who came from countries where the idea was established didn't always see the connection. One American woman who heard about our work in Fushë Kosovë said she wanted to help somehow. 'My particular passion is for supporting women and children,' she said.

So I told her how heavily-pregnant Hatemja had been taking her children out begging; how none of them had been in school; how we were now supporting the kids through their mother. Would she like to buy some soap?

'Well, I don't like giving money,' she said. 'I'd like to give something that's useful. Can I buy the children pencil cases for school?'

'You could buy the soap and then the women could buy pencil cases themselves for their children,' I suggested – thinking, too, that Hatemja had told me there was no flour left in the house for making bread tomorrow.

The lady from Kentucky never did buy any soap.

But others did, and the run-up to that Christmas was a whirl of trying out new moulds, tying on the cute labels we'd had designed by our friend, Su, on homespun recycled paper, and slipping soaps in bags. One woman placed a bulk order for the soaps on condition that we customised the label to say 'Happy new year' with the names of her family printed there, and we dashed in taxis to the printers to collect her special labels, and spent our team meeting tying them onto the soap bag drawstrings as we talked. Time was running out − I felt it with a growing sense of panic about the presents my family would be receiving from me. Had I made myself so busy fulfilling orders for other people's Christmases that I was unable to show my own relatives that I cared for them? I wondered whether the Christ child might keep some cosmic balance sheet and I could somehow transfer some of the thoughtfulness of our customers as a gift to my parents.

The pre-Christmas rush was made all the more surreal by the fact that we were preparing for our Christian celebration in a particularly Muslim neighbourhood. Kosovo as a whole is a majority Muslim country, but as many Kosovars are keen to point out, the roots of this were 'for tax purposes' under the Ottoman Empire when the historically Catholic population was convinced − usually by incentives rather than force − to convert. The extent of the conversion, especially when overlaid with 50 recent years of socialism, leaves most heads − and indeed knees − uncovered. Alcohol is freely drunk, few of my friends had ever been inside a mosque, and Christmas was generally seen as a great Hollywood tradition that everyone would like to try out. But nevertheless, 25 December was not the focus of traditional celebrations − instead, these had been transferred to New Year's Eve, when presents were given, relatives got together to celebrate with a big meal, and a familiar figure in a red coat with a white beard came to visit children; he was called 'Father Winter'. For most of Kosovo's

Muslims, this benevolent figure and the 'turning of the times' as the translation of the traditional Albanian name rather apocalyptically put it, was a secular way to bring a welcome glow to the darkest month of the year.

However, a small but growing Muslim population was rejecting the legitimacy of this dear old man and his festival. They pointed out that it wasn't 'the turning of the times' in the Muslim calendar, and that even if it were, they considered the celebration of something without religious significance to be *haram*. I caught a glimpse of Oliver Cromwell's po-faced government round Fushë Kosovë sometimes.

A charity in the UK had said they'd like to buy Christmas presents for the children. 'Hmm,' said one of our volunteers, *por nuk është festa jonë*, – 'but it's not our festival'. We debated whether activities should be held on the Saturday which fell in between two national holidays over New Year, or whether we should give all the volunteers – and Hysni, our employee – a break. *'Por nuk është festa jonë,'* argued Ezel.

Finally, when all our soap orders had been delivered, my suitcase packed, and I felt my Christmas holidays had arrived, I had my last meeting with the team in Fushë Kosovë before setting off for the airport and my family. I'd stopped worrying about Christmas shopping either for me or anyone else, and was starting to get excited about the Christmas that really mattered; time with my parents and sister and grandfather, with Rob's family; time to sleep and to eat well, as if throwing down a challenge to winter's cold clutching famine fingers. I said my goodbyes to the group in Fushë Kosovë, a little giggly even on just the promise of mulled wine that awaited me in a Cotswold village.

'Goodbye, Hysni,' I stopped myself from wishing him a happy Christmas. 'Have a happy new year!' Hysni smiled.

Off to one side Ezel was muttering, *'Por nuk është festa jonë.'* I waved cheerily at him and lurched away, with a heavy suitcase full of soaps wrapped up for my friends and relations, and Hatemja's precious gift to me snuggled into a pocket within my luggage.

24 Home birth

Early one Sunday morning Agron called me, his voice tight with tiredness or emotion.

'Is everything alright?'

'Yes, yes it is! Hatemja's had a baby boy!'

'When? When was he born?'

'Just now!' Agron said with a laugh in his voice.

'Are you in the hospital?'

'No, he was born at home.'

My heart sank. I thought of that little dark space, with no hot water. I wondered where the other children had been. I remembered asking Haxhere, the birth attendant, whether there was anything she needed that we could give her to help with her work delivering babies. 'What equipment do you use?' I'd asked, with all the ignorance of a childless woman who had never been present at a birth.

Haxhere hadn't seemed sure what I'd meant; it seemed her role wasn't dependent on much equipment. The tools she took with her, she'd said, were a 'Gillette' – razorblade – and some string, for the umbilical cord. She had smiled indulgently at my wide-eyed response. Surely this was not the best a man could get.

Kosovo's hospitals were not well-staffed or well-equipped, but they had more than a *Gillette* and string to welcome the newest citizens to the country; I wished Hatemja had been able to get to a hospital. But I had known this might happen – a survey done a few years ago in Fushë Kosovë by an NGO called Health for All had found that 38% of births in

Hatemja's neighbourhood in the year of the survey had been at home.

These occasions are what set phrases are invented for – while my mind was racing on razor blades I was able to say just the right thing; the same optative phrase I'd used when Hatemja had told me she was pregnant.

'May he have a long life together with his parents,' I muttered, in a blessing. Agron thanked me.

'And can I come and see Hatemja and the baby, soon?' I asked, wondering what customs and superstitions I might be trampling in my enthusiasm.

'Yes, yes; come when you want. You can come now,' Agron said. But I didn't like the idea of intruding so early – I thought about the family scene, Agron with the five children clustered round their crumpled new little brother, Hatemja needing sleep; the children suddenly understanding their ties not just as an abstract relationship or an accident of accommodation, but as a bond of blood. I had no place in the animal heat of their family home today.

'I'm going out now, through the bins,' said Agron, 'because we need money.'

Ok, so I was going to visit Hatemja and her very small son.

I wondered what I should take for her, aware that I owed Hatemja at least a pair of silvered slippers for this day. I stopped my taxi at one of the supermarkets on the road out to Fushë Kosovë, and while its engine was running I rushed in. How should I welcome this child, who should have been born to a woman in sapphire shoes?

In the end I rejected the soft toys and was ruthlessly practical about what Hatemja's son was going to need for a good start in life. A clean soft blanket, a babygrow and cotton hat, and some nappies. *May he have a long life together with his parents.*

As the taxi approached the house I realised I was nervous. I had never seen a baby this new before. In fact, with the exception of my little sister, born when I was five, I don't think I had ever seen a baby younger than a week or so. I imagined a little gobbet of a thing, red and bawling in an embrace of milk and talcum powder.

But when I got to the doorway, I realised we had not yet reached the milk and talcum powder stage; this was a room that was still recovering from its recent throbbing with pain and blood. The air was meaty.

Inside Hatemja lay awkwardly on one of the mattresses. She struggled to her elbows when she saw me but gratefully sank onto the pillow when I told her to lie back. She was pale and looked terrible, but she clung to a chrysalis-shaped bundle and when I asked if I could peep at it, her drawn face transformed into a smile.

I peered in at this new member of the Krasniqi family.

He wasn't crumpled at all; he was perfect. Eyes closed in a deep sleep, he had soft cheeks feathered with fine lashes, and a little mouth pursed as if in a kiss. Despite what I knew of the statistics about antenatal care; what I knew of his lifechances already slimming through Hatemja's poor nutrition during pregnancy, his birth at home, even what I remembered of Hatemja's regret at another mouth to feed in the family ... right now, in his mother's embrace there was no room for scepticism; this was a new human being, plump with potential, and already generating so much love. Toddler Elhame tottered over to me as I knelt in contemplation of this miracle that Hatemja had brought forth, and with a curious but proprietary hand, she stroked her little brother's cheek.

All of us wanted to protect this piece of magic, the ruby in the rubble of the Krasniqi's home. And I remembered, a little late, the other imprecation I should have uttered to keep the baby safe from the evil eye. The word is used across Arabic lands, but the accompanying action I've seen only in Fushë Kosovë — I swiped my finger down the bridge of my nose like I was swatting away a fly or some other dark preying presence. *'Mashallah,'* I muttered, and Hatemja smiled weakly back at me.

And how was she feeling, I asked Hatemja.

'I'm so hungry,' she said.

She hadn't eaten? I checked I'd understood. Well what about the rest of the family — what had the children had to eat today?

'Nothing; it's why Agron's gone out through the bins.'

My mouth was open as if I was hungry myself.

'What about the neighbours?' I had imagined solidarity — the Fushë Kosovë equivalent of a cottage pie left in the porch. But I realised the baby meant one more mouth not just for Agron's family but for this whole community to feed.

Even the vegetarian could see that Hatemja needed something bloody; iron-rich and protein-filled. I had a deep instinct calling to me, a collective memory from before lettuce was farmed, that I should feed this exhausted new mother some meat. So I excused myself from the pieta on the mattress and went to the nearest source of animal protein I knew — the kebab shop fifteen minutes' walk away. There I ordered warm bread filled with as much meat as could be stuffed in it, with salad and fruit juice for some quick sugar. One for Hatemja, one to keep for Agron when he returned, and one each for Gjelane, Vehbi, Labinot, Ramadan and Elhame. I had never bought kebab before, but then I'd never seen such a new baby before either. And this tiny little boy had never done anything before; a big day for everyone.

25 A boy named Elham

A few days after the baby was born I drove into Fushë Kosovë to find Agron waiting at the centre. As soon as I got out of the car he came up to shake my hand,

'Mrs Elizabeth, we want to invite you to the baby's naming ceremony.'

Ceremonies are about belonging and this one would be a way of demonstrating that this child belonged – to this ramshackle, populous, seething, rich, poor community and its extended family. But the leap of my heart at Agron's invitation was because it would be a way of showing that I belonged – not just the outsider shuttling in with a text book in hand, but taking my place in the row of other members of the community sat in Agron and Hatemja's dark little room, to welcome a small boy to our world. I wondered when the naming ceremony would take place – on a Friday, when the men would go to mosque? One evening?

I thanked Agron for the invitation, assured him it would be a pleasure for me.

And when would the naming ceremony take place?

Well it had depended, apparently, on when Dashnim, who knew the Koran, was free.

Aha, so when was it now due to be?

'Now, now!' Agron pulled at my arm. 'Come on – we've been waiting for you.'

But... I gestured futilely at my unceremonial clothes, at the bags I was carrying, at my diary that I knew sat within them – a symbol of all my plans, the reasons I'd been coming to the

centre today, my doomed sense of control over my time....
And with a shrug from Agron at all these irrelevant issues I set
off with him in a rush. If I wanted to belong here there were
some things I would have to let go of.

I entered the house down the dark puddled alley with Agron,
manoeuvring my shoes off at the door almost adeptly. Peering
in, I could see the room was full of bodies. Men and women,
but no children, apart from the baby, swaddled on his mother's
lap. They were sat quietly, not with the gigglesome chat of a
wedding; this was more like the meditative calm of a funeral.

They all budged up along the mattresses when I came in, and
I smiled at them apologetically – sorry for squashing them
in the tight space, sorry to have kept them waiting. It was
evident that Agron's claim that they were waiting for me was
not merely a form of etiquette – the ceremony really was
going to start just as soon as I arrived.

I recognised Dashnim as a man I'd seen around
Neighbourhood 29. I thought he might have been one of
the men who'd come to hear me not singing hallelujah at
the beginning of our project – he was certainly as bearded
as those men had been, and he wore a little white knitted
cotton cap which was unusual in Fushë Kosovë – more like
the Muslim headwear I'd seen in the Maghreb. He took the
baby tenderly (the man's name means 'love') and then gently
raised him up to the level of his head, half singing, half saying
words in Arabic. As he lifted the boy up high, he pronounced
his name – Elham (the male version of the name that had
been given to his sister Elhame) – and repeated the action
until Elham had been lifted, named and blessed three times. A
gentle mutter of 'Amin' went around the room.

And now Elham was passed to others to do the same. Agron
took his new son between his hands, and raised him up three

times, high above his head. Each time he said the boy's name, and murmured something as he did so. I wondered what he was wishing for his child.

Then it was Hatemja's turn, and she took her boy back and raised him up slightly self-consciously with a prayer which she ended with a kiss.

Then the baby was passed to Haxhere, the birth attendant whom Hatemja had told me had been with her during her labour. She's a small woman who's economical with her movements and her words; I had rarely heard her speak but her voice came out confident now,

'O Elham, welcome to our community, where you will grow.'

I had a lump in my throat. And also a clutch around my heart because I was beginning to understand the rhythms of this ritual, and I could sense that they were getting closer to me. I didn't know where I would come in the fine taxonomy of men and women, Muslim and atheist, local and foreigner, those who had known the family all their lives, and the newcomer. But since Agron had waited so particularly for me to join them, I was pretty sure Elham would be handed to me soon.

I was well aware of the privilege of being part of the defining of a name and a person. Until now I had only helped children transcribe the names they had been given by their communities, holding the hands of Gjelane and the others as they learned to twist and loop a pencil into the particular shapes which signified them, but in that I was only turning speech into text; this was turning a nameless baby into a known and labelled citizen of Kosovo and of the world. I didn't want to get it wrong.

I was panicking over the optative form of Albanian verbs, a grammatical oddity reserved only for blessings and curses; but more than that I was wondering what I should say in any language to tiny, perfect, Elham. Could I bless him with wishes of bounty, when I knew the mean, desperate scrabble of his family's economy? Could I wish him an education and then not stick around to make sure he had shoes to go to school in first grade? And to whom was I addressing this appeal anyway? Dashnim and the other bearded, headscarved members of the community here knew to whom they were talking. But I didn't have a God to call down blessings from, and it seemed a dodgy start in life to bless Elham with hypocrisy; I wasn't going to pretend. So whom was I invoking? I looked around me at the faces in the gloom: at Hatemja anxiously tracking her son's progress round the room, at Agron's proud smile. I thought of Gjelane, of Elhame's wondering curiosity about her new brother on the day he was born; I saw Haxhere's eyes … These were the people I was invoking; this was as close to God as I could get.

So yes, I wished Elham vaccinations and vitamins, a home where sewage didn't wash in during the rains, a mother who had the skills to help him with his homework … I knew all the things that were missing and much missed in this cobbled-together shelter for a family. But this wasn't a Unicef moment, and looking round the room I also saw the form of prosperity in which Elham would grow up. So when it came to my turn and I held tight the swaddling around a patient blinking Elham, and lifted him as a light offering to the heavens, the best blessing I could find to say was this: 'Elham, you are lucky because you are loved. May you always be loved.'

26 Drums and diplomas

Love was not enough, however. In some ways, love was the easy bit; the surge of endorphins which had kept us going on no money and no sleep in those busy first days in Fushë Kosovë. Now we needed to think about something more systematic than love; more sustainable than a handful of foreigners in a flat above a mini-market. And I needed a rest.

I rather grandly declared a 'month of me'. For four weeks I wasn't going to take any paid work, and I was going to do the absolute minimum in Fushë Kosovë.

'So what *are* you going to do?' people asked me, and I didn't really know the answer.

'Drink ginger tea,' I'd explain, hoping I could spin the cuppas out for thirty days or however long it took to come up with a vision for the rest of my life.

The other thing I told people I'd be doing was reading, and I had a stack of books I wanted to lose – or find – myself in. One of them was *The Tipping Point*, subtitled 'how little things can make a big difference'. It was inspiring stuff, and one of the references which caught my eye was to a sociological study of how many professionals it takes to live in a New York neighbourhood before there is any perceptible correlation with a decrease in school dropout rates in the area. Immediately I thought about Fushë Kosovë and how many college graduates it would take to 'tip the rubbish tips' into a community whose children routinely attended school.

The question seemed ridiculous at first. I'd read the statistics so I knew that the number of Roma, Ashkali and Egyptian students from all of Kosovo attending the University of Prishtina would fit in one classroom. I only knew of one person in the whole of Neighbourhood 29 who was going to university; I could only think of a handful of people who would even have the high school certificate to be eligible. Were there the raw materials to try to tip this community into aspirations of tertiary education?

But there was that one person to start with, and he was living just below our classrooms: Idriz, the landlord, was the single college student I knew of, routing some of the money from our rent back into getting an education. I wondered how we could inspire others to join him.

As it turned out, I was looking at the question the wrong way round. But it took Jeton to show me that.

Jeton is a strikingly tall and handsome Roma guy in Neighbourhood 29. The children's nickname for him was *kajushë* which is their dialect word for 'stork' and he loped with the effortless grace of the long-limbed. With his brothers he was a musician in a traditional group who were often called on to play at weddings, and he'd come for some of the sessions with Mergim to teach the children to play his *surl* pipe (the one that sounded like a duck. He'd told the wide-eyed children, and me, their wide-eyed teacher that he'd got the reeds for the pipe from the river that trickled at the back of Neighbourhood 28. I'd wondered then whether he had some magic to steal the voices of the birds down there too). I'd heard his playing – lively (his name means 'he lives') and anarchic. Was it that which had made me deaf to the idea that he might be interested in education – as if drums and diplomas didn't go together?

Thankfully he set me straight, coming to ask me whether The Ideas Partnership could pay for his evening classes so that he could get his high school diploma. Perhaps the issue wasn't finding students willing to study, but just the wherewithal to fund them; and this suddenly seemed an easier task. The classes cost 150 euros a term which there was no way he could pay, but as it happened we'd just been given 150 euros – and more – by a family in Austria who told us they didn't buy presents for each other at family celebrations, but instead pooled the money and gave to a charity. So, walking alongside Jeton on a dusty Fushë Kosovë street one bright day, I passed on a Christmas present from Austria – the gift of further education.

But, I said to Jeton, we'd need something back. His personal goal might be to get his education, but we wanted him to be a rising tide, lifting all boats. I had to look up at him as I said it. A condition of us paying his tuition would be a few hours of his time every week supporting his community through us. I offered that he could help us sort the clothes that were increasingly being donated to us for distribution to families in need. Or perhaps he could teach children at our Saturday activities?

When Jeton started teaching on Saturdays it seemed a win-win-win situation. The children were brought face-to-face with an inspiration to education from within their own community, while we had another person to help with teaching in the crowded Saturday classrooms, and Jeton was fulfilling his personal dream.

Others heard about the idea, including two men – one of them Haxhi Bashkim who had been so generous with his whiteboard and desks – who wanted to join Idriz at university, and asked whether we could support them with a similar small bursary each month. Other potential donors heard too – a university friend of mine who offered to collect money instead of presents for her fortieth birthday, to be donated to the bursaries fund, and a visitor from Cyprus who came to see our work. Within eighteen months, our 'bursaries programme' as we grandly named it, had thirteen students who were supported in further studies and offering work back to their community through football clubs, computer classes, office admin, a free trip each week for members of the community to hospital in one guy's dented van, and teachers of women's literacy as well as Saturday classes. We had a waiting list which overran the space in Hysni's notebook with the names of potential students wanting to join them.

I wondered how Benjamin Franklin had felt – this was like tapping into a source of power we'd never realised existed – the unseen crackling currents of aspiration that had been in the air all around us.

Sometimes, I could even see them take shape, like flashes of lightning. With Hysni I saw it when he went to his first conference. It was held at one of Prishtina's nylon-and-laminate hotels; an event to discuss inclusion in the Kosovan education system. I was used to these meetings – low-budget versions of the training events I'd attended in England – all name badges and plates of biscuits. Though the Kosovan biscuits made me long for custard creams, the conferences in Prishtina always had one feature which gave them a greater sense of glamour than their British equivalents – they had headphones for simultaneous translation. Somewhere behind a screen would be a Table of Babel with interpreters translating between English, Albanian and Serbian. In the main part of the room, the delegates would – unless particularly cocky and demonstrating their competence in all three languages – sit with their headsets on, tuned to the appropriate channel to hear all proceedings translated into their own language as if they were at the UN.

Jeton (right), with Hysni (middle) and our volunteer, Fikret (left)

Hysni shook his head half in wonder, half in dismay, when I told him to pick up his headphones as we came in. We were becoming comfortable with each other's position as guides to our different worlds. He'd saved me from social disaster at the weekend in Fushë Kosovë. One of our young volunteers, a sixteen year-old lad, had bought some pretzel sticks and was handing them round to the team during a break between the Saturday classes. He'd offered one to me, and I'd politely declined since I'd just had a snack.

There was a shocked silence among the others, and Hysni explained, 'But you have to, Elizabeth.'

Why? Was this more of the aggressive hospitality I'd come across elsewhere in Kosovo which force-fed guests? Of course I didn't want to offend, but was it so bad to turn down a snack offered by a work colleague in the office when you weren't hungry?

'He's unmarried,' Hysni had explained. 'If you refuse food offered by an unmarried man he'll never get a wife.'

I had taken the pretzel stick, wishing young Jashar a long and happy marriage as he grinned.

I'd shown Hysni how the 'bcc' on emails worked (he had shaken his head in disapproval at what he considered to be 'like talking behind someone's back'), and he had helped me in the correct navigation of a Fushë Kosovë family's tragedy, when a seven year-old boy had been killed by stray dogs when he was out scavenging through the garbage. I'd gone to pay my respects to the shaking family and although Hysni hadn't been able to come with me, he'd talked me through it on the phone beforehand – 'there will be one room for women and a separate one for men,' he'd warned me. When you arrive, they'll show you to the right entrance.'

Now it was my turn again, and Hysni was patient with my explanations about how conferences operated. I showed him where to collect his name badge, and we stood surveying the crowd, to see whether there were people from other NGOs we knew. Balkan Sunflowers would be there, but I couldn't see them yet. I shrugged and turned to Hysni, gesturing at the tablecloth where pots and cups were laid out – 'would you like a coffee?'

No, he said, he was fine.

I couldn't believe it. Hysni was a working man, with a working man's instincts for hot drinks; I had never known him turn down a cup.

'Um, you know, Hysni, that it's free?'

His eyes widened. I guessed it was the first complimentary coffee Hysni had ever been served in a hotel. With a smile he headed towards the cups.

I remembered his neighbour coming to visit the centre that week. She was asking for money because, she'd said, they had nothing to eat. She'd made the gesture I'd learned meant that reserves were at rock bottom. This flick of thumbnail out against upper canine was something I'd only ever come across with the women in Fushë Kosovë (maybe it was just that these were the only people I knew in such straits). It made a click like the sound of a scoop in an empty flour bin, a spoon in a sugar pot with no sweetness left.

I looked around me at the sleek, well-fed conference guests smoothing their ties against their shirts as they bent over the coffee pots and dropped in sugar cubes. It wasn't only a thought-provoking conference for Hysni, fiddling with the channels on his first set of headphones, but also for me seeing the world of advocacy in Prishtina through Fushë

Kosovë eyes. I'd never wondered before about how it was that free coffee was served to those talking at conferences about inclusion, but no coffee to the families struggling to integrate their children in school. Like the test Gjelane had had to pass to show she already knew the things school should teach her, the only people who got free lunches were those whose jobs made sure they weren't hungry.

Soon after the conference, we lent Hysni a laptop to use to create lists of the children we were supporting to stay in school. It came in a faux leather case and he swung it gently from his hand as we walked down the stairs from the centre together. 'Like a professor,' he said, as if daring me or himself to laugh at his pretension. I smiled, but I didn't laugh.

The next time I saw him, Hysni told me that he, too, wanted to go back to school. Gjelane and her friends were proving to be powerful role models.

27 The haunting

Coming out from my Month of Me I had to acknowledge that my relationship with Fushë Kosovë was probably not coming to an end any time soon. I'd thought it was just a place to hand over some clothes I didn't need any more, and then just a family whose son I could help with burns cream, and then just some kids to get to school. But now I wanted to know how those stories ended – I wanted to check that Gjelane stayed at school; I wanted Hysni to get his school certificate; I wanted Bashkim to graduate. And even if none of these things happened, this was a place where I was happy. I felt like I had friends here. The relationships were complicated but the warmth was genuine.

So I tried to get a little more practical about how we were going to fund what we'd started here. From that first fundraiser at Zsofia's house with Laura's donations box, through Eleanor's dinner, we had mainly been dependent on the one-off generous impulses of people we knew. Sometimes that was a folded twenty-euro note; once it was a guy who asked me to lunch to talk about our work and at the end passed me an envelope which turned out to contain two thousand euros. Rob ran the Prishtina half marathon raising money; my brother-in-law kayaked around the UK and asked for sponsorship for The Ideas Partnership; the Austrians gave us their Christmas present money. But next month, maybe no-one would feel generous; maybe there would be no marathon; our families' attention might be elsewhere – we had no guarantees of any money coming in. Our financial planning was about as sophisticated as Hatemja's. If we had money we would spend it immediately – and like her, on things that seemed essential. Knowing that we had that 150 euros from the König family, it would have been morally indefensible to tell Jeton we couldn't afford to help him through school. So although I tried to tell Hatemja and the other soap-makers about the importance of keeping some money back each month, when they looked at me disbelievingly and said 'but we have to eat and the boy was sick…' I was no role model for them.

But, like Agron rooting through the scraps for something useful, as a group of volunteers we kept our ears open for grants we could apply for. I was learning from Aurélie how to write them, and how to win them, and when we heard that there were grants for promoting cultural heritage particularly among excluded groups we applied to take the children from Fushë Kosovë on a summer trip.

Cultural Heritage Without Borders – CHWB – granted us the money: a few thousand euros to pay for transport and food to take six separate groups of children to a restored century-old *kulla* in the west of Kosovo. The *kulla* was fully equipped for guests – CHWB had restored it with a modern kitchen and bathroom, and the former stable on the ground floor (the heat from livestock traditionally kept there would have risen to warm the family living above) converted into a meeting space.

Our visits there would be a symbolic activity for the concept of cultural heritage without borders as the *kullas* were the most closely defended core of Albanian heartlands. They're a form of architecture unique to Kosovo and northern Albania. They are three-storey houses, though the word in Turkish means 'tower' coming from an era when all building was low-rise, as in Fushë Kosovë today, and three floors was dizzying.

There were still children in Neighbourhood 29 who told me they were scared to come to our centre because of the stairs, as none of their houses or those of their friends had these jagged trip-hazards to be navigated between entering and going to sleep. The *kullas* are fortified, with walls high and thick enough for you to feel safe and their upper floors pierced only with tiny windows just big enough for a rifle to aim through. The reason for the need for defensibility was traditions which were drawn from the Albanian *Kanun* code and which required a family to avenge any case of murder in what quickly became tit-for-tat blood feuds. Tradition stipulated that any male family member old enough to hold a gun was liable, and as a result, Albanian boys whose families were in feud were kept safe at home (and out of school, just like the Ashkali kids) behind these heavy stone walls. To have them stormed by a posse of Ashkali children would be evidence of deep penetration of the idea of a multiethnic Kosovo.

The visits would be a signal, too, for the acceptance of the Ashkali. The reasons for their discrimination and exclusion were subtle and layered and not easy to pin down. Some had their roots in historical moments when the interests of the Roma or Ashkali (Albanians rarely distinguished between them) were at odds with the Albanians – one of our Albanian volunteers had shivered when she first came with me to Fushë Kosovë. 'I'm sorry,' she'd said, 'but the last time I saw someone who looked like these people, they were carrying loot out of a burned-out home in my village during the war.' I'd heard such cases referred to before – when, during the war, Serb paramilitaries would burn down an Albanian village or expel its residents at gunpoint, and then notify local Roma that the abandoned houses were ready to be picked over. It was a vile reputation and of course it was reinforced every time it was mentioned – the same volunteer said to me that as a child, her mother would threaten her that if she didn't behave, the Roma would come and get her.

So in Albanian tradition, the Roma were frightening bogeymen, or by-words for filth – one liberal Albanian friend of mine described to me how when his toddler had covered herself in tomato sauce, and he was mopping her up in irritation, he was horrified to hear himself telling her she'd made herself into 'a *magjup*' with that mess, using the offensive word for the Roma. Those messages muttered by your parents as they mop ketchup from your chin are the hardest to forget, and when the Roma, Ashkali and Egyptians' poverty and exclusion kept them living differently and looking different from you, there was fertile ground for prejudice to flower; it was no easy task in front of CHWB.

But we were happily part of the project for inter-ethnic harmony, and our volunteer, Kelsi, got in touch with the woman who had the role of caretaker, based in the nearest town to the *kulla*. We confirmed that Teacher Avdil would take his group of students – hungry lads who'd fingered the pages of their exercise books with stubby fingers rough from manual labour, as they dreamed of dinner – to have a village lunch there; others would stay the night.

Kelsi and I set off with a group of ten girls in the minibus. Driving us was one of our bursary recipients, Elvir, who was always up for new adventures – whether into textbooks or old buildings. He was a lively conversationalist, always interested in passing on something he'd seen on the news or some gossip from a neighbour. If something funny happened, or someone came out with a bon mot, it would be Elvir who'd remember it, store it up, and bring it out later when he was with a different group. When you met him you'd get a digest of the best witticisms Elvir had heard that week. What those who had smartphones did with photographs, Elvir did with anecdotes, 'liking' and 'sharing' better than any social network site.

We arranged that we would stop off to buy food on the way and we'd cook together in the evening. I'd worried about what else we'd do – whether we should take books and balls and games. I'd worried about quite a lot of things; we'd packed a first aid kit and I'd charged up my phone.

In the minibus on the way down the girls wanted to know more about where we were going. I told them that the *kulla* had been built at the beginning of the twentieth century and they stared – for most of them it would be the oldest building they'd ever seen. A hundred years is unimaginable antiquity when you are ten and your country is only seven years old, particularly when guerrilla and paramilitary activity, and other destructions unleashed on Kosovo in the war from 1998, had destroyed about half the homes in Kosovo. And that war had been only the last in a line of conflicts where buildings had taken as much damage as the soft flesh of human beings. In Fushë Kosovë homes weren't constructed to last anyway – many were still built out of mud bricks, and others were nailed together boards and sheet metal that would never endure as the stone *kullas* had.

'Is it haunted?' they wanted to know. Of course I told them it wasn't – aware that we would all need our sleep that night – but I was lying. Everywhere is haunted, every building carries the scuffs and stains and damage and repairs of the lives and deaths within it. Old buildings are a nation's memories, and that's why I, like CHWB, believed they were important to protect. If your home is new and made of PVC and laminate and freshly poured concrete, there are no corners for dust nor for other ways of remembering the past. It's understandable that after the trauma and ruin and dirt of war, people wanted wipe-clean surfaces, but I didn't want Kosovo's next generation to aspire only to plastic.

In the minibus the children told me, with shy looks, that this was for most of them the first time they had spent a night away from home. They didn't have teddies or comfort blankets, but some of the girls huddled into one another on the journey.

When they arrived at the *kulla*, though, they jumped out to meet this new experience. They scampered through the rooms, poking dark faces out of the windows and waving to me in the garden. Elvir paced curiously behind them. I wondered what the Albanians who built this stronghold would have made of this occupation of their defences.

The girls paired off, some sitting in the smaller bedrooms, and others spreading out in the top floor *oda*, originally the men's meeting room and traditionally where the *pleqnar* council of elders would meet to judge cases of civil law. I had heard that the *pleqnar* was still used to resolve minor disputes or in cases where both parties were distrustful or impatient of Kosovo's judiciary and its backlog of cases. In fact, the one case where I had been given a first-hand account of the *pleqnar* being used was not by Albanians but by one of the girls' Ashkali neighbours. He and his wife had wanted children for some years and when she still was not pregnant he decided he wanted a divorce. The *pleqnar* was called with representatives from his community and the community where she'd grown up, in another town in Kosovo, to decide whether to allow the divorce or not. The husband was allowed to attend but not to speak.

In the end, the *pleqnar* concluded that the divorce should be allowed only if the husband repaid his wife the equivalent cost of her years of labour serving him, at a rate calculated as if she had been a waitress. He discovered then that he couldn't afford to lose her.

Opening the door to the room where such decisions had been made, I found a group of girls plaiting each other's hair.

'Elizabeth, are we allowed to use the bathroom?' they asked.

'Of course', I told them, and they jumped up, calling to the girls in the other rooms,

'Did you know there's a shower?'

I hadn't been into the bathrooms of many of the homes in Fushë Kosovë. But in some cases – like Hatemja's – that was because they didn't have one. And if you were used to washing from a standpipe in your yard, splashing water under the curious gaze of your brothers and neighbours, the white ceramic privacy of the *kulla* bathroom and shower must have been as good as a spa. Before long, the girls had discovered the scented shampoo that had been left there, and they took it in turns to wash their hair. I heard shrieks and giggles and splashes from the bathroom, and the wet patter of feet on the floorboards. The corridor filled with the perfume of artificial strawberry, and past the windows dark shiny bodies flitted with a flick of slick long black hair.

I was foolish to have worried about bringing games equipment with us so we could pass the time.

'Can we make dinner now?' they asked me. I had thought this would be a chore, but I had misunderstood the training that girls get in traditional societies, in homes with lots of children, no PlayStations, and sisters-in-law used to working together to produce meals. I was accustomed to working with these girls on the edge of their comfort zone, forcing them to reading and writing for which they had diligence but no flair, and where success brought them the dubious currency of school certificates, but no respect from their families. Usually, I would leave the chaos of my kitchen – dirty plates crowded in the sink – to travel to Fushë Kosovë and share the areas of my expertise with illiterate children … now it was payback time. I poked my head into the kitchen to tell the girls what they should be doing, and no-one even looked up. Two of them were washing vegetables, another pair were chopping – fast and expert, as if making food for twelve was a more regular occurrence than doing their maths homework. Others were organising cutlery and plates or portioning food into serving dishes. There was no messing around; a quiet practical hum of collaboration. And nothing I could teach them. I closed the door quietly and let them get on with it.

The food was great, and the washing-up was organised without a murmur. And then in twos and threes the girls came down to the former stable where we sat chatting. One girl asked if she could wash her hair again, and she and a friend went to experience once more the miracle of hot water on tap. The others discussed weddings, and talk led to dancing, and before I knew it they were up in a traditional Balkan dancing line, moving their joined hands in tiny rhythmic circles while they followed the repetitive steps in unison, making a sinuous thread of dancers which moved round the room, dodging furniture, and turning back on itself to make full use of the space. I watched their bare feet on the boards, tempted to join them, but then watching more carefully I realised that the moves were not the step-right-together-back-together that I'd learned at Albanian weddings here, though the basic dance structure was the same. This was an

Ashkali variation, and I knew from the time it had taken me to learn the Albanian version, that I would need to watch for longer before I could get up and take a place in the line. So I sat at the side like a matriarch, clapping in time and watching. The girls at either end of the dancing line snatched up tissues which they twirled in their free hands to replace the traditional red scarves used by the dancers at real weddings. I'd always assumed these represented the bloodstained sheets of the virgin bride's wedding night, but I'd been corrected by one anthropological fellow guest at a wedding, and told that there were ancient Illyrian traditions of sacred snakes, and that the whole dancing line represented the slithering of a snake, with its darting tongue flickering out of the hand of the lead dancer. When the Illyrians were charming their snakes round young brides in Kosovan territory, these Ashkali girls' ancestors would still have been in India, and I had no idea how they would have been dancing, though it would presumably have been some ancient version of the steps I saw here, with footfalls that tramped across Persia, and found their way over mountains and over centuries to this unlikely dance floor. This was what I had meant by haunting.

It was a long night, and when the girls finally got to sleep in the early hours, they abandoned their plans for separate rooms, and created a nest – recreated the squash and reassuring presences of their homes – with mattresses on the floor and duvets thrown above, and all ten of them squeezed together in one room. Hysni taught me a new word to describe the cosy huddle – 'gullumuq'.

The girls tidied up and got ready for our departure (none of them had brought more than a plastic bag, most of them without a change of clothes. I asked, 'what about your toothbrushes?' but not a single child had brought them, so we had stopped at a shop to get them all a toothbrush as a souvenir of the weekend) and Elvir drove us back in the bleary companionship of people who'd stayed up most of night together. We dropped the key off with the caretaker en route and before we'd even finished our journey home, Kelsi had a phone call from her.

She was angry, and talking too fast. There was a broken plate, she said, and a cigarette end under the bed. And the toilet seat was broken. 'I don't want any more of those Ashkali kids coming here,' her voice was relayed in irritated scratches through cheap phones.

Kelsi narrated the conversation to me and we looked at each other in confusion. We were sure we would have heard a plate being broken, even if the girls – those competent domestic managers – hadn't come to tell us. And we were both ready to swear that no-one had been smoking. I asked Kelsi whether she'd seen the toilet seat broken, and she was sure it hadn't been.

But it was only the caretaker's word against ours; the Albanian against the *magjup*… And perhaps we'd been stupid not to ask her to check us in and out so that we were all in situ and could look at the state of things together, be clear whether a broken seat or a left-over fag end predated our visit or not. But either way, this couldn't be grounds for not allowing any Ashkali group to come to the *kulla* again.

This wasn't really about a cigarette butt. This was the sharp end – the red-hot end – of attempting to have cultural heritage without borders.

And luckily the CHWB office understood that. We rang them, and told them about the phone call. They said they would contact the caretaker and get back to us, and when they did it was to say that she had conceded that the other visits should go ahead as planned, and agreed that we should do a check-in and check-out together.

'There was one other thing that she mentioned,' the girl from CHWB said, 'Apparently all her strawberry shampoo has been used up.' That, we knew to be true, and I offered to buy a replacement bottle to leave in the *kulla* on our next visit.

So we were able to set off again with a van full of lads from Fushë Kosovë, ready to spend the night. They were as excited as the girls had been and full of questions too.

'Is it haunted?' they repeated. The echoes of the past, still making people jittery today. Yes, it was haunted.

28 Begging

I went away for a couple of weeks, and felt the usual tug to come back to Kosovo. I kept in touch as best I could when I was in England – beeping electronic conversations on Skype or Facebook. Hysni got a new phone which enabled him to send me messages from the field though he put an inexplicable full stop between every word, giving them the feel of phone calls clicking through a distant telephone exchange. Whichever way we tried, Kosovo seemed a long way off.

So when I got off the bus in Prishtina one Sunday I was happy to be home. I would be going to Fushë Kosovë the next day, but for now I was just pleased to be back in my Kosovo life; a place where I felt I was doing something useful. I was proud to the point of vanity of the children who we'd registered for school, of our efforts to keep them in school, the soap-making project, the way people were turning their lives around. When I was in England I spent much of my time talking about Fushë Kosovë to curious friends, and it was exciting to be back in the plot, reminding myself that this was not just a story.

So when I spotted Gjelane in the courtyard of a block of flats between the bus station and our home, my heart lifted. Her face was momentarily clouded – I guessed from confusion at seeing me here, rather than in Fushë Kosovë – and then she, too, broke into a huge smile. She ran towards me and gave me a tight hug. As a welcome to Kosovo it was pretty much Hollywood perfect.

Except … my own face clouded. What was she doing there by the flats? Where were her parents? It took me a few minutes to take in what Gjelane had understood right away. I pulled away from the hug and held her at arms' length.

'Where's your mum?'

She looked down and answered with a monosyllable; 'home'.

'So what are you doing here?' I knew, and she knew I knew. She wouldn't say it.

'Gjelane?'

'I'm with my grandmother,' she muttered. And it was probably true – I knew Agron's mother went out begging, and I could see that taking pretty little Gjelane with her would be more likely to bring in the euros. I felt heat building somewhere between my belly and my heart.

'Mum's out with the wheelbarrow because Dad can't work at the moment,' I knew that was true too – we had recently paid for the hernia operation for Agron, and he'd been told that he had to rest for a few weeks while the mesh embedded. I hadn't thought that Hatemja would be replacing him. And now Gjelane was replacing her. And this was somehow our fault for paying for Agron's operation?

As well as my own feelings of implication, there was the terrifying vision of gorgeous young Gjelane wandering up to the doors of strangers' homes and asking for money. I knew from my consultancy on human trafficking that Kosovo was becoming a source country for trafficked women; I felt like I was watching a case study unfold. I remember my mother trying to explain to me as a child why she'd shouted at me when she'd found me after I wandered away in a shop. 'I sounded angry because I was so scared that I'd lost you.' I was sounding angry now; I was so very scared.

'You mustn't go to the homes of people you don't know. It's not safe.' I wanted to snatch her myself, away from all these dangers. I hadn't believed that poverty could continue to threaten her despite all the safeguards of school and some regular work for her mother, and healthcare for her father – even because of the healthcare for her father.

'I don't go to homes; only to shops,' she told me, and I wondered who had taught Gjelane how to be a careful beggar. I was still furious.

Gjelane needed to know that, but I think she could tell already. I let the anger boil in me, adrenaline seething into my twitching fingers and a pink face. I looked around for Gjelane's shambling grandmother, but she wasn't to be seen; I don't know what I would have done if I'd found her.

I kept my voice steady and looked straight at Gjelane. My voice came out in a frightening hiss.

'You know that children shouldn't go begging,' I said to her hearing a strange tight urgency in my voice. 'Your grandmother shouldn't take you, and you shouldn't go with her. And you can tell your mum that I'm going to come and see her because I'm not happy. Not happy at all.'

Gjelane looked at me wide-eyed. I tried to sound less frightening.

'I'll see you at our Saturday activities, love.' The last word caught in my throat.

I thought we had stopped this. I wasn't foolish enough to believe that the meagre sales of soaps would substitute all Hatemja's earnings from begging, or that getting her kids to school would be an instant way out of poverty. But I thought she'd understood that there was a better life possible for her family. I thought I'd made some changes to the childhood of the six Krasniqi children. That was the story I'd told myself, but this was no fairy-tale. I was certainly no heroine. I had pretty much been wasting my time.

The next day I went to see Hatemja. I could tell immediately that Gjelane had told her I was coming; both she and Agron were nervous, placating, embarrassed.

Despite having had time to think about it since I'd seen Gjelane, I hadn't prepared a speech. I was still feeling too angry to think subtly or to think of how best to persuade them of Gjelane's right to a childhood. This was not going to be a Save the Children workshop; it was going to be blunt and cruel – it was going to be heartfelt.

'I guess Gjelane told you that I saw her yesterday?'

They nodded.

'You know that it's against the law for children to beg. You know that children have the right to a childhood.' *There you are, Save the Children – I tried.* 'And it's dangerous. Anyone could snatch Gjelane and … exploit her.' The image of what could happen made the rest come out in a rush.

'If I see or hear that Gjelane or any of your children are out begging again, I won't ever help you again.' This was ugly, and I hated myself for saying it. I wondered whether I really meant it, but right then I did.

'There'll be no more place in the soap-making, no more cleaning at the centre,' I wondered whether I had the right – whether moral or legal – to fire a woman from a job just because the job didn't pay her enough and she was sending her children out to beg. 'No more help with operations.' *Would I really do that?*

They nodded, as if I was being reasonable. I felt miserable, and said goodbye as politely as I could, and left.

I went round to see Hatemja the next time I was in Fushë Kosovë. She held me hard as she greeted me, and then ushered me inside. Some of the children were playing around Elham, strapped into his crib and somehow managing to remain asleep, but Agron was out. 'With his wheelbarrow,' said Hatemja when I asked about him.

The acknowledged absence of her husband created an intimacy. Hatemja had never criticised Agron, never complained, but now she said,

'I've told him that I'll leave him if I lose you.' She was talking about my ultimatum about begging; she was offering me the only bargaining chip she had, saying she would risk everything − not only her relationship with the father of her children, a good man, but her economic well-being.

'I'll do what Ragip's wife did,' she went on, referring to a woman on the other side of the railway line who had left her husband with three children to bring up. 'He needs to make sure the kids go to school, stay safe.'

Agron returned a little later while Hatemja and I were still talking. He greeted me formally, not meeting my eye. We sat down while he asked me how Rob was, asked after my health, but Hatemja was still standing, ready to serve us tea, and I sensed also asserting her position as she looked down at Agron while he spoke.

Sure enough, when the rituals were over, she brought up the issue again.

'You know you've got to make sure the children go to school and are safe,' she repeated, and Agron nodded meekly and wordlessly.

'Gjelane has to go to school, and it's your responsibility to make sure she's safe,' she said with a new strength in her voice. Vehbi was listening to the conversation,

'And you, Mum, what's your responsibility?'

Hatemja's stern face and furrowed brow opened into a spontaneous smile.

'Ha!' she said, picking up a frying pan that happened to be on the stove next to the *xhugym*, and waving it cartoon-style at her husband. 'It's my responsibility to make sure everyone else does what's their responsibility.'

We all laughed, longer than we might have done because we were grateful to be laughing together, and Agron and Vehbi and I all looked up with wide eyes at their ferocious mother hefting the frying pan with a slim arm.

I never did hear of Gjelane going begging again, even though I told Hysni what had happened and put him on alert. But children from other families still went out. One of them was Edonis, only seven years old and not going to school, despite us having registered him. I saw him frequently in Prishtina, sitting on a square of cardboard by the cathedral, or walking the pavements with a heart-melting asymmetric smile and his hand out.

One day, Hysni came to tell me that Edonis had been out in Prishtina as usual, begging for money, when he'd hit by a car. He had survived, but his leg was broken, and he had a huge bruise over one eye, where he'd hit the tarmac.

The same anger came back – fury with the people who should be caring for Edonis: who'd sent him and his older sister out to Prishtina, and who collected (and spent) the money he was given. It was because of them that Edonis had lost his childhood to beggary, and it was because of them that he had been on the road when that car had hit him. When I spoke to them they blamed Edonis for not having been good, not having been more careful as he crossed the road. I reminded them that Edonis was seven.

My fury was also directed at those who weren't implementing the law against child begging but also at ordinary caring citizens of Prishtina – the people who gave Edonis money, and thus give encouragement to his parents. If Edonis' begging didn't bring in any money then his parents would let him stay at home, and he'd be safe from those dangerous cars. I understood why people gave Edonis money; his smile was worth at least the casual donation of fifty cents – it would light up your day, and you'd feel you'd done something generous through your donation. But actually what you'd have done is to have collaborated with Edonis' parents in keeping him on the streets; made yourself complicit in their crime.

When I'd asked Edonis about coming to our Saturday classes he'd sighed and his face became old before its time. 'Oh, but I've got to go to Prishtina,' he'd grimaced. His parents could work out exactly how much it would cost them in lost revenue for Edonis to be sitting at a desk rather than on the pavement.

And of course most of all I was angry at how ineffectual I was, apparently unable to give these children a childhood.

Someone challenged me when I said that, pointing out that just to take the children off the streets didn't necessarily give them a childhood, and that in fact they might have more chance at a childhood if they had money from their begging. They taunted me with the suggestion that all I wanted to do was remove the kids from parading their poverty in front of me on the street in Prishtina, and that sending them back to sit at home on a barren floor with no money and no food gave them no more childhood than they had on the pavements of the city. But as Zsofia had said right at the beginning of our work in Fushë Kosovë, 'you do both'; I wanted them off the pavement in Prishtina, but so that they could be at home or school in Fushë Kosovë learning something meaningful.

In fact, the meaningful things on offer for children at our centre were growing by the week. We now had dance classes, up to three times a week, in the centre, run by a volunteer from the community. We'd started a 'quiet play' afternoon drop-in for children to draw, browse books, make Lego cities. We'd run a photography project that had produced cheeky, beautiful, funny, poignant photographs by the children presenting their community to the world.

We'd needed to find money for many of these projects. Surprisingly little money because we had the centre and we had the children, and the work was done by volunteers, but there were still materials needed, transport to be paid. I was getting better at asking people for help than I had been in the dusty attempts in Haxhi Bashkim's shed. I learned the ridiculous tricks of the donor world – when we discussed with one donor that we would like to get an administrator and rent a space for him or her to work, he advised us not to write a request for an office because they wouldn't pay rent. 'But I see that you need some office space,' he said, especially after we'd discussed the laborious receipt-keeping arrangements needed. As Aurélie said, the scraps of paper I pulled out in grubby origami from the bottom of my bag were the equivalent of money because unless we stored and classified and presented them properly we wouldn't get the money to cover them from donors.

'So how can we get money for our office space?' I asked plaintively.

'Ah, well we would be able to give you money for a training space. Might you use the same room for some training sometime?' Of course we would.

Another international donor said they'd like to help, and invited us to submit a proposal for what we needed. I did the maths, and calculated that what we really needed was something towards the rent of our centre in Fushë Kosovë, some money towards an administrator's salary, and the funds to pay for the snacks we offered the more than one hundred children who came on Saturdays to additional learning activities. I wrote a compelling narrative for why these things were important for ensuring the right to education of these children, and a reasonable budget of a few thousand euros that would cover everything we needed for a year. We were learning what we needed to do in writing detailed narrative and financial reports to donors and filing returns at the tax administration – and what the penalties were for not doing those things well. Having some time from an administrator each week would make sure we got the most out of the rest of the money donated to us. Meanwhile, the need for rent was self-evident – without a space where the children could come to our academic support activities, or where the women could make their soap, none of our volunteer time to support these families could make a difference.

Our contact at the organisation sent their guidelines through to us and asked me to make sure our proposal reflected them. When I read the guidelines I saw that only 12% of any grant application could be for resources that didn't go directly to beneficiaries. The Saturday snacks would be fine, but apparently the rent of our centre wasn't considered to go 'direct to beneficiaries'. And I could see that our administrator's salary wasn't going straight to the beneficiaries either – the organisation wanted to be putting apples directly into the little brown hands of malnourished children. Well, I could think of another 12 000 euros' worth of things we could ask for and distribute to families but that the community didn't need very urgently, and that would bring the total up to something where the 2000 euros we really needed would be the appropriate percentage. People sometimes me ask why aid budgets aren't making a difference where they are most needed.

Before long we had a bank of statistics, photographs showing the children in action, and case studies crafted by me to use when we were sending out our letters or funding applications. I realised it wasn't just Gjelane's grandmother who knew the benefit of a plaintive looking child when you were asking for money.

One day I was in the UK, doing a talk at the prize-giving ceremony at a private school where open-mouthed sixth-formers and their well-heeled parents had listened with touching attention to the story of the community in Fushë Kosovë. One of the mothers in the audience had offered a generous monthly direct debit donation to us as a result, and students were offering to come as volunteers in their summer holiday; it seemed to have been a successful evening. I caught a taxi to the station at the end of the night and got chatting to the driver. He asked what I'd been doing, and I told him about the talk, and the outcomes.

'And what do you do with the money you get?' he asked. I told him about education and soap-making and schoolbags and vaccinations and changing lives and opportunities, and he was interested. 'So what's your real aim for these kids you work with in Kosovo?' he asked, as if I were being offered a coaching session free with the ride.

'Well, I guess I want them to be in school, and I want to stop them begging.'

The taxi driver laughed. 'I see – so you've just taken over their job. The Kosovan kids don't have to go out begging because you do it for them round posh families in England.'

29 The tank drivers

''en ca' I s'art 'kool?'

Agnesa had a hearing impairment. It affected her ability to communicate – the challenges of articulation combined with the challenges of being laughed at or ignored; the challenges of her then hitting anyone who laughed at or ignored her. Where other children made friends and created allies and cliques with chatter and whispers, Agnesa barked and shouted half-words which were often met with no response.

I concentrated hard and hazarded a guess at the missing phonemes. She wanted to know when she could start school. Me too.

I thought what we'd done was so easy; we'd found 62 children who wanted to go to school, and had persuaded the school to accept them. The problem was solved.

But it wasn't: it had turned out that there were more children – some of whom had moved into the area only after The Sixty-Two had been registered. Others had been below our radar – never coming to our classes, nor to the Balkan Sunflowers centre, nor to school, but now growing in confidence, or making friends with a child who came to us, and suddenly turning up on Saturdays and shyly saying they'd like to start at school. Agnesa had been kept at home and not registered for school (her mum said with apparent embarrassment – which seemed focused partly on her daughter's disability, and partly on how she herself had dealt with it – that she hadn't thought the girl would be able to learn) but now found her way to our centre where she shouted at me her slurred claim to a place in a classroom.

And not all of those first 62 children had stayed at school. Some had found it too difficult to shift from a childhood without timetables or alphabets to the routines and behaviours of the classroom, especially when the other pupils had been there many years more than them, and the teachers didn't want them there. In some cases Hysni negotiated the children back into class and they returned successfully, but after a certain point in the autumn term the teachers said that any child who had dropped out had missed too much to be taught with the others. The Kosovan curriculum was a terrifying tank of a thing, tearing through childhoods with no regard for where natural paths lay. Moreover, it was a tank with a timetable, and if the timetable had specified page 37 yesterday then today was page 38. And if you'd missed page 37, or if you hadn't understood page 36, then that was really not the fault of the tank, and you were asked to get out of the way.

At least Young Rob's idea of the Saturday activities gave us a chance to go through some of pages 36 and 37 with anyone who needed it. We didn't turn anyone away from the activities, so as well as the kids we'd registered for school we had children coming who'd always been at school but wanted some extra tuition, or children who had never gone to school and for whom this was the only education they received. We regularly had over 130 kids in a day, and had to extend to three shifts to accommodate them all. Adults drifted in to help, too, and soon a quarter of our volunteer team were people from Neighbourhood 29. Saturdays were the distillation of all the energy we'd had within a full week of the lessons before the kids started at school, together with a weekend sense of freedom and playfulness. There was a surge of chatter, a flurry of distributing exercise books when the children needed new ones, and at the end of every session a tumultuous miru-miru-PAFSHIM! The children would then stream out, pausing at individual volunteers for a farewell hug.

This was hard for a well-trained British teacher used to encouraging physical distance between myself and the children I taught. We'd worked on a child protection policy to try to make sense of the cultural differences between myself and the Fushë Kosovë team, and volunteers from all around the world. Hitting a child was out. Grabbing a child's cheek because they were cute was also out. But if a child came up to hug you? We agreed that we should be multiplying such affection, not restricting it.

But the children's puppyish physicality always caught me unawares. Some of the younger children would linger and cling and clutch, kneading my flesh, hands on my belly, pulling at the fatty part of my arms. Some of these children were kids without mothers and I sensed a hunger for some part-time ownership of at least some piece of a mother substitute. Others had loving mothers shared between siblings, and there was always a younger brother or sister at the breast monopolising a Fushë Kosovë woman's attention; if you were eight then you had little chance to cuddle up. But in lots of cases I concluded it was sheer wonder at the nutrition that could produce a body that was as abundant as mine, enriched with vitamins and calories and protein. I had excess weight on my hips where Fushë Kosovë women had bones, or a baby. I had long natural fingernails, proof of the luxury dairy products' calcium I ate and drank, and the fact that the hardest labour my fingers did was touch-typing. I had a stomach swollen with last night's warm dinner, not with childbearing. The children were doing perhaps what I would have done in a stately home, feeling the weft and the quality of fabric, knocking on luxury furniture, amazed by the workmanship, and the expense of something the visitor could never afford to own.

More importantly, these encounters with the children on Saturdays gave us a chance to find out whether they were going to school, or whether there was mediation needed by Hysni with teachers or parents. There were still battles being fought – one little boy, for example, had come with me to register in the normal way – at the correct age – in September. When the sullen secretary had asked him for his birth certificate he had calmly told her that he didn't have one. The calm belied the mess of his childhood – a father who had died and a mother who had left, so that he was now being brought up by his older brother. In such circumstances, it was hard to get a birth certificate, when the parents were not around to swear to when the child was born.

'Well, with no birth certificate you can't register for school,' the secretary had lied.

We had raised the question with the Director, but he was adamant, even though we could find no law to support him and he himself didn't even bother trying to prove that he was acting within the law. So for several busy months we rushed around making contact with an NGO specialising in civil registration, and with the municipality's registration office. Finally we got a birth certificate issued and took Muhamet to meet his teacher.

'Ah, but he's too late now,' she said. 'He's missed out all the work we've done on the alphabet. We're at S already. And I won't sacrifice 35 other children just to help him catch up.' I looked hard at the slim, pretty tank driver in front of me.

In the end we had persuaded her to accept Muhamet, and he had attended classes for the remaining six months of the year. But she had been as good as her word, and hadn't given any help for him to catch up, and at the end of the year she predictably failed him and told him he'd have to repeat the year.

For children out of school but without Muhamet's special circumstances, the Director gleefully waved a law at us to say they would have to attend 'intensive classes' and then rejoin mainstream school in September. According to this law, the 'intensive classes' were the responsibility of the municipality. But the municipality wasn't running them. So in fact from November onwards, children out of school – the deaf child, the newly-arrived child, the child who had dropped out – had been no better off than they had been the previous year when we had started our enthusiastic attempt to transform the opportunities of Fushë Kosovë's children.

And this year we were not going to run our daily classes again. We would still be there on Saturdays, we were managing to fund Teacher Avdil offering academic support, and our daily quiet play drop-in, but – like the law said – those 'intensive' classes were part of the responsibilities for which the municipality received a budget, and we felt that in the long term we wouldn't be solving any problem by offering teaching to these children; we turned our attention instead to lobbying for the classes to start.

Nevertheless, it was haunting to think of what we could be achieving in the short-term if we had directed our energies at the enthusiastic children instead of their unenthusiastic state institutions. Every time Agnesa, the hearing impaired girl, lurched up to me to ask when she could start 'kool', my heart lurched with her. Because we could have started right there.

And it would be close to home; she would probably come every day, and no-one would shout at her.

But this year we were trying to do things the grown-up way, trying to learn from Agnesa's pester power to make some difference at the Ministry or the Municipality. We were not alone in our calls for the municipality to put on the intensive classes that were their obligation by law – we had been joined by the Balkan Sunflowers organisation who ran the centre where Rrahmon worked, and by other NGOs. Some were more enthusiastic than others. One member of local staff who was from the same ethnic group as the children, though living some way away – in the smarter area of town, in a neighbourhood mixed with Albanians – had said to me at a meeting,

'You know they're just going to drop out again even after intensive classes?'

Well yes, I had acknowledged, it was likely that some of them would. But what about all the ones that didn't – there were still a majority of the 62 children we'd registered for school who were regular attenders.

The local guy had shaken his head, 'You're making us look bad. We used to have really low drop-out rates, and now the rates are going up.' So he would prefer that the children wouldn't even 'drop in'? With activists like this in their own community, there wasn't much more that racism could do to harm the kids trying to get into school.

Finally at a meeting with the municipality they had acknowledged that they should run the classes but … ah – they were so sorry – there was no space.

Really? We had offered the use of our centre.

They were sorry, but it would not be appropriate to use an NGO's space.

We were sorry, but it was not appropriate for children to be out of school.

Well, until municipal-owned space could be found, there would be no chance of having the classes.

And was there no space anywhere in the entire municipality of Fushë Kosovë?

Well, yes, there was one small school in a village thirteen kilometres from the community where we worked. But the municipality had no budget to cover the transport.

An international organisation who was at the meeting had stepped in. They would pay the transport.

At the next meeting, the municipality regretted to inform us that the village in question was an Albanian village and they felt that there would be strong feelings against a group of Ashkali children coming to learn there. They were sorry to say that they couldn't guarantee the safety of any children bussed to that school for intensive classes.

The conversation had gone on from November through to June. Then with the school year over and the schools empty, there could be no excuse of a lack of space. 'Ah,' said the Municipal Director of Education, 'but we now don't have any budget to pay the teachers.'

In the end a budget was quietly found for him by one of the bigger NGOs. We all officially disapproved – if what we'd been trying to establish was a sustainable model for the children, then magicking funds for the municipality to pay their teachers at the last minute was not useful. But by then we had all had enough of Agnesa's questions as to when 'kool' would be ready for her and were just grateful something could start.

I was learning that I had a limited appetite for the abstract struggles of advocacy. What fuelled me was seeing children learn, and I charged myself off their energy. Too many meetings with the Director or the municipality or with other NGOs and I started wondering why I was bothering.

After one day full of such meetings, I made my way back to our centre, tired of the challenges of education; tired of trying and tired of giving; tired from the heat and the lack of power. I realised I was heading to our classrooms from a sense of duty, with no love in it. As I turned the corner into the street I was scuffing the dust in a sulk.

'E-LIZ-a BETaaaaaaa,' came a call from a hundred metres away. And a little figure hurtled towards me, calling out my name all the way till I smiled back at her. Sometimes I wondered whether Gjelane and her friends knew just how much I – and their community – needed them.

30 The goddess of bicycles

'Is there a problem?' I asked. The father of one of the children
needing intensive classes had arrived at our centre for the first
time.

'No, *motër*,' Naser began – using the respectful form of address,
literally translating as 'sister', that had something of the cloister
or the hospital ward about it. I'd learned that as much as a
sign of respect, it was an assurance of the sexual purity of the
intentions of the speaker. Men telling me intimate medical
details before they asked for help with buying tablets for
urinary infections or any similar potential embarrassments
would always preface their narrative with this honorific. 'No,
motër, it's that I was wondering if you could help me with a
bike?'

At first I assumed he had trouble – a puncture perhaps – with
a bike he'd left outside, but the trouble turned out to be that
in fact he didn't have a bike outside – or anywhere. Naser,
like Agron, went out with his wheelbarrow every day. 'But,'
he said, 'with a wheelbarrow you can't get far. The best stuff is
in the skips in Prishtina.' I had thought back to my morning
with Agron, hunting for the plastic pastures; it was true that
the search would have been easier in Prishtina, but also that
the eight kilometres you'd have to travel to reach the city
would be impossible with a wheelbarrow.

'If I had a bike then I could have a trailer and carry more
scrap and I'd earn more money.' Naser had grinned – 'maybe
one day I could get a *motokultivator*. Then I'd have all I could
ever want.'

Motokultivators are vehicles I have only seen in Kosovo – the most basic form of motorised locomotion possible, like a tractor engine mounted on wheels without any housing. Sometimes the basic seat is supplemented with an armchair which gives it an air of raffish luxury, but usually they are barebones contraptions driven by hardscrabble guys – often Roma or Ashkali – hauling mean loads of scrap metal, or surplus vegetables needing a quick sale.

Whether consciously or not, Naser had been outlining to me – his potential investor – a business plan. I was impressed; it was the first time anyone in Fushë Kosovë had ever approached me like this. So I said yes – though not to the *motokultivator*. But surely we could buy him a bicycle.

We'd been given a grant to enable us to move The Ideas Partnership from totally volunteer-led administration to something more robust and sustainable, with an Executive Director at its helm. Our volunteer, Aurélie, had been one of those who applied. On the day of the interviews temperatures had been sub-zero and we had only one heater in the room at the centre where the panel sat. Aurélie's nose was pink and we were all bundled against the cold but it seemed her energy was undimmed. Her face lit up, eyes wide, as she described how she saw The Ideas Partnership growing, and the practical skills she had from having been director of a French charity in Kosovo. We appointed her to the role, and within a few weeks we had donor funding for that office (or 'training venue') and a part-time administrator.

Aurélie put together a plan for a total of eleven men like Naser to be given bikes, and even to be given the contacts for organisations who'd like their recyclable rubbish collected, offering their staff the chance for discarded Coke cans to end up directly in the smelter at the depot, rather than rusting among mixed waste and awaiting the tender scavenging fingers of a child rubbish-picker.

We got funding from the Kosovo Foundation for Open Society, part of the international network of philanthropic foundations financed by George Soros, and sent out announcements about the project. We sent notes home with each of the children who attended our activities, and put up signs on the telegraph poles. We knew not everyone we were trying to reach could read, so we spread the word along bush telegraph lines too – our volunteers and the children's families. We told everyone that if they were interested in being part of the project they should come to the centre at a certain time when we would give out application forms and have volunteers on hand to help people complete them.

I remembered the meeting for the applications to be part of the soap-making project: six brave women showing themselves to be willing to learn, to strike out, to become *biznesmenja*. I wondered how many men would be as brave for this project.

When the taxi carrying Aurélie and me approached the centre I saw a cluster of men outside. It was what you see when there's been a death and the community come, all within the 24 hours allowed by Islam between death and burial, to pay their respects. My heart sank.

If it was not a death then it must be some other problem – perhaps the key had broken in the lock again. What a day for it to happen....

'I don't think it's that,' said Aurélie, and when we got out of the taxi I realised my mistake – the dozen men crowded at the door were the overflow from our centre. The hallway was choked with more, and we could hear noise within.

The meaty smell of an unwashed crowd hit you as soon as you opened the door. The centre was dark with faces, black jackets, dirty clothes – men who had come from going through the garbage; the bottom of the heap and yet – these were those who were willing to see and to seize an opportunity. These were the top of the heap – the Nasers who could see how hard work could be transformed into more, when it was coupled with two wheels. This could be the industrial revolution happening right here. I counted the heads – there were eighty!

I made my way to the front of the room and used my best teacher's voice. I didn't have to say much, but it needed to be really clear. I needed to tell them that we didn't have bicycles for them all. I needed to convince them that this was a fair process of application – that they should fill in a form and answer our questions and we would call to interview those who showed the most motivation, but also those whom we could see were most in need. I said those things twice, while Hysni and Aurélie scrabbled in the office for photocopier and paper to produce additional copies of the form for so many unexpected people.

I looked around me at the faces. Almost all were male and most seemed older than me, though if you've spent your thirty-something years shinnying in and out of rubbish bins then your face may have gained some lines that mine had been spared. The expression on the faces was of hope. In some cases scarcely daring to show it (if you've spent your life shinnying in and out of rubbish bins then dashed hopes may be familiar) but everyone who was there had come with an aspiration for progress. I remembered the trudge behind Agron's wheelbarrow, the backache even on my short half-day of rubbish-picking tourism, and I ached again. I wished we had more than eleven bikes to distribute.

Meanwhile, there were people needing help with the first stage. The form was – we hoped – simple. We asked questions about name and age, number of members of the family, whether there was family abroad, whether the applicant already had a bike – or a car (of course none had, or admitted to, either). And then a few questions about why the applicant thought they were suitable for the position, and why they wanted to do it. Even those who had confidently stabbed at the paper with the one word answers to the earlier questions were awkwardly coming to ask for help with formulating the responses to those more searching final questions about why…. And the answers they wanted transcribed were heart-rending. Hardly any could give reasons or articulate their motivation, or any skills that would make them better for the bikes than others. All they could repeat – I transcribed dozens of the same response – were the details of their misfortunes; children dependent on the scavenging from the bins, parents and wives who were sick. It was moving, but it was not what we needed – I tried to encourage the men not to convince me by telling me of the bad things that had happened to them, but of what they were going to do about it. Was it only Naser who understood?

This, then, was another kind of begging that Fushë Kosovë needed to learn. Not the whine of the women outside the mosques, with their stories – however honest – of the terrible hand they'd been dealt, but the business pitch, the tug at their own bootstraps and not just a donor's heartstrings.

I faithfully transcribed what each of the men told me (the 62 year-old – almost the age of my own father – who told me poetically 'bread can be found only with a bicycle') and around the room I saw our other volunteers doing the same.

'And then,' I said to each of them when we'd finished the form, 'we'll look at what you've written and work out who fits our criteria best and then we'll get in touch.'

Behind me, I heard Hysni finishing up with a guy whose form he'd completed.

'We'll be in touch with whomever it is who's the fortunate one,' he said, using the Turkish word for good luck, 'nafak'.

'Hysni,' I corrected him, 'it's not about *nafak*; it's about the criteria.'

'Yeah,' he said, with no hint of irony. 'Fulfilling your criteria is what we call *nafak*.'

When the men had left and our team huddled round the ghost-written application forms, the choice was hard. We asked Hysni for a background check for the economic status of our shortlist, and a confirmation that they were the most deserving causes.

Just as importantly, we had to assess who was likely to be reliable enough to work within the model we were offering of connecting the bicycle-owners with businesses or organisations generating waste. My morning with Agron had given me a tiny insight into the terms of his profession: it was grim work, antisocial in its hours, in its location, and in the smears and smells you brought home with you. It paid badly and carried risks to your health and safety. It had only one thing going for it: the satisfaction of the self-employed. You may have to work on a rubbish heap, but when you got there you could feel king of that heap. No-one could tell you where to go or what to do; you chose whether to get up early and work all day, or take a break for mosque or to relieve your wife from childcare so she could go and do her cleaning job at the learning centre. Our project was going to take away the one perk of Agron's job.

And then we had the hard job of telling all the others that they hadn't been successful in their search for bicycle – or bread. In a bid for transparency we wrote out a list of the names of the successful applicants and stuck it outside our centre. It was ripped down twice in frustration by those who hadn't been chosen.

Making visits to families or even travelling to and from the centre was stressful, stopped at every turn by people wanting to know why, why…? 'O Elizabeta, how could I be thought to be better off than…' *O Motër…* Eventually I would invoke the Criteria and people would back away in incomprehension.

Meanwhile Aurélie was busy hunting down bikes and trailers. The best bikes we could find for our budget came in silver with a discreet pink flash and the name 'Afërdita' written on them. None of us could understand why men's bikes would bear this common Albanian girl's name (in fact, goddess name – divided into 'afër' and 'dita' the name means 'near day' and it's argued that the Greek goddess Aphrodite, who gave her name to the morning star, was borrowed from the Illyrian ancestors of today's Albanians). But we didn't think the men would mind – proverbially, they were in no position to be choosers.

A few weeks later the name revealed to me just how closely I'd become identified with the bikes in the minds of the community; as I walked through the streets on the way to visit one of our kids at home, a man called out to me. I didn't realise he was talking to me at first, but when he repeated what he'd said I realised he'd not been shouting my name but 'O, Afërdita!' If I had ever dreamed of being referred to as the goddess of love, I had never imagined that it would be from a rubbish-picker seeing me as the fleet deity of his improved scavenging power.

The enthusiasm for the bikes made us think of other ways we could help the community to generate income. Over the next months, and with Aurélie's skill in turning ideas into projects, and finding donors to fund them, we started another initiative for turning unrecyclable glass jars into candle holders (five more women in Fushë Kosovë sharing in the profits of their labours), making paper-bead jewellery, and in a village in Lipjan municipality where we got to know a smaller Roma community, we made an attempt to kickstart a tourist industry, advertising the skills of a woman known for her excellent *burek* pastries to run classes for foreigners interested in learning the fine art of filo pastry-making, stuffing and coiling for the perfect *burek*.

With the registration of the soap-making as an official business, I was surprised to find myself a certificated *biznismenja* myself. This had never been part of my dream – I was at best suspicious and at worst ignorant of business. But I did know some decent business models from a childhood inspired by Port Sunlight and Titus Salt. This seemed a more sustainable way to be helping Hatemja and the other mothers in our projects, and we started to consider a social contract. So they would have their share of the profits every month. But in exchange? I'd heard that Tito's Yugoslavia (perhaps a strange role model) had required workers in its Socially-Owned Enterprises to demonstrate their children's school attendance each month before they got their pay cheque, and I wondered whether we could set the same requirement for the women in our programmes.

But also … what would they like from us? Support with the medical needs of their families, they said, and we established a small monthly medical fund that could be used for requests that were urgent or serious. No ongoing prescriptions, we ruled, but we helped with one child's hernia, tests for another's possible diabetes, and contraception for those of the women who asked for it.

And, they wondered, would we be able to teach them to read and write? Vjollca, who had been to school, checked our maths when we told the group how many soaps had been sold and how much they'd earned. But the others signed only with a cross, a shy symbol of absence, like a wrong answer. I wondered what it would take for Hatemja to learn the string of letters in her name, and thought of her helping Gjelane with homework, and Vehbi and Labinot – and one day Ramadan and Elhame and Elham….

We found a volunteer who was a gifted educator – Sarah was an American who had been in Kosovo for some years. She'd learned to speak Albanian like a Kosovar and, together with Iliriana, her friend from Prishtina, she threw herself into a relationship with her group of nervous students. The classes expanded, until the women had learned not only the rudiments of reading and writing but also ideas of how to use mayonnaise to deal with headlice, how to discipline their children without hitting them, games to play with their pre-schoolers, and any other questions the women brought to Sarah and Iliriana. One day Kelsi went round to Hatemja's house and found her recreating a phonics game that Sarah and Iliriana had played with the group, giggling as she taught her children letter-sound correspondences that she hadn't been able to fathom herself only a few months before.

I was better prepared for this part of running our business than I was for selling soap. But we still managed to shift the products, and the women took home an envelope – either slim or bulging – each month and I knew that the alchemy which had turned olive oil with lemon into bars of soap was now turning the soap into bread for children's dinner.

When a researcher from the University of York asked to come and study our soap-making project as an example of a social enterprise, we arranged for a volunteer to translate for him, and let him interview the soap-makers, our staff, and volunteers, as part of an evaluation of the project. He asked whether he could interview me, too, and we sat together in the little office we'd rented in Prishtina, where we could store our paperwork and where customers for the soaps and bags could drop by to purchase. The office was above a cheap restaurant and the smell of frying peppers floated up through the poorly insulated walls every morning in time for lunchtime orders. We sat there together ignoring the amuse-bouche and he asked me a question he said he had put to everyone,

'So what do you think is the most important element of being part of this project, from the women's point of view? Is it the money? Their status as breadwinners? The skills they've learned? The healthcare for their family? Or something else?'

I thought of the wooden crib Hatemja had bought for Elham with her earnings from the soap, the smooth plastering over the mud bricks of Haxhere's home which she told me she'd paid for with what she'd saved, and of the women's hungry eyes when the envelopes were given out each month; of course that was it. The other parts were nice to have, but this was a business, right?

The researcher smiled and wrote down my answer. At the end of the interview he thanked me and said,

'I've got to tell you something that you've got wrong, you know.'

There were no doubt many things.

'I asked all the women, and not one of them said that the money is the most important thing. Not even the healthcare and the rest – they say that what they most appreciate about this project is the chance to come together as a group of women and talk. They say there's nowhere else they can do that.' Of course that was true – Hatemja had no meeting place apart from the homes of her friends, thronged with children, and which she'd make disproportionately busy if she visited, as her own youngest kids would have to come with her too. The women in our projects weren't near neighbours – it might take fifteen minutes to walk from Fitore to Hatemja, and longer with a babe in arms.

I thought of how the women would boil up some tea to drink together at the end of their soap-making sessions and how I'd heard them bicker (with Hatemja's gentle refrain – 'lejë, lejë' – above the quibbling of Vjollca) and tease and exchange news, fret together about their health, their children. Perhaps they talked about other things, too, when I wasn't there; things you couldn't talk to your sister-in-law about on family visits. Things you didn't share with your husband or your kids.

So perhaps ironically, when we'd thought we were giving these women employment, what they actually most appreciated was the fact that in between their new work obligations we gave them unaccustomed leisure. At first I couldn't see that looking good in a funding application or business plan, but that just showed how little I knew about business plans. I guess that's all they ever are at heart – a bid to have better quality leisure time and richer friendships.

31 What now?

Which begged the question of what I myself most appreciated about all this activity I'd got myself involved in. Of course there was the professional satisfaction I was used to from classrooms and school staffrooms in London and Prishtina of watching learners and teachers blossom. There was a glow from knowing that small injustices were being challenged, but being an injustice junkie wasn't an attractive role, and it probably wasn't sustainable.

The richer friendships the soap-making women were astute enough to have identified were definitely a factor for me too; friendship with Hatemja and with the others in the soap-making co-operative, but also friendship with our team of volunteers like Zsofia, Elena, Iliriana, Jeta, Kaltrina, Kelsi, Sarah – people from all over the world whom I would never have had the chance to meet or work alongside without a joint interest in the centre in Fushë Kosovë. I loved the company of Aurélie and also of our new Kosovan administrator, Anemona. She had studied English Literature at Prishtina University and at her job interview had revealed that she was one of the group who had produced a booklet I had been handed in the street early in my time in Kosovo. The booklet suggested words which were etymologically Albanian as the alternative for Albanianised English words that had started to come into use. Anemona would never have used the word 'biznesmenja'.

We had received a grant now, too, for someone to help with marketing the women's soaps. Arta's father had a shop in Gjakova, and she had completed a marketing diploma as well as her degree at the American University of Kosovo. She brought experience and professionalism and knowledge I'd never had, and turned a kitchen-table enterprise into something that now had a desk – and a native Albanian speaker and dedicated time. We now had an office 'team'.

But there was another way that the work in Fushë Kosovë was making for richer friendships: the dimension it added to my relationships with people back home. All my friends and family had heard about the battle to get Hatemja's kids to school, and the response had been generous. Friends had transferred money in envelopes of cash or the silent dignity of e-banking transactions; they had sent over boxes of nit combs, or got their kids' schools to collect old shoes.

To show our gratitude, we'd showed the children how to write thank you letters. They were usually in simple felt-tipped capitals with the donor's name and the child's name – 'FALEMINDERIT JOHN NGA ELVIRA' – and bright, botanically implausible flowers and hearts around the words. When I returned to the UK on trips to visit friends, almost every kitchen I drank tea in had one of these letters stuck to their fridge; it seemed the children would go with me wherever I went. Everyone I cared about had 'bought' into the work in Fushë Kosovë; it was a cushioning bubble of love and cash that I felt pillowing me as well as the children in Neighbourhood 29.

But it also raised the stakes. If I pulled out or gave up; if I failed, then the people I was accountable to were not just an alien community at the end of a taxi ride; they were in the place I called 'home' too. Donor reporting was not just a paper exercise on the intricate template of the Austrian Development Agency; it went on over each cup of tea or glass of wine, whether with friends in Prishtina or in London.

Not just my time and my relationships, but my home was brimming with Fushë Kosovë; the exercise bike which had so excited Labinot and his brothers was in a room now choked with donations of clothes and office materials. I would come back to the house and find plastic bags bulging with donations left at my front door. I feared coming back one day to find a baby left there.

When I visited England the experience was the same. The most precious donations were shoes – the gift of the journey to school in scuffed pairs of Clarks, handed on for Ashkali children to walk them out of the *mahalla* and into education. But shoes aren't light; it didn't take many of them to build up to the 23 kilograms of luggage allowance for Rob or me. And without a car in the UK, every kilogram donated was by one route or another carried back to Kosovo in a rucksack on our backs. Drifts of shoes started to collect at the points we visited in England – silting up the back room of our flat in Cornwall, piled in my parents' spare bedroom, stored in the basement of kind friends in London.

Harder still were the choices I had to make when packing up for the journey to Gatwick. The local word in Fushë Kosovë for an aeroplane was 'ballon' and making the decision on what to take with me, and what should be jettisoned was like a literal balloon debate. I vacillated between the shoes for barefoot Ashkali children, and the cheddar cheese and Hellman's mayonnaise treats I'd bought for myself to take back to Kosovo. Of course it should have been no contest, but sometimes back in Kosovo I hungered for that cheddar. I had to choose between the children's shoes and copies of my own books, which I brought back to sell in Kosovo. The books felt like pure greed when I could be getting another child to school... But I had to make my money somehow, I thought

– aware that each one of the books sold for more than the price of a day of Agron's muscle and sweat. Bending over my rucksack was an identity crisis.

And if every flight from England was a guilt trip, the days in Prishtina were fraught in a different way. We had Hysni now, doing a better job than I had of the community liaison I'd started with my awkward home visits right at the beginning of our work. We had Aurélie working on a diverse list that included funding applications alongside the purchase of axles for the bicycle trailers we were giving with Aphrodite's bike. We had Anemona doing a far more fluent job of the translations I'd bodged where necessary. And yet … I was still busy. I had lunch one day with our Kosovar Albanian volunteer, Zyrafete, who'd been sharing her skills in sewing with the group of women trained in making cloth bags.

'My husband says I have too much work to do with my own dressmaking business and I should leave all this stuff with TIP,' she confessed. Yeah, I wondered whether Rob had sometimes thought something similar.

She went on, 'but I tell him that when I see how much you do, and you're not even from this country like I am – how can I not make a contribution?'

It was a kind compliment. But it terrified me. So Zyrafete's contribution depended on mine? It was like a 'matched funding' model where someone would donate the same as I did. It was a wonderful multiplier of all the effort I was willing to give to Hatemja and her neighbours … but what happened if I took a holiday?

The idea of a holiday scared me; it was partly that I was frightened to find out who I was when I wasn't E-LIZ–a–betaaaaaaa – a persona I now seemed to have not just to the children racing up to me along a dusty street, but even to the friends and supporters who were showing their appreciation of my new role. Would people still like me if I wasn't part of making those education miracles happen?

But it was also a question of what I would do if I wasn't busy with things I cared about. Other activities seemed pointless or wasteful compared to the tangible achievements of what we were busy with in Fushë Kosovë. And yet I was working hard to make myself dispensable there – to let Aurélie and Hysni and Anemona do the work in a way that was higher quality, and more sustainable. And anyway, the initial crisis was over – after the shock discovery of all those children wanting to go to a school that was closed to them, we had succeeded at getting children registered, establishing intensive classes run by the municipality, employing some women to earn a small income for their families.

So what now?

32 The *hoxha's* cure for tuberculosis

Emine, whom we'd registered for school with her dad when she was still eight years old, had sustained her bouncing enthusiasm into school, and she ricocheted back to us from there every weekend to attend our Saturday activities. One day when I was talking to her about school I noticed a thickness in her voice and I asked her whether she was feeling OK. She said she was fine, but she had some lumps in her neck. She stretched back her head to show her slender throat, and I could clearly see the swollen glands under the skin.

'Are you sure you feel OK?' I checked, but she assured me she was well.

The next week, Emine didn't attend our activities, which was unusual, but didn't worry any of us. However, when I sat down with Hysni during the week to go through the list of children we'd registered to check on their attendance and whether there was anything we needed to do to support them in school, he told me that she had missed class too. It didn't surprise me, given the state of her neck, but she was obviously suffering from some kind of bug that would hopefully quickly pass.

The next week she came to our activities but was still not in school, she said. And looking at her neck I could see why – the glands had now swollen to distinguishable little spheres – two on one side, and one on the other. They were red, and the skin across them was flaking and cracking as if it was stretching further than it could give. I imagined that Emine had been scratching too. I winced just to look at her,

'Have you been to the doctor, love?' I asked her.

'*Go*,' said Emine, her throat choking the 'y' sound of the Albanian word for no.

Go indeed – I told her that she needed to tell her mum to take her to the doctor straight away for some antibiotics.

When I saw her next, things had not improved. She was still out of school, and when I persuaded her to take off the scarf she was wearing self-consciously round her neck to cover up the glands I could see that she had got no better.

'Have you been taking the antibiotics?' I nagged. She shook her head and managed another strangled '*go*'.

'Mummy hasn't taken me to the doctor. But she took me to the *hoxha*'.

Emine's mum didn't wear a headscarf. I remembered fondly the day that we had been talking about *Shëngjergj*. A man nearby had said that he thought we shouldn't celebrate it, and Fitore – with the stubbornness of the unschooled, had uncharacteristically spoken out,

'Look at the weather!' gesturing at the soft sunshine outside the window and the lush foliage of a pale green tree. 'It's the coming of springtime. I'm going to make baklava anyway.'

Evidently her bravery at gainsaying the *hoxha* when it was a matter of pastries had not extended to her daughter's health.

So what had the *hoxha* said?

The *hoxha* had told her to comb the glands three times a day, and then they would subside and the infection go away.

The *hoxha* told people in Fushë Kosovë lots of things I didn't believe. He said that if they prayed five times a day they would go to paradise, and I had never suggested any disagreement. To do so would be disrespectful; it was not my place. So what should I say now?

I shut my mouth, and gave the *hoxha's* remedy a week to take effect, and I told Emine that if – by chance – the daily combing hadn't made a difference within seven days then, together with her mum, I would take her to the doctor. I even took a photograph of Emine's neck (along with another of her smiling coquettishly at the camera, which is how I guessed she preferred to think of herself, rather than being defined by her glandular system). It was going to be my baseline data if there was any discussion about the effect of the combing on the glands. As I flicked through the images on my camera I wondered at myself; was I challenging Allah to a medical experiment?

Sadly, the baseline data wasn't needed: when I went back to Emine a week later it was indisputable that the problem hadn't got any better. The glands were discoloured and spreading, huge and angry.

The doctor we went to asked Emine's mum whether there were animals in their house (there weren't), and about all kinds of apparently unrelated symptoms. She said that tests would have to be done for scary-sounding conditions like tuberculosis and tularemia. Google Translate helped me find the English words for what she was suggesting Emine might be suffering, and Wikipedia translated the medical word into something I understood; the doctor thought Emine might have plague.

Apparently the tests weren't available from the state system so we were told to go to a private laboratory. There are dozens of these just opposite the hospital entrance, and I'd passed their shiny front doors as I'd walked to the state clinic. The inadequacies of the Kosovan state health system were spread out on that row like an indictment – the stalls of nappies and sanitary towels for the ObGyn ward, and other essentials that patients had to provide themselves in this underfunded system, then, for the full cradle-to-grave service offered by the free market, the funeral operators at a discreet distance with hearses parked up and plastic flowers and wreaths on sale. With the Islamic requirement for burial within twenty-four hours of death, when the hospital had completed its eventual inevitable failure to keep patients alive, valuable time could be saved by hiring here the next round of services required.

And surveying them all with the glassy grin of private money were the shop fronts of those labs across the road, staring unflinchingly at the collapse of their neighbours' state-funded services. It was convenient to have them close to the hospital, not just for the patients but for the staff – it was to these little earners that the doctors ran after turning up for their state hospital shifts. It was because of these labs that there were no staff to be found if you went to the hospital after midday.

Clutching the tests we went back to the hospital and saw a doctor who gave us a referral to the ENT department. We headed off to another building, passing the doctor smoking in the corridor, and found the ENT door. When we knocked and entered, the staff inside told us we'd come to the wrong place and that we should go downstairs. We went downstairs where we were told this was not the right place for Emine's test results to be considered. But they were curious about us and asked where I was from.

When they heard I was from England, they beamed and called my country *'miku i madh i Kosovës'* – the great friend of Kosovo. I smiled, a little impatiently.

An old man got up from the group and said he would escort us to the right room, taking us all the way back to where we had been. The staff there who'd already seen us once disputed with him whether they should be the ones to look at Emine's test, but my elderly escort reminded them of the *miku i madh i Kosovës* and they agreed to see us – in front of all the others waiting.

When we finally saw the doctor he said we should come back on Wednesday and turned to his nurse to book us in. She quibbled that there was no space for an appointment on Wednesday, but '*miku i madh i Kosovës*' hissed the doctor – now we were part of the problem presented by Kosovo's healthcare system – and we were sent to a new queue to be registered for the appointment. In front of us was a woman who seemed to be a friend of one of the nurses, and the nurse's colleague was trying to work out how to let them off paying for her appointment. She apologised that she couldn't absolve the woman of all charges but got it down to five euros. Then it was our turn to be registered, with extreme bad grace. I was just about ready to go the *hoxha* myself.

On Wednesday when we came back for the appointment, the doctor interpreted the results. The good news: Emine didn't have plague. The bad news: she had TB.

The fact that it had taken us – the combined and contradictory forces of Emine's mother, myself, the *hoxha* and the Kosovan medical system – nearly two months to find this out made me scream with impotence and frustration. It reminded me of how I'd felt when I'd taken the case of another nine year-old round Kosovo's institutions and traditions. Except that with Gjelane I was dealing with an area where I had some expertise – I know what good teaching and learning looks like, and I could prove that I did. In Emine's case, part of the problem was my ignorance. If I'd been as experienced a doctor as I was teacher perhaps I would have spotted the signs of TB right away. I wondered whether I would have dared to challenge the *hoxha* then.

I learned more about how this *hoxha* worked and discovered it wasn't my old absent friend, the man I'd never met from the local mosque. This was another *hoxha*, and part of a group who were only visiting in Fushë Kosovë. Some said they were from Arab countries, but others told me that they spoke Albanian; perhaps they were Arabs operating like good missionaries do everywhere by learning local languages. Or perhaps there were more than one of these groups and the people I asked were describing different medicine men.

I started hearing details of cases, such as when I was invited to Ganimete's house because she wanted to ask me for help with her daughter. I'd seen the girl hanging around in the street outside their house, with a severely twisted spine. She was mute and her mum told me she also frequently lost consciousness or hallucinated. The girl was now nineteen and eligible for invalidity benefit, but they said that the benefit could only be claimed by getting a stamped declaration from three doctors. The doctors might charge nothing, but could charge up to twenty euros. I explained that we would be able to help with this if they could show us a receipt for the fees they'd paid, and Ganimete looked at me as if she was trying to decide whether I was hard-hearted or just stupid; you don't get a receipt for a bribe.

Could they not find some way to fund the cost for these declarations themselves? No, they assured me, gesturing round their stark sitting room, where we sat on blankets on a concrete floor.

I tried to offer some other way to show support – had they found anything that helped their daughter?

Well yes, the girl went regularly to a *hoxha* in Prishtina who chanted the Koran over her for an hour and a half at a time. It had been his suggestion that she now wore the headscarf, and she had apparently felt better ever since putting it on. They paid the *hoxha* twenty euros a time.

I wished them all the best and left, wondering at the power of the Koran.

Someone else said that the new *hoxhas* in Fushë Kosovë didn't charge, and gave me other details of their treatments. One devout young man who worked as a volunteer with us didn't come to the Saturday activities one week and his colleagues explained he'd been having headaches. The headaches had now gone, but he'd had to shave his head and have 'six cups' of blood removed, so he was embarrassed to be seen in public for a while.

He seemed to have had a particularly severe treatment – others sounded less hard-core, involving pins on your hand and perfumes from Mecca. Someone added that although you didn't have to pay the *hoxhas* you did have to buy the oil and honey they prescribed which they'd brought from Arabia with them.

Valdete told me another story, having been to visit the *hoxha* in a basement of a house in the *mahalla* for her depression. The *hoxha* had apparently said some holy words over her, and she narrated having 'woken up' to find herself in the mosque with a veil on. I wasn't sure whether she was speaking metaphorically; maybe she wasn't either.

But perhaps it didn't work; the next day she came to me with a prescription for diazepam from the doctor. We had established some rough criteria for the medicines we would reimburse. Children had priority (and Valdete wasn't a child), and mothers second priority (she wasn't a mother either). We'd said we wouldn't pay for ongoing medication either, and our funds were to be focused on emergency cases which could be resolved through one-off interventions; I told Valdete we couldn't cover the cost of the diazepam. Was I playing into the *hoxha*'s hands?

The decisions about supporting people's medication were always fraught, and the stakes were high. The cases where there were the least discusson were those of inguinal hernias, causing boys to have horribly distended scrotums and enormous pain. One boy was nine when his mother finally came to us to tell us he needed it to be operated on 'because he can't walk properly.' Elena was the first to try to negotiate the hospital system for the operation to be done, persisting in the face of Kosovan medical bureaucracy with all the skill that had got us the negotiated price for Idriz' flat at the beginning of our work. The operation cost less than a hundred euros in blood tests and transport, and with that the problem was solved forever, and the boy was able to go back to school. As soon as the word got round that we'd help in such cases we had seven more boys, from babies to school age, for whom we were able to organise operations.

But other cases were harder to judge; one day during our weekly activities with the children a man came to ask for us to pay for pills for his wife. They cost only seven euros, but the woman didn't fit our criteria, and I worried about justifying the expense that could go towards another case that was in greater need, and where a child would directly or indirectly benefit by gaining access to education. Hysni looked at me, 'the family is really in need, Elizabeth, and the case is urgent.'

I trusted him, and rang the pharmacy to tell them that the woman's husband would be coming, and that the cost of these pills should be added to what we'd now set up as a monthly tab. A few days later Hysni told me that the man's wife had died. He looked at me when he gave me the information, and as I muttered the correct 'may Allah take her to paradise' response to such news, I knew that he knew what I was thinking. Such relief – an irrational gratitude that we'd made that decision, and her ghost hovered over every subsequent patient who came to us. What if they were to die during the week, but after we had refused medicine; how would I feel?

It was from Hysni, too, that I learned about the alternatives people would use if medicines weren't available. For bruising or sprains you put an egg yolk on the affected area; the yolk 'will immediately know where to go'. Then you cover it with flour – 'like making plaster'– to stop the egg running off. It sounded like a fancy cake. One day one of the women cut herself very badly on a piece of corrugated metal on her way to a meeting with the soap-makers and me. We arranged someone we knew in the community to take her to the doctor, but when they'd got to the health centre they'd found the doctor on his break.

'At least the bleeding had stopped with the sugar we'd put on,' the woman said.

'Er, the sugar…?' I queried, thinking about the Victoria sponge ingredients for a sprain. Hysni confirmed that yes, sugar sprinkled on a cut would stop bleeding. 'You can use tobacco too,' he added. 'Or spiders' webs,' someone added.

'Or,' said Hysni drily, 'you can go to the doctor. But he'll probably be on his break.'

When I went to visit Hatemja next she told me she had heart trouble. My own heart sank at the idea of this slight, strong mother becoming incapacitated or being taken from us. I thought of her poor children, and knew that if she needed operations there was no way that she could afford any of the costs.

'Oh, Hatemja,' I clutched her shoulder. 'What's wrong with your heart?'

'Well, I've had diarrhoea for a few days now,' she explained.

Hatemja had never sat in a biology lesson. She'd probably never seen a model of the human body – the circulatory system shaded one colour, the digestive system another. How should she know that hearts and guts were unconnected? I struggled to explain. And I realised that if you thought that gastro-enteritis might be linked to the pounding you felt in your chest, it was pretty easy for a guy with a holy book to convince you to comb your tubercular daughter's neck each day: health education was the correct response to help these families make good choices to prevent and treat disease. If I'd thought the need in Fushë Kosovë had passed, these conversations reignited something in me. I believed in perfumes from Mecca and pins on your hand in as much as I had paid for aromatherapy and acupuncture sessions; I knew they could help with headaches, or depression, and many other ailments. I was pretty sure they were not the best choice for curing tuberculosis though, and people needed to know they had choices.

But education was too slow – how many years would it take of our project before the mums of the nine year-olds in this *mahalla* would be fully educated about the best health choices for their children? Perhaps a generation. There were too many school days to be lost and children's lives threatened by TB in the meantime.

So we needed a new approach – something more sustainable than women sidling up to me in the street with overfolded bits of paper to show the money they owed at the pharmacy, and my non-expert opinion on what the serious health needs were. I didn't even recognise the brand names of the medicines they were being prescribed so it was rare that I could distinguish paracetamol from something more urgent. One day I did spot a word I recognised though – the patient was being prescribed Floradix. It's available at chemists and health food shops in the UK – a mixture of vitamins, minerals and herbal extracts in an iron-rich tonic. I'd bought it myself in Kosovo when I was feeling run-down so I knew how much it cost: eleven euros. More than a day's wages for Agron or others like him.

I asked the woman who'd shown me the prescription and had asked me to cover the cost, 'What will this Floradix help you with?' She didn't know; it might as well have been perfumes from Mecca to her. The medicine man – whether *hoxha* or GP – had told her to take it in order to feel better. If she took it, she probably would feel better, but it would cost her and her children all that they had for the day.

'Go and buy spinach and beans,' I said. 'It will be just as good for you, and a tenth of the price,' and I handed back the prescription.

I realised we needed expertise to help educate people on their nutritional choices, on vaccination, on basic biology that might help mothers diagnose the difference between more serious cases that needed the doctor right away, from those where bed rest and fluids would cure a passing virus in a few days with no extra expense. The more I spent time in the community, I knew that these fierce slim mothers – like Hatemja who had first thrust her scalded son at me – were the key to changing the health, and then the education, of the community. So we needed a woman who could work among the families.

Maybe I couldn't diagnose tuberculosis accurately, but there was one skill I could contribute: I could write, so I started drafting begging letters asking donors to fund the 250 euros we'd need each month to pay the salary of a community health worker.

33 Lessons from Hikmete

Meanwhile I told Hysni he should spread the word that I could help women with accessing the state health services. It meant offering money, but also knowledge (telling Hatemja not to worry about her 'heart problem' diarrhoea) and sometimes just a supportive presence (*miku i madh i Kosovës*). Women started arriving at the centre for quiet consultations with me. Usually, eventually, it was about babies. We had a rule that we wouldn't help with fertility treatments of any kind, not least because it seemed always to be the woman who was considered to be in need of 'treatment', irrespective of any evidence, but also because the treatments usually involved 'cold' women being taken to hot springs or to healers outside the medical system. But if women had come to whisper their need for the opposite kind of help, preventing them from getting pregnant, we were happy to be useful; contraception seemed to me to be a way of ensuring the welfare of the mother and all her existing children, and I believed that the sustainable solutions to poverty would only work when couples could make decisions about the size of their families.

One of the first women to come to me was a woman bringing up ten children – six of her own and the others of her late brother-in-law. We had had the conversation when she was pregnant with an eleventh child. *'Boll,'* she said – with this one on its way I've got enough. So we agreed that when the time was right after the birth we would go together to the doctor.

Some months later we made it to the family medicine centre about a mile from her home. When we knocked on the doctor's door, he came out frowning (looking behind him into the room I saw we had disturbed his game of solitaire on the computer) but when he saw a foreigner (the experience at the hospital came back to me) he smiled a greeting,

'What can I do for you?'

'I'm here with my friend,' I said, pushing Hikmete forward.

'Well she can wait outside,' he replied, ushering me in.

The challenges of inserting an IUD into a woman who is not physically present in your surgery did not seem to have registered with him and I wondered what I should do. To go in was to leave Hikmete outside, to reinforce apartheid. But to argue with him on the threshold seemed unlikely to achieve what we needed for the women we were working with. Hikmete shoved me – 'go in, go in; I'm fine here'.

So I went in alone.

I explained what we were there for and the gynaecologist said he had run out of their supply of free coils, and of condoms and everything other than oral contraception or injections; what did I think would be best? I suggested, with an irony that seemed lost on him, that we should ask Hikmete in.

When she came in I suggested I could leave while they discussed it, but they both said they wanted me there. Thinking about the doctor's disrespect for Hikmete earlier, I agreed to stay, feeling like a pimp as I sat next to the doctor asking Hikmete for her reproductive history.

We established that the pill would be no good for her because of its effect on her breastfeeding,

'So then we can buy a coil at a pharmacy,' I suggested, 'since you don't have any free ones in stock. We'll bring it here for you to fit.'

The doctor cleared his throat. 'Unfortunately,' he said, looking straight at me and ignoring Hikmete's presence completely, 'the women from her community don't keep clean enough for me to fit a coil, and there will be a risk of infection. They need to keep extremely clean, and I won't suggest it's feasible to change your underwear frequently if you're living in...' at last he acknowledged that Hikmete was there, 'the conditions you have.'

I opened my mouth to shout, half got up from my chair, cleared my throat – ran through a range of useless responses in anger and outrage and embarrassment...

But Hikmete was quicker than me.

'Oh no,' she said, 'I'm an observant Muslim. And you have to change your underwear every time you pray' – this was news to me – 'so I change my underwear five times a day'.

Now the doctor was speechless. And I sat feeling filthy next to defiant Hikmete.

The gynaecologist didn't try any more excuses, and we fixed a date for us both to come back for Hikmete's coil to be fitted.

On the way home I was furious with how she had been treated, but like Emine over school registration, she shrugged. He was just ... she used a word I didn't know, so I asked her what it meant. It turned out to be a Roma word, which surprised me because I'd only ever heard Hikmete speaking Albanian.

Oh yes, she said – she'd been brought up speaking Roma, and only when she married an Albanian speaker had she switched to using Albanian as her main language. I asked her how she'd come to be married to him and learned that they'd been introduced in the traditional way through a *mësit* – a matchmaker. She told me they'd gone out together for a while and she'd decided she'd have him because 'he'd listen to what I told him'. Remembering her tone with the ignorant gynaecologist I thought that was just as well. Getting in Hikmete's way would be a frightening experience.

She was fretting a bit about the coil fitting, and since I'd told her I'd had one fitted a few years before she asked, 'Is it going to hurt?'

I – the childless woman – took a punt, 'Not as much as childbirth.'

I tried to take her mind off the procedure ahead of her and remembering what she'd told me about her mother-tongue asked her to teach me some Romani. She taught me the words for 'black' ('kali' – later I heard that some say it's linked to 'Ashkali') and red and blue. She taught me 'come and drink coffee' and the words for different domestic vessels. 'A pot' – I asked whether she meant a pot 'like that one' since we were passing the market.

'No, a pot for washing clothes'. I had only recently learned – and forgotten – the word in Albanian, and I had never used one of these slope-ended zinc troughs. I realised I wasn't just learning Romani, I was being taught the vocabulary of Hikmete's days.

The coil was fitted successfully, and soon other women were coming to ask for one like Hikmete had. I took Hatemja to have hers fitted too, and we sat together afterwards at the doctor's desk while he filled out a card to note what he'd done.

'Now I hope you're going to keep it in, especially since Elizabeth has paid for it,' he said.

'Of course,' Hatemja muttered obediently.

'I don't want you coming back to me in a few weeks like that other woman, asking for it to be taken out,' he said. I looked at him.

'What are you talking about?'

'Oh yes, that Hikmete – she came back a few weeks after it had been fitted. Apparently the *hoxha* had heard that she'd had the coil put in, and he told her husband that this is not our religion, so she had to have it taken out.'

The familiar feeling of being lost for words in front of this gynaecologist returned. For a start, it was a terrible breach of patient confidentiality. But I was also stunned by what he'd told me.

When we got back from the surgery I went straight to visit Hikmete, and she confirmed that what he'd said was true. 'I didn't want to tell you,' she frowned, checking to see my reaction.

'It's your choice, Hikmete,' I said, 'it's not for me to decide – you don't have to worry about me.'

Her choice though – hers, not the *hoxha*'s.

Driving back to Prishtina I wept with frustration. I was the closest I had ever been to giving up all our work in Fushë Kosovë. I was not going to go head-to-head with this *hoxha*; I was not going to pit myself against the full machinery of Islam. I wondered how he'd found out about our visit to the doctor; I wondered how many other women he knew about, and how much further he would interfere. I wondered what hope there was for addressing long-term poverty in Neighbourhood 29.

A few months later, Hikmete came to ask for our help again. She needed a scan, she said; she was pregnant. I wondered whether the *hoxha* would be making more visits to her house to help out when the twelfth baby arrived.

We wouldn't stop offering to support women with contraception, but I realised we needed to be more subtle. We would have to make it clear that we weren't promoting contraception, but we would continue to make it possible for women to access the state services they were entitled to. It was the same philosophy we were applying to education – although I had views on what teaching should be like, it was not my place to promote those; I just wanted the Ashkali children of Fushë Kosovë to have access to the same education services that every other child in Kosovo had.

But what about our volunteers and staff? I wondered whether I was putting those of them who attended mosque in a difficult position. I didn't want them to feel they had to choose between the activities of their *hoxha* and the activities of The Ideas Partnership.

Not long after this demonstration of the *hoxha*'s opinions, one of the team came to speak to me in private. I stiffened; I knew this guy was a mosque-goer and a devout man. I hoped this wasn't going to come down to him – or me – having to choose sides.

Sure enough, he began, 'Elizabeth, I've heard that you've been helping women with contraception.'

Well, there was no denying it.

'Yes. If they want it then we'll help them to get it.'

'Aha.' He seemed to consider this for a moment. 'So you could help my wife?'

I breathed out.

In fact, in the end, there were three women who wanted to get contraception at the same time as his wife so we set off for the doctor together. We'd picked a Tuesday for the appointment which was market day so on the way to the surgery we bumped into plenty of the women's neighbours, bulging with bags, holding out trays of eggs, all curious as to where our little group were heading. Everyone we met knew at least one of us. With the men they met, the women in my group were evasive in answering questions and the men hurried on, looking like they knew better than to ask more. But with the women we encountered, long conversations were held, the newcomers sharing gynaecological issues.

Halfway there one of the women realised that she didn't have her ID card. 'Well, do you know your date of birth?' I asked. Nope, she didn't know that either, though she said her husband did. She couldn't read or write, so I guessed that that string of numbers was a complicated code to memorise. We agreed that it might be better for her to find to out before we arrived at the surgery so she used my phone and we called her husband whose number I had.

As he was telling her the date when she was born she turned to me, 'I don't think I'll be able to remember,' she said nervously, so the phone was passed back to me and I memorised the date I was told. Her birthday was only a week away so when I'd hung up from the call, I told her this and she beamed gratefully – like the child she'd been reduced to. The interconnections of education, health and women's rights had never been more real for me.

With a bigger group of us this time, once we got to the surgery it was easier to suggest I stayed outside the doctor's room while each woman went in. They each came out with different recommendations, and on the walk back home they compared notes. One of them had had a coil fitted there and then and she related how the doctor had asked, 'is your husband heavy? If so, make sure it's not him that's on top'. They all giggled and I grinned awkwardly too. All three of them were modest women – all wearing headscarves – and as we strolled home laughing I was dizzied by the idea that I was out with a group of covered women discussing sexual positions as we walked home from market.

The woman with the new coil told the others that she'd been told that the coil was valid for five years, and I frowned at her. 'Seven years, I think?' I corrected her gently, remembering what my own doctor had told me when I'd had mine fitted. But she was adamant that the doctor had said five, and I decided that it was better to err on that side of the correct expiration date so I said no more. When I got home I looked it up online and discovered that she was right. I did some hasty maths and realised that with my misremembering of the date I'd in fact been unprotected by my coil for some months now. Mexhide and her group of new friends might have saved me from an unwanted baby just as much as I had saved her.

One of the others in our group was not so lucky. She'd been told to come back for her coil at a better stage in her monthly cycle, and she and I did some intimate maths as we walked along – her contributing the facts, and me doing the adding up to calculate when she should have her next period, later that week.

I was walking past her house a week or so later and she was standing outside.

'How are you doing?' I asked meaningfully, but she shook her head. No period yet.

We saw each other again a few weeks later and she was still shaking her head at me, and before long she was sure of it; she was pregnant.

It was the same feeling I'd had with Emine's TB treatment: I should have moved faster; we should have made it easier. I had been in her home and I knew the effect this new baby would have on strained space, on eking out the coins her husband brought back from his rubbish-picking. I knew that another mouth to feed would mean that the older brother would be likely to drop out of school as soon as he was old enough to lift sacks of salvaged scrap metal and help his dad. We needed that funding for a community health worker.

And then we got it!

A succession of good people came together, with the same sense of the world listening to the muttered prayers, the half-formed wishes, the labour pangs and the raw bleeding need of Fushë Kosovë that I had experienced when we started offering classes in the centre. Suddenly the money was available; the Southampton Hope and Aid Direct group gave us a grant which would be enough to cover half a salary, at the same time as another grant from the Austrian Development Agency, and we were able to advertise for a local health worker to do some of the work I'd been doing, but with the advantages of being based in the community and knowing the women in advance. Even better, LiveLink Kosovo, the charity run by Mary – who had first advised me on Ramadan's burns – offered to pay for a Kosovan midwife, Ilmije, to come out to Fushë Kosovë one day a week to work alongside Bajramsha, the community health worker we appointed, and to run ante-natal classes for pregnant women.

Suddenly we had a team, and expertise and a sustainable way to address the needs in Fushë Kosovë in a properly holistic way, with education supporting health, and health contributing to quality education. Leaving our centre one day after watching Ilmije and Bajramsha at work I felt a strange lightness, which felt also like emptiness. There were properly trained people in place to lead these things now; perhaps I had at last reached the limit of what I could offer Fushë Kosovë. But I didn't want it to end – there were friendships here I didn't want to walk away from. I could no longer avoid an uncomfortable truth: I now needed Fushë Kosovë more than it needed me.

Bajramsha, our community health worker

34 The private gardens and the public meadow

What if we could turn Neighbourhood 29's wasteland into a meadow? It would be a symbol of the education and the iron–pink cheeks of the pregnant women we were supporting, the soap simmering in the SaPunë women's saucepans.

We discussed the idea at a team meeting; of buying seeds and bedding plants, and creating patches of colour and beauty in the dust and garbage of Fushë Kosovë's alleys. The faces of Hysni and the volunteers in Fushë Kosovë blossomed into smiles at the idea, and when we told the children we were thinking of holding a gardening day, the group half rose from their seats, with grins at each other and hands fluttering as if spring had come to the classroom, and they asked when? How? Could their families come?

Arta and Anemona spent a hundred euros on over a thousand seeds and plants and we set a date for a bright Saturday to plant them. By eleven o'clock the wasteland near our centre was filled with a jostling crowd of children, some with parents and older brothers and sisters, plus volunteers from Fushë Kosovë, Prishtina and beyond. Once we'd distributed what we had to be planted the children broke away into crouching groups, huddled over the mud, some of them using spoons to make holes in the pebbled dirt where they could press the plants in to the ground.

It was a warm day and we wiped damp hair from our foreheads until we were all streaked with mud. But the muddier we got, the more beautiful the land we were working became: studded with jewels of flowers, and the promise of more; the air already scented with the virtuous smell of turned earth. People helped one another – larger hands helping inexpert little fingers; people from the *mahalla* showing the foreigners the best places to plant, volunteers sharing out the packets of dahlia and sunflower seeds. People smiled at strangers and everyone looked with new appreciation round their changed environment.

'*Sa mirë*, Elizabeta,' said the people who passed me, with approval. Old men nodded in careful evaluation; children rushed up to ask me to come and admire what they'd planted; teenage volunteers were quietly proud when the kids they'd helped stood back and clapped at each clump of petunias that was bedded in.

I looked around at the people I knew here – almost all of them I knew as faces, and many by name. Women I'd taken to the doctor; children I'd taken to school; volunteers I'd watched grow from high school students to adults. One of the volunteers who had started working with us as a teenager was now holding his baby. I realised that there was no community anywhere else on earth who could come together on one piece of wasteland where I would know so many people. I could look at the houses which surrounded us and know which ones had someone who was sick, or where the new baby had been born; where there was domestic violence or where someone had just started school. Over there was the woman whose husband was in prison; this here was the house of our volunteer's brother where I'd been given a welcome fizzy drink on a hot day. That was the family with twins, here was the woman who'd brought a sample of a glass candle holder her husband had found in the rubbish and who'd suggested we could copy it as a design for sale…. Nowhere near our flat in London could I tell you the names or the lives of more than half a dozen people in a street; in Islington where we'd been paying a mortgage on our house for years, how many people would invite me in for a cool drink when I walked past looking tired?

This, here, was a community like I'd never known, its fragile petals flowering in wild patches between the drifts of garbage. And under the ground were more seeds, and behind the doors of homes I hadn't visited were children almost of school age who would come to our classes soon; in the bellies of women attending our ante-natal classes were children soon to be born. I felt connected by deep roots – deeper even than you could dig with a spoon in the mud – to this place, and I felt a surge of love for the people who made it up.

And by the next day, it had gone.

The children – always the best early-warning system, with ears to the ground – told me first: every single plant that we had bedded in had been stolen away.

Our volunteers confirmed it, and when I went back to see the space, all that remained of our glorious joint effort, our shared dream of a meadow, was an ugly rash of patches of darker earth where the children had dug, each with a ragged torn hole where the precious plants had been ripped up.

I stood looking round again at the homes that encircled the wasteland, and one of the children pointed a finger – 'it was them'; one of the neighbours.

I tried to comfort myself and our team. 'At least the seeds can't be stolen', I said, as if it was a metaphor. But the children around me had faces as stony as the ground we'd been digging.

'And if they've been stolen it shows the flowers are valued,' I persisted. 'I'd rather they were stolen than that they were trampled. They'll still be planted somewhere, so Fushë Kosovë will still be a greener place.'

Some of the kids still had earth under their nails, the ache in their slim arms from digging; still had in their minds the vision we'd shared with them of what the future could look like here in their *mahalla*, and they shook their heads at my talking. I'd let them down – I'd encouraged them to believe in their community, and then their community had let them down.

I drove back to Prishtina in the silence of pursed lips. One of our volunteers from Fushë Kosovë was with me in the van and I saw him stealing a glance at me every so often. He didn't try to make conversation. Finally, as if my grim expression had forced it out of him, he said,

'Er, Mrs Elizabeth, if you want to know where one of the flowers is, I – er – I'm looking after one of them in my garden.'

I glared at him. 'You stole it?'

'Well, I guessed that one of those neighbours would thieve the plants if we left them there, so I thought I'd take one back to my house...'

'You stole it,' I said in confirmation. 'It wasn't yours; the plants were there for everyone to enjoy.'

Perhaps it was an inappropriate concept I had been trying here. Apparently you can't redefine the concept of public space – from somewhere where you dump your waste, to a community garden – in one day, armed just with a group of kids and some spoons. I thought of Hatemja's horror at seeing me keeping my rubbish in the house. The outside land that belonged to 'Others' was for your unwanted garbage; anything pretty you had for yourself should be treasured for your family and in your house.

And this guy had been proved right – by trying to redefine a public rubbish heap into a shared meadow we had left nobody but the thieves with anything. But by liberating one begonia (yes, he swore – just one) he had something beautiful for his kids to look at when they looked out of the window.

I had entered Fushë Kosovë through meeting just one family. If it hadn't been for drinking tea in Hatemja's home, would I have cared about getting Gjelane to school? And without her certainly none of the other kids would have had classes, vaccinations, clothes, healthcare.... None of the other mothers would have had the chance to earn money making soap. I wondered whether the only way a community can change is by each member first planting a flower in their own backyard and watching it grow.

35 Invitation from a shoe-shiner

Mother Theresa Street – named after the most famous Albanian in the world – leads through the centre of Prishtina, thronged with the smartest shops and smartest people, who parade every evening in the pre-dinner *shëtitje*. As if Mother Theresa's boulevard has been spotted as a vein of charity running through the capital's public life, it is also a centre for beggars and peddlers, with battery-operated dogs yapping round the feet of their hawkers next to huddled figures muttering prayers with outstretched hands. There are other street sellers too – in winter, roasting chestnuts on braziers and wrapping them in sheets of used A4 office paper, which you can unwrap when you've finished eating to read the discarded photocopies of minutes of meetings from the Ministries which line the boulevard. One day when I was walking there I spotted a shoe-shiner, too, and checking the mud-encrusted scuffs on my boots, I stopped and asked him for a shine.

In the awkward intimacy of his polish cloth massaging my toes, and his head butting around my calves, we made conversation. Where was he from? Janjevo – a place I'd visited a few times, about 45 minutes from Prishtina. I didn't know much about the town, except that it was a fully multi-ethnic community (Albanians, Croats, Roma, Ashkali, Bosnians and Turks) and the only community in all of Kosovo where there had not been a single inter-ethnic killing or burning of property either before, during or after the 1999 war. The guy shining my boots seemed a gorgeous interethnic mix himself, with the dark skin and hair of the Roma or Ashkalis, but startling green eyes. I asked him and he confirmed that yes, he was Roma. I asked whether the Roma children in Janjevo went to school, and he shook his head sadly. It was a terrible shame, he said.

I told him about our initiative in Fushë Kosovë and asked him whether he thought we might be able to support the kids in Janjevo to school. He stopped brushing at that point. Yes, he said, we should definitely come. No-one was interested in Janjevo, he grumbled. There was no investment – the metal factory had employed 1200 people in a town of 11 000. 'Now the town is three thousand people, and the abandoned factory site employs just a couple of guards.'

'No-one's interested in us because we've kept quiet and got on with our lives. Maybe it would have been better to have flare-ups of crime between communities every so often, and then the international donors would pay us attention,' he said ruefully. I thought of our lessons in Fushë Kosovë and the energy expended by the teachers on kids who were always out of their seats, distracting their classmates or calling out instead of putting their hand up or waiting their turn, while others leant over their work in silence with no adult help. He was right.

'Can I have your phone number in case we come to Janjevo one day?' I asked on a whim.

When I told Aurélie and Zsofia about the conversation, they were enthusiastic. We'd proved that something extraordinary could be done in Fushë Kosovë. They said we should go and see whether the approach could be transferred to other places; they were sure that we'd be able to find a donor to fund another project if we selected an appropriate community to run it in.

I was hesitant, thinking back to my first chance meeting with Hatemja, and how she'd raised her son up to meet my gaze, asking me for help. You couldn't replicate those meetings and the trust that had been built between me and the family as I'd sat in their front room, teaching their children clapping games and learning the names of the neighbours on my visits to drop off tubes of cream for Ramadan. Was the secret of our success that we had been volunteers, working to help Fushë Kosovë's kids into school just because we cared – and the children and their families had known that? Maybe it would be different to turn up with a budget and an action plan and a model. This felt a bit like we were Starbucks.

'Yes, maybe the randomness and the volunteerism was the secret of our success,' said Aurélie. 'But maybe it wasn't. Maybe it wasn't important how we came to be there, but just the way we dealt with the kids and their learning. Or perhaps it was some other factor that we haven't even identified yet; we'll never know if we don't try replicating this.'

Zsofia agreed, 'Is a conversation with a shoe-shiner not a random enough start to a new project?'

Perhaps I was looking for excuses. And anyway, there could be no harm in visiting; and it would be an interesting trip to make. As it happened, we chose the most beautiful day of the year so far for the drive. Zsofia drove us under blue sky, past fields of glossy new grass where sun shone on the blossom on the trees, though the mountain called Luboten was still snow-white in the distance.

As we reached the first houses of the town we saw that others were as energised as we were – rugs were being beaten or soaped or hung out like flags, water was sloshing into the roadway and it seemed that everyone was busy cleaning. I realised that we were only a few days from *Shëngjergj* or St George's Day – celebrated thirteen days later than the UK's St George festivities, because of the Orthodox calendar. I thought of our volunteer in Fushë Kosovë this time last year, preparing to flick people with water from nettles, and Hikmete's memories of processing to the river, and what I'd heard of bathing babies with flowers ... these are rites that go back much further than Muhamed or Jesus, to something that runs deep in the blood of all mammals stretching out into the warmth of the first sunny day of the year, and thinking that it's time to beat out the dirt of winter from your carpets.

It was an auspicious day for new beginnings. And when we'd parked and started walking around the town, looking for the house of the shoe-shiner with the green eyes, and being directed along cobbled alleys and past the Catholic church and the birthplace of the nineteenth century Kosovan folklorist Shtjefën Gjeçovi, to the mosque, and the first post office in Kosovo, we had started to fall in love with the town and its old buildings clinging to the hillsides. If Fushë Kosovë felt distant in place – Africa to my Europe – then Janjevo felt distant in time; medieval to our modernity.

We were led up to the home of the Roma community's headman, a residence built at the top of one of the hillsides as if it were a metaphor (had the house come first, or the role?). We had already been convinced by the barefoot children who clutched our hands as we walked up. But when we sat with the Roma chief and his wife in their yard looking out over the valley, and in quiet voices they sketched for us the facts about school attendance in this community, we were certain that there was a job to be done here. So now we just needed to find some funding to do it.

With Aurélie's skills it seemed easy. No drinks parties and donations boxes this time, but a neat project proposal to the Dutch Embassy, returned with a neat contract to sign, and a neat note from the bank to confirm that funding was in our account. It would be a three-month project running over the summer so that children who were normally in school wouldn't lose their knowledge over the long summer break; and children who were out of school would be set up for an easy transition if we could get them registered at school for September. And this time we could pay someone to lead the project, so we advertised for a co-ordinator and soon had a young Serb, Katarina, who started creating a learning centre out of an empty building on Janjevo's southern hillside. I watched her at work with a mixture of sympathy, admiration, and jealousy. I heard about what she was busy with – commissioning local carpenters to make tables, meeting with the lady with the big blonde hair-do in charge of the minority children at the school, knocking on the doors of every Roma family and peering into the darkness of crowded homes and smiling at the mothers and children there even when what she saw inside gave little to smile about, coming to agreements with the shop by the bridge to provide a piece of fruit for each child every day … and I observed from the 'cc' line of emails with the cluck of a grandmother. It was fun seeing the project unfold, but it wasn't my project. That, of course, was the point: we'd wanted to look at replicating the model, not replicating my experience (sleeplessness, headaches and all).

Once we had a centre set up, we organised a team trip to go and help Katarina. Hysni came, to share his experiences with working with families in Fushë Kosovë. And, since this community spoke more Roma than Albanian or Serbian, we brought Jeton, the Fushë Kosovë night school student whom we were supporting to get his high school diploma, and who spoke Roma so could help us with translations. In fact, the translations that day were giddying – Katarina spoke not only Serbian and English but also German. Aurélie spoke not only her native French but also English and German. Faik, our driver, spoke his native Albanian but also German, so he and Aurélie and Katarina communicated in German – the first language of none of them, while Jeton and I struggled through in Albanian.

As our little Babel van came into Janjevo, Faik commented on the beautiful town, 'vairy nice', showing off some of the little English he knew.

'*Çka është* very nice *në gjuhën rome?*' I asked Jeton in Albanian for a translation into Roma.

And that was just the beginning. We were all children again – pointing and asking, and laughing and being laughed at for our splutterings and imprecisions in this strange new tongue. I'd read that Roma is cognate with Hindi, but I didn't expect the similarities to be obvious. I've been to India twice, and hardly learned any of the language as I travelled around, but words came back to me. Jeton taught us to count, and we all obediently held up our hands and stuck out fingers in time with his chanting. They were longer fingers, with rings on them and more creases around the knuckles than they'd been when we'd first done this on our mothers' knees, in our own languages, but it was the same exhilarating process we were engaged in now. *Yek, duy, trin…* There were some old friends here from other Indo-European languages I'd learned. Jeton stuck four fingers out and we followed, repeating, '*shtar*'. And then the final finger – '*panj*'. It was one of the few words of Hindi I remembered, thanks to the five rivers that give the PUNJ-ab its name, and the five ingredients required for the Anglo-Indian drink of 'punch'. Later, gesturing at my glass of water in a home where I was given a drink, I was reminded of another word I'd needed to ask for repeatedly as we made our way around the dust of Delhi – '*pani*'.

We weren't the only people excited about learning – there was a collection of children waiting outside our centre even though lessons weren't due to start until the following week. The word had spread.

Katarina and Hysni were here to meet with potential helpers for the lessons, and the children milling around were getting in the way, being told off and shooed to one side in at least four languages, and obeying in none of them. They were enthusiastic about the project that was about to begin here, and they knew that in some way it couldn't happen without them, but right now there was nothing for them to do. I knew how they felt.

'Hey, why don't you all come in here!' I said in Albanian. None of them responded. Jeton had taught us 'here' and 'there' in Roma and a few key verbs like 'come' and 'know' so I said it again, with a self-conscious smile, but in their language – 'come here'. They looked up from their giggling in the hallway and they came to me.

Afterwards I discovered that in fact I had said to them 'Know! Here!' but it wasn't a bad mistranslation in the circumstances, and I herded the children into an echoing room (the tables were still being assembled). I got the ragtag bunch of perhaps a dozen children of different ages sitting on the floor. One of them spoke Albanian so he became my translator. I spoke slowly for him. 'Here, we will have a school for children for three months. You can come every day, Monday to Friday. It starts on Monday at ten o'clock.' I gave an encouraging welcome smile and waited while my helper gave a conscientious translation. There's always a time lag when speaking with a translator – like talking on the telephone with a bad satellite delay.

But now he had finished his sentence and the grubby little faces looking up at me burst into grins, and looked at one another as if they couldn't believe their luck. 'We're going to have lessons?' They started clapping.

Maybe I was the grandmother, not the parent of this project, but who says grandmothers don't get some of the best bits?

With the laborious hours spent by Aurélie and Katarina over spreadsheets as well as carpenter-produced tables, we had kids flocking to classes and many if not all of them were registered for school in September. I visited to see how it was going, of course (pulling into the town in the van and watching children running towards us, calling, 'Katarina, Katariiiiina!' This really was not my project), but soon I was busy with another opportunity. We were approached by an international NGO (they approached us! I thought again of the fundraising evening at Zsofia's house) to try a similar project in two more municipalities. By now, sadly Aurélie had moved from Kosovo – into the heat of Africa's refugee camps, with another organisation – but Anemona was still with us, and we had promoted her to be our Programmes Director. Grandma was here, too, but increasingly I was handing over.

As part of the new project we had funding to pay for an additional teacher – a clone for Teacher Avdil. When Anemona and I spoke about the interviews for the post, we couldn't find a date when I was available to be part of a panel. If we waited for me, the recruitment process would be held up; it soon became obvious what I had to say,

'The thing is … I'm not actually needed for these interviews. You could do them yourself with someone else from the team.' It would be the first time that I wouldn't be part of the

Janjevo

selection panel. To be more positive, it would be the first time that this complex, wonderful organisation that had grown up with me as part of it would be generating itself. It was a miracle. And I felt a bit lonely.

Then I spoke to Hysni at one of our weekly catch-up meetings. How were things going with the school? He smiled, proud but too kind to be triumphant. 'Something's changed you know. That Deputy Director doesn't shout any more when I come in to see her about a pupil. Last week she invited me for a coffee and she wanted to talk about some other cases of children who'd dropped out of school that she thought we could work together to get back to class.' I was open-mouthed, and newly in awe of Hysni for the working relationships he'd managed to build once I'd stopped complicating things.

It was therefore very good timing when Rob was offered a new job – four hours away from Prishtina. In fact it was not only four hours away but in a different country, although Albania seemed like it should be familiar territory with its shared language, and all I'd learned about its history from my time in Kosovo.

Four hours was a manageable enough commute that Rob and I could come to an agreement: I would still spend four days a week – Friday to Monday – in Prishtina, meaning I could help where necessary, and be around for the flagship Saturday activities in Fushë Kosovë, and Rob could join me for the weekend. In theory that meant he and I wouldn't spend a single night apart. We planned that after six months or so, I would start leaving Kosovo with him on Sunday afternoons, and spend only three days a week in Kosovo. Anemona would have time to grow into her role, and I would not be needed.

I would not be needed. This kind of built-in obsolescence was the right thing to do, but – as I mused on the jolting bus which left Tirana at six o'clock on a Friday morning – it was not always a comfortable process. That day I got off the bus in Fushë Kosovë, before even reaching Prishtina and the little bungalow we'd kept on in town. Friday mornings were the team meeting, and with some delays to my bus journey they would already have started without me. From the bus stop I hurried through the streets of Fushë Kosovë, my ears still popping from the journey across the 'Accursed' Mountains, and waving brisk hellos to kids and mothers who greeted me in the streets. When I entered the centre I could hear the voices of Hysni, Bajramsha, Ilmije, Anemona and some of our volunteers, and I went to the door of the room where the meeting was taking place. Opening it quietly, I saw the group deep in discussion of the plans for the following week.

Anemona was steering the conversation, carefully taking notes, her hand out like a conductor before an orchestra, acknowledging members of the team waiting to give their opinions. They were all looking at her to be sure of their chance to contribute and no-one saw me standing in the doorway. After a few seconds I stepped back and pulled the door shut.

There was nothing I was needed for there; I put my rucksack down, and went out into the road to talk to some of the kids I'd rushed past on my way in.

36 The lace mats

However pleased – and liberated – I could feel about the complicated music played by the orchestra in our centre in Fushë Kosovë; the melodies floating out through the windows, and hummed by Gjelane and the other children learning to read and write there; Hatemja and the other women earning a basic income as they stood stirring their pots of soap sludge … there was still one jarring note. I would walk away from those meetings, drumming my fingers in time to the triumphant tunes we were playing, and take myself back to where all this started, and the squalid makeshift home where Hatemja's family lived, and feel that nothing had really been achieved.

The poverty which had burned little Ramadan as he'd played scaldingly close to the stove was still there. Yes, Vehbi and Labinot and Gjelane were all at school. The children were all vaccinated. Hatemja had a small income, but it wasn't enough of a difference. We had done everything the Unicef way, looking for long-term change, and supporting people to help themselves. We knew that if you give a man a fish you feed him for a day; teach him to fish and you feed him (and his family) for a lifetime. But Agron and his family were still – and not just metaphorically – hungry. The soap sales were unpredictable. Every soap sold for two euros, of which fifty cents went on the raw materials, and the remaining 1.50 euros was divided between five women. In the best month – when we had bulk orders from brides offering the soaps as wedding gifts to their guests – the women took home a hundred euros each. In the worst months, when we sold single soaps to a few people passing by our stall or our office, the women's pay was less than ten euros.

Whenever I talked to Hatemja or Agron about it, they said that all they wanted money for was a decent home. And from what Agron could scrabble in the dirt of Kosovo's garbage, together with what Hatemja made from helping the country keep clean, they were never going to save enough to buy or build somewhere new. I'd known Hatemja for more than two years, and over all the time I claimed to have been helping her family, the only change I'd seen in their living conditions was a room crowded with one more body, now that baby Elham was taking up space on the floor when they all went to sleep.

That Christmas, I was back in England and with Rob and his family I attended a carol service in a chilly Dorset village church. The familiar hymns and the poetry of the words ('earth stood hard as iron, water like a stone') echoed round the vaulted ceiling, and we all listened to that extraordinary story of a precious baby born, like Elham, into the unsanitary conditions of a rat-infested stable. In the middle of the service the vicar asked us to pray quietly by ourselves for a few moments, and I shifted on my pew, wondering quite what I should do now. It was the same dilemma I had had at Elham's naming ceremony; asking an atheist to pray is like inviting someone to shout in an empty room. If I believe in people, then praying can't be done in silence and alone; it's conversation and Twitter and writing books that people will read. I fidgeted a little more and stole a look at those kneeling either side of me, faces frowning in thought and communication beyond themselves.

Well, it was nearly the new year – maybe I could use this time of silence to set some intentions, some commitment to changes in my life. That seemed appropriate, and I wondered what it was I really wanted to have changed in the 365 days before I came back to this village church for another carol service.

I thought again of those babies lying in their unhealthy beds. That was what I wanted to change – a house for Elham and for Gjelane; for Agron and Hatemja and all their children. When he explained the need for it, Agron would say 'somewhere for the children to get ready for school' and I imagined Gjelane pulling on her trousers in the midst of seven other people pulling on their clothes at the same time, trying to brush her teeth at an outside standpipe; *water like a stone*. So I prayed for health and for education: a living space that could be kept clean, for an indoor toilet, for an area where the children could play without the scarring splash of boiling water.

Early on in my visits to Hatemja's family they had asked me if I could help get them on a television programme called 'I'm From Kosovo Too.' The programme took a case each week of a family fallen on hard times. Lingering close-ups of the family's children, interviews with the parents describing their life – preferably in between sobs – and violin music played in the background were accompanied with a 'donate now' banner along the bottom of the screen. The programmes were apparently hugely successful in raising money for the families, but they turned my stomach. People in Neighbourhood 29 complained that they only ever showed Albanian families, but that wasn't my main complaint – it was the unsophisticated approach to charity, the reinforced helplessness of the beneficiaries to do anything to solve their own plight; the idea that the more you cried on national TV, the more money you would get (a broadcast version of what Hatemja had done outside the mosques on Fridays). I had told Hatemja that they shouldn't go on the programme; that there should be other ways for them to get themselves moved out of the stinking unhealthy home where her children were growing up.

And yet … the families who had learned how to cry on camera were now in homes that didn't leak when it rained. The next time I had seen Ramadan, he had had a mark on his cheek. 'What happened?' I had asked tenderly.

'The rat bit him in the night,' Hatemja had told me undramatically.

A few weeks later I had been invited on television to talk about my latest book. It was the same channel that aired the 'I'm From Kosovo Too' programme and when I'd seen Hatemja at the soap-making the following week she'd told me she'd seen me on TV.

'Could you not ask them to put our situation on the programme?' she'd said again. And I could. I knew the people there and if I asked they would probably come and film the family – what genteel sensibilities was I so bothered by offending?

I'd asked Agron whether there were people in the municipality who could help – political leaders perhaps? Or social services? He had laughed at the naiveté of the question. 'I went to one of the leaders to ask for help with getting a new house, and you know what he told me? He said I should come back at election time – you know, when they buy the votes – and he'd give me a cubic metre of firewood.'

I had contacted social services and filed a formal request to them for decent housing for a family living in unhealthy conditions. They had said they would have to send a team round to assess the family and would then report on it. Their report had come back some weeks later – they had confirmed that the Krasniqis' living conditions were unacceptable. But they had no budget for any housing issues in Fushë Kosovë so were unable to help.

Sitting in my pew that Christmas Eve I wondered what else I could do? I was wary of taking this on, but was that just cowardice or laziness? I knew there was one reason which did stand up to scrutiny as to why it was not a good idea for The Ideas Partnership (and maybe even me as a familiar symbol of The Ideas Partnership) to help Hatemja's family with a house: even if we were to have the money – even if someone donated the perhaps 12 000 euros we estimated it would cost to buy land (itself about 4000 euros) and build a simple one-storey home – how could we justify spending all of that on one family? It was more than it had cost to teach 62 children for six months and get them all registered for school. Although the Krasniqis were reckoned by everyone to be a family in one of the most desperate situations in the whole neighbourhood, I still wasn't sure we could explain to other desperate people why we chose one family and not another. And if we did it for one and then opened the gates for other housing requests, there would be no end to it. We were not a housing organisation; we had no expertise in buying land or contracting builders.... And what about our liability; if we raised the money and paid workmen, and the house then fell down. Would we be legally responsible for injuries to the family? Would we be morally responsible? It wasn't something we could take on.

If I wasn't very good at praying, then I resolved that the only thing I could try was the humanist's alternative: I would make sure that everyone I could think of would know about the conditions that Hatemja was raising her children in, and hope that someone else would know a way out of the rat-infested mattresses.

In the new year, when visitors came to Fushë Kosovë, I took them to meet Hatemja. She and Agron got used to telling their story, and at least they didn't cry to camera on cue, and could explain what they were doing through their own efforts to make a better life for their family. They were visited by groups from the UK, the Netherlands, the US; ambassadors and journalists, friends and potential donors. Hatemja concentrated when I introduced people, looking intently at them as I explained who they were or how I knew them. On the occasions when someone came back a second time she always recognised them even if she usually struggled to recall a name, whether it was Kosovan or foreign. I realised she was much better at remembering faces than I was, and I wondered about the curse of the literate.

My friend Nicola came to see us in Kosovo and we took her round our favourite sites. 'Would you like to see the work with the kids in Fushë Kosovë?' I asked and she pulled a face,

'Of course it would be interesting, after all I've heard. But … I have to warn you, I'm not great with kids.'

The next afternoon she was sitting with Elham in her arms, taking photographs of him as he played with her necklace and giggled into her lens.

The picture went on Facebook and one of her friends saw it and asked Nicola who the baby was. As Nicola told her about Elham's living conditions, and with Nicola's friend Andy helping brainstorm what could be done to help, they came up with an idea for fundraising for the family. Nicola's Facebook friend, Ali, led a charity registered in the UK and offered to set aside a sub-account with its accompanying JustGiving page to raise money for the family's home. With Nicola and

Ali on the case the cause was led from outside of The Ideas Partnership, and I hoped avoided setting the precedents that had bothered me. The fundraising started to gain momentum: Ali's son Dani was in a band and used his online presence to raise awareness, even coming out to see the family for himself (when the TV company did come out and film his visit with Elham in his arms, and his promise to help the family get a new home); a group in our village in Cornwall organised a fundraising lunch; a local glass designer donated a large lump sum. Nicola crafted an exquisite nativity scene which was auctioned... Would we really raise 12 000 euros though? As offers of direct debits trickled into the inbox, and messages of support on Facebook, it seemed possible, but still a long shot.

And then one of the British visitors I'd brought to see Hatemja's home sent me an email. He'd been touched by what he'd seen of the family and had mentioned it to a friend who worked in Kosovo with the international NGO, Mercy Corps. Mercy Corps were building houses for 'returnees' to Fushë Kosovë, like those we'd visited in Srbobran. And although the Krasniqis weren't eligible for such houses, the plan that Mercy Corps had devised included what they called a 'balancing component' where a smaller number of local families who had stayed in Kosovo – like the Krasniqis – and were in extreme need (like the Krasniqis) would also have homes built for them. After some more emails and some visits by Mercy Corps to confirm the family's situation it was official: if we could buy the land then Mercy Corps would build the house. Raising 4000 euros seemed like a real possibility through the generosity of friends and friends of friends; perhaps we could do this.

Anemona and Arta wanted to help too. Kosovo had no infrastructure for JustGiving or online pledges, but they proposed running an event with a friend called Rema to raise money. A funky café in Prishtina (whose name, appropriately, meant 'The Door') agreed to let us use their space. A local drinks company donated refreshments, and a local bakery gave trays of cookies. A singer gave her time for free and a dress designer and hotel offered luxury goods for auction. Zsofia's husband ran a marathon for the fund, and soon we had enough money in the dedicated bank account to be able to go and tell Hatemja that the family would eventually – we estimated it would be within the year – have a new home.

I found her sitting with Ramadan on one of the mattresses, stroking his hair. He was sick, she said – weak with diarrhoea and vomiting. I looked at his frail little body and suggested they should go to the surgery straight away.

That evening I got a phone call from a doctor at Prishtina hospital. He said he'd been given my number by Agron as Ramadan had been admitted and was on a drip. But they needed money to pay for the prescription and Agron didn't have any, or even credit on a mobile phone to call me. Could I come, and bring with me some money.

In the hospital bed, Ramadan was dwarfed by the paraphernalia of hospitals. Hatemja and Agron were both standing over him, watching him as if their gaze alone could transfuse nutrients into his body.

'What's the matter with him?' I asked the doctor, but he said he couldn't tell how the gastro-enteritis had started.

'Do you have animals at home?' he asked Agron, who shook his head.

'Er, well…' I intervened, aware that I was going to embarrass Hatemja. 'There are rats…'

'Well that's why then,' the doctor said briskly.

The money for the Krasniqis' new home was in the bank account, and while we worked on finding the land for the new house, and while it was being built there was really no excuse for them to continue living in a place that was making their children sick.

When I spoke to Ali and Nicola they agreed that this was the priority. Zsofia said 'it's not a move; it's an evacuation'.

The house we found to rent as a short-term measure had two rooms, plus an indoor bathroom and a huge overgrown garden. I imagined a rug outside during the summer and the children playing. I took Agron to see it and he stood in the empty space with a goofy smile that made him look like Vehbi, his son – like an overwhelmed eight year-old.

I rang the landlord after the weekend to arrange signing a contract and making payment so Hatemja and her family could move in.

'They're in already,' said the guy who owned the house. 'Have you seen what that place they were living in was like? I told them they shouldn't spend a single night more there.'

I hurried to the new house, hoping Hatemja would be in to receive a guest.

At the door I could tell that they were at home, but I could also see the first sign of upward mobility. Where at the old house shoes were scuffed off at the threshold and left in jumbled piles half in, half out of the pools of waste water that collected at the door, here the Krasniqis had a little shelf for shoes like I'd seen in middle-class Kosovan homes. Arranged in neat pairs I could spot Elhame's little sandals, three pairs of trainers for the older boys, some girls' shoes that Gjelane had left there, and Hatemja's own trainers. Only Agron's were missing so I guessed he was out with his wheelbarrow.

I knocked on the door (a real door – not a piece of corrugated metal) and Hatemja came out with Elham at her hip. Her face lit up to see me, and mine to see her huge smile.

'Come in, come in,' she ushered me as I was taking off my own shoes. She gestured at the shelf at the door – 'I've washed all the shoes'. Mine looked scruffy at the end of the row.

In stockinged feet I stepped carefully over the threshold, making sure to do so with my right foot first in the Kosovan tradition of respect. Inside, the children were giggling together on an enormous sofa. Where were the mattresses? Where did she get a sofa?

'An Albanian gave it to Agron when he was going round the houses at the weekend,' said Hatemja when she saw me staring. The huge saggy embrace of the old sofa represented not just all the dozens of people – Kosovars and foreigners – who had come together to provide some decent living conditions for her family, but also a rising upwards from the dirt of the floor, up through Maslow's hierarchy of needs.

Elhame came up to me and tapped my thigh. 'We have a new house,' she announced, rather unnecessarily, and I hugged her. Behind us, Gjelane was spraying air freshener in the spick-and-span new space. Air freshener!

'Do you like the house?' I asked Gjelane, and her eyes rounded.

'It's fantastic!' she said. 'And my teacher asked me today at school why I looked so smart, and I told her it was because of my new house.' What she was saying didn't really make sense. But it made complete sense – the chance to put your trousers on in the morning without treading on your brother; the pride, the sense that you were worth something.

I tried to see her home through her eyes, and as I scanned the room, I saw another detail that made me turn to Hatemja again. Lace mats! These are the pride of every bourgeois home in Kosovo; traditionally crocheted by every unmarried girl in preparation for her trousseau, and then set out over television sets, frothing over tabletops, given as presents to visitors, and dotted over furniture like a benign cancer. There had been no place for them in the grim minimalism of their last home. Yet here they were on every surface; how on earth had Hatemja suddenly got so many lace mats?

'They were in my trousseau,' her eyes danced with pride. 'But when I saw the house that Agron was bringing me to when we got married, I didn't want to put them there, so I asked my uncle to keep them for me. He came round at the weekend and gave them back to me for my new house.' I thought of Hatemja the young bride, being brought back by her doting husband to his horrible house, with the frightening mother-in-law, and the fine mats folded away like a promise of a better future one day. I realised I had underestimated Hatemja. Somehow, for all that I had learned about her, for all my attempts to support her, and for all our friendship, I had thought that the damp mattresses and sewage-soaked rugs of the house where she'd lived had defined her. I had never imagined that she had aspirations of suburbia squirreled away in hand-crocheted mats.

I thought about what I had dared to do in the time since I first met Hatemja; she had taught me what friendship could make you brave enough to try. I wondered what else there was hiding here, waiting to be brought out if the conditions were right, when we believed that others would not laugh at the incongruity of our handcrafts, when we trusted that no-one would dirty the fine lace of our dreams.

Hatemja and her family – (from left) Vehbi, Hatemja, Elham,
Elhame, Gjelane, Ramadan, Labinot and Agron

The Ideas Partnership continues its work in Kosovo. We are always in need of volunteers and of funds, so if you think you could donate your time, your skills or your money or other resources, please get in touch.

f   Read about what we're doing right now on Facebook (www.facebook.com/theideaspartner.ship)

y   @kosovarngo

🏠   www.theideaspartnership.org

There's a button on the homepage of the website for donations via PayPal, and The Ideas Partnership has both a UK and a Kosovo bank account:

Kosovo	ProCredit Bank
	Account No: 1110 305926 0001 15
UK	The Co-operative Bank
	Sort code: 089299
	Account No: 65492860
	BIC: CPBK GB22
	International Account No./IBAN: GB54 CPBK 0892 9965 4928 60

A note on the pronunciation of Albanian

Albanian is an almost entirely phonetically regular language. This means that once you have learned the sounds made by each of the Albanian letters (very similar to English in most cases) you would be able to read a newspaper out loud – even if with very little clue of what it means.

For the Albanian words or names in the book, the following alphabet equivalences will be helpful:

A like *ar* in *car*

B like *b* in *begging*

C like *ts* in *rats*

Ç like *ch* in *children*

D like *d* in *daughter*

Dh like *th* in *mother*

E like *e* in *education*

Ë like *er* in *teacher*

F like *f* in *friend*

G like *g* in *garbage*

Gj like *ge* in *garbage*

H like *h* in *headscarf*

I like *ea* in *teach*

J like *y* in *yacht*

K like *k* in *kids*

L like *ll y* in *fill your boots*

Ll like *l* in *lace*

M like *m* in *mother*

N like *n* in *name*

O like *or* in *for*

P like *p* in *soap*

Q like *ch* in *teach*

R like *r* in *rubbish*

Rr a rolled *r* that we don't have in English

S like *s* in *school*

Sh like *sh* in *shoes*

T like *t* in *teacher*

Th like *th* in *filth*

U like *oo* in *book*

V like *v* in *volunteer*

X like *ds* in *kids*

Xh like *ge* in *garbage*

Y like the French *u* in 'tu'

Z like *zz* in *buzz*

Zh like *s* in *leisure*

If you enjoyed *The Rubbish Picker's Wife; an unlikely friendship in Kosovo,* read Elizabeth Gowing's first book, *Travels in Blood and Honey; becoming a beekeeper in Kosovo* (Signal Books, 2011) available in Kindle and hard copy.

The book was described by *The Times* as

'A sheer delight; a beguiling, bittersweet story of a lively love affair with a traditional world, as ancient as apiculture, in transition to new nationhood'

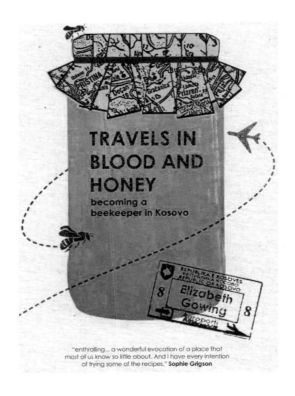

TRAVELS IN BLOOD AND HONEY
becoming a beekeeper in Kosovo

Elizabeth Gowing

"enthralling... a wonderful evocation of a place that most of us know so little about. And I have every intention of trying some of the recipes." **Sophie Grigson**

Elizabeth Gowing's second book, *Edith and I; on the trail of an Edwardian traveller in Kosovo* (Elbow Publishing 2013) is also available in Kindle and hard copy.

The book was described by *The Times* as

'The most delightful read of the summer'

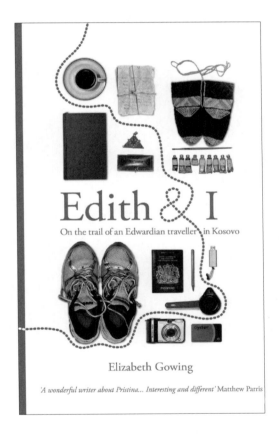